THE ART OF TABLĀ RHYTHM

Essentials, Tradition and Creativity

New Vistas in Indian Performing Arts

No. 1 **Hindustānī Music and the Aesthetic Concept of Form**; by Anjali Mittal (ISBN 81-246-0134-8)

No. 2 **Hindustani Sangeet and a Philosopher of Art** — Music, Rhythm and Kathak Dance — *vis-à-vis* — Aesthetics of Susanne K. Langer; by S.K. Saxena (ISBN 81-246-0180-1)

No. 3 **Speaking of Dance** — The Indian Critique; by Mandakranta Bose (ISBN 81-246-0172-0)

No. 4 **Performing Artistes in Ancient India**; by Iravati (ISBN 81-246-0207-7)

No. 5 **Ritual as Ideology** : Text and Context in Teyyam; by T.V. Chandran (ISBN 81-246-0275-1)

No. 6 **Tantra — Mantra — Yantra in Dance** : An Exposition of Kathaka; by Ranjana Srivastava (ISBN 81-246-0268-9)

No. 7 **Hindustani Music** : A Tradition in Transition; by Deepak Raja (ISBN 81-246-0320-0)

New Vistas in Indian Performing Arts, no. 8

THE ART OF TABLĀ RHYTHM

Essentials, Tradition and Creativity

Sudhir Kumar Saxena
Formerly Professor of Music
Faculty of Performing Arts
M.S. University, Vadodara

Sangeet Natak Akademi
New Delhi

D.K. Printworld (P) Ltd.
New Delhi

Cataloging in Publication Data — DK
[Courtesy: D.K. Agencies (P) Ltd. <docinfo@dkagencies.com>]

Saxena, Sudhir Kumar, 1923-2007.
The art of tablā rhythm : essentials, tradition and creativity / Sudhir Kumar Saxena.
xv, 184 p. 25 cm. — (New vistas in Indian performing arts ; no. 8)
Includes bibliographical references.
ISBN 13: 9788124603680
ISBN 10: 8124603685

1. Tabla — Methods. 2. Musical meter and rhythm — India. I. Title. II. Series: New vistas in Indian perfroming arts ; no. 8.

DDC 786.93 22

ISBN 13 : 978-81-246-0368-0 (HB) ISBN 10 : 81-246-0368-5
First published in India in 2006
Second impression in 2008

Published by:
Sangeet Natak Akademi
National Academy of Music, Dance and Drama, India
Regd. office : Rabindra Bhavan, Feroze Shah Road
New Delhi - 110 001
Phones : (011) 2338 7246; 2338 7248; *Fax* : (011) 2338 2659

and

D.K. Printworld (P) Ltd.
Regd. office : *'Sri Kunj,'* F-52, Bali Nagar,
New Delhi - 110 015
Phones : (011) 2545 3975; 2546 6019; *Fax* : (011) 2546 5926
E-mail: dkprintworld@vsnl.net
Web: www.dkprintworld.com

Printed by: D.K. Printworld (P) Ltd., New Delhi.

To the memory of

Ustad Habeebuddin Khan

my main mentor in the art of Tablā rhythm

and

Madhukar N. Gurav

a pupil unforgettable

Plan of Transliteration

(Not strictly in accordance with the standard practice, but with an eye to easy following by the average lover of Tablā rhythm):

त=t ट=ṭ; so धित = *dhit* and धिट is *dhiṭ*

धि and धी are *dhi* and *dhī* respectively;

Similarly, ति and ती are *ti* and *tī*.

Where they appear as the last letter of the *bol*, तिं; धिं are written as *tin* and *dhin* in English;

but तिंना and धिंना are put as *tinnā* and *dhinnā*, hoping that the letters *nn* will enable the nasal tinge required by a dot over the Hindi letters to help the continuity of flow which is implicit in resonance.

ड़ is ḍ, as in kḍedhā (कड़ैधा).

Contents

Preface

THIS book climaxes a lifelong interest. Rhythm has fascinated me from my very childhood; and so this academic fruition of my commitment to the art, at the age of eighty-three years, is very satisfying. As I grew up, I had the privilege of nurturing the interest in every possible way, namely, the following: first, years of systematic and dedicated learning under the doyen of the Ajrāḍā gharānā of tablā playing, the late Ustad Habeebuddin Khan, at Meerut (in U.P.); second, serving the A.I.R. (Delhi, Calcutta) as a staff artist (1945-48); thirdly, participation in most of the important music conferences of the country, mainly as accompanist, to almost every leading exponent of music (both vocal and instrumental) and Kathak dance of my day (1945-1995) including such legendary maestros as Ustads Faiyaz Khan, Bade Ghulam Ali Khan and Amir Khan (vocal); Ustads Vilayat Khan and Abdul Halim Jaffer Khan, and Pandit Nikhil Banerji (sitar); and Sarvashree Acchan Maharaj, Damayanti Joshi, and Roshan Kumari (Kathak dance).

What is more, I had the privilege not only of listening to live performances of, but of also having intimate dialogues on the art with, almost every leading tablā player of my day including the following maestros of yesteryear whose revered names and artistic skills I cherish to this day: Ustads Ahmad Jan Thirakwa and Amir Hussain Khan (Farrukhabad); Ustads Abid Hussain Khan and Wajid Hussain Khan (Lucknow); Pandits Anokhey Lal and Samta Prasad (Varanasi); Ustads Feroze Khan and Allah Rakhā Khan (Punjab); Ustads Gami Khan and Inām Ali Khan (Delhi); and Ustads Abdul Karim Khan and Habeebuddin Khan, both pioneering exponents of the Ajrāḍā gharānā (traditional family-school) of tablā-playing.

Above all, I have trained generations of aspirants in the field of tablā rhythm during my tenure of thirty-three years at M.S. University, Vadodara (Baroda), from where I retired as Professor and Head of the Department of Instrumental Music in 1983. To this self-education as a teacher I attach as much value as to my own thorough training under a maestro of undisputed merit, whose name has rightly appeared as one of the Music Makers (percussion) of the 20th century in the January 2001 issue of *Śruti* (Madras), India's leading magazine of music and dance. It is indeed this long spell as a teacher which has given me the ability to analyze what I myself learnt as a pupil; to discover not only the essentials of Hindustani rhythm, but the principles and devices that determine both composition and effective practice in the region of tablā playing; and so to compose quite a few patterns of my own in the different idioms of rhythm.

My pupils in the field abound. Quite a few of them are excellent performers themselves. Some are serving the A.I.R.; others, the very institution where I myself worked as a teacher; and all are held in esteem for their proficiency in the art. Happily, this is quite as true of those of my old students who are teaching tablā in foreign lands. But so far as this book is concerned, the main impulse to work it out — in spite of my general indifference to writing, as against my penchant for performance and practical teaching — has come from my occasional articles and talks on the subject. It is these which made me realize that I could do some clear thinking and writing on the art which has not only won me a fair measure of recognition as a player of merit, in the form of quite a few Awards, but has nourished me in spirit and kept me cheerful and fit all along. One of my talks, "Appreciation of Tablā" first recorded by A.I.R., Baroda — and later translated into our different regional languages — has been broadcast all over the country; and my article in *Sangeet Natak* (Nos. 117-18, July-December 1995), "The Art of Tablā rhythm: Past and Present," has also been well received. It is to these essays in analysis and to my reverence for the art and for its masterly, if unlettered, exponents of old; and, above all, to *my concern for preservation of the art in its purity*, that I owe the present offering, in print, to this magical art of sheer sound, variform pace, structure, articulateness, and flow.

Peter Kivy's well thought out book, *Music Alone* (Cornell University, 1990) is today regarded as a pioneering essay on "*pure* instrumental music, *sans* everything" (Ibid., p. IX). But, if "purity" in art be taken not only as utter freedom from both verbal meaning (and so from representation) and expression of emotions — *and* (in *sangeet*) from multiplicity of notes as arranged in a scale — *yet without any detriment to art's capacity for giving us what has been called* "disinterested delight" by aestheticians, no art can claim to be "purer" than the one I speak of in this book, with love and regard, and not a little wonderment at its creative potential.

The truth that aesthetic delight is by no means inseparable from representation and expression of emotion was first brought to my notice by my brother, Professor Sushil Kumar Saxena, who, I happily acknowledge, has also taken pains to improve the language of this book. Indeed, on looking at the Taj Mahal for the first time, when we vent our instant shock of delight by exclaiming, "How lovely" — or as a sheer gasp of wonderment — is not our reaction determined simply by the impeccable symmetry of the structure and its semblance of a primal, organic singleness, as against the thought of having been constructed by degrees?

Be that as it may, the completion of this work, I repeat, gratifies me. How its readers will react to it is quite another matter. My own effort has been all along to make it easy for them to follow what it says and presents to the ear. This indeed is why the notation of every rhythmic pattern has been given in both English and Hindi letters.

As for the select patterns recorded in the CD, the listener should find it easy to follow them with the help of recurring 'announcements' which have been kept minimally brief, so as not to interrupt the relish of listening unduly. Reading alone will not do. The ear has to be tickled; and one's feeling for articulate form and flow, quickened and gratified.

I am naturally happy to see that this labour of love is going to take the definite form of a book. But I would have been happier had Madhukar been there by my side as I write this preface. Unfortunately, he passed away, quite unexpectedly, on 9.7.2004, well after recording the compositions for the CD accompanying this work, but well before its appearance in book form. His help has been invaluable, and I cherish the memory, fondly and sadly.

However, he has not been the only source of help to me. Prajna, my wife, has all along taken excellent care of household matters and my personal comforts, releasing me thereby for exclusive attention to the practice and teaching of tablā. My daughter Hinā deserves my gratitude not only for continually goading me to get on with the writing of this book, but for providing the fitting 'announcements' that go with the compositions recorded. And how can I fail to acknowledge the many-sided help given by Mr K.K. Goswami, always happily, in the last thirty years or so? Unluckily, he too is now a memory, though a fond and recurrent one.

It is not easy to bring out a book of this kind. The printing of tablā *bol*s (mnemonics) can be tricky. So D.K. Printworld must be thanked most heartily for producing the book presentably.

I indeed feel mellowed in gratitude as I bring this preface to a close.

5th January 2006 **Sudhir Kumar Saxena**

Acknowledgement

I hereby acknowledge, very happily, the help given to me by MADHUKAR N. GURAV, my topmost pupil and former head of the Department of Instrumental Music, M.S. University, Vadodara, for notating the rhythmic compositions provided in this book; and for recording some select compositions, with the requisite measure of accuracy and finesse, under my supervision.

I also take pleasure in expressing my gratitude to the following:

- Prof. G.N. Sharma (Canada) and Samskritiki Shreyaskar (Rani Karnaa's Dance Academy, Kolkata), for financing the many rehearsals preparatory to the recording;
- Ms. Pooja and Smrti Srivastava for carefully putting the needed arcs under the patterns notated when the manuscript was typed for the first time. Later, when it had to be re-typed, arcs were replaced with straight lines;
- Mr A.N. Sharma for typing even the notated mnemonics with loving care and accurately;
- Mr A. Chatterjee, editor, Sangeet Natak Akademi, for all along taking a very kindly interest in the work; and, above all,
- Sangeet Natak Akademi, New Delhi, for agreeing to publish this book.

1

Introductory

I think I should begin by explaining why I have phrased the subject the way I have. Under the word "essentials" I propose to discuss such details as the basic alphabets of tablā rhythm and the common principal numbers of an authentic solo tablā recital. "Tradition" should enable me to speak of the different gharānās of tablā; and when I turn to "creativity," I shall speak, first, of some principles that determine creation in rhythm; and then provide some compositions that the exercise of these principles can produce.

But what is rhythm itself? Various answers have been given to this key question. But what is common to most of them is an explicit emphasis on the idea of regular recurrence. Thus, we speak of the rhythm of seasons, of day and night, rise and fall, and even of the different phases of human life, namely, childhood, youth, old age, and death. As against such common ways of looking at rhythm, quite a few aestheticians have related it to our sense of the flow of time — not, of course, to time as marked by watches and clocks, but to time as we experience it in daily life, say, as in waiting for the outcome of an effort or for the arrival of a friend, or as the sense that one's whole *long* working day has been packed with meetings and interviews.

My own concern with rhythm in this book is not so wide and various. It is limited to *sangeet*, a word which covers not only music, both vocal and instrumental, but dance as well; and even in this pretty extensive area of enquiry, I am going to focus on tablā rhythm regarded as an autonomous art. It would be wrong to think that I am trying to *confer* autonomy on rhythm. In north India, good solo tablā[1]

---

1. The word "Tablā" has two meanings, one basic, and the other subsidiary, though quite common. Basically, it means a set of two drums, called the →

recitals have always been due objects of aesthetic attention. Even theoretically, our rhythm may be said to be an art in itself, because it has it own unique material — that is, beats and *bol*s (or rhythmic mnemonics); and some quite singular criteria of evaluation, such as immaculate arrival at the *sama* or the focal beat. No other art can claim to build upon such singular material, or to provide so very clear criteria of evaluation to the critic.

However, a question is yet possible. The sceptic may turn from the word *autonomy* to *art*. How is rhythm an art at all? Here, I may offer the following answer, strictly in the light of what makes the substance of this book:

(a) All art builds upon something abstracted from reality. A painting may not present figures, things, or happenings. But even the most abstract work shows some shape, maybe merely geometrical, such as a square; some volume and size; and a measure of proportion, or balance, say, of lightness and depth, or of glowing colour and shade. Now, from where does the maker of such a work acquire his sense of these formal features, if not from his experience of everyday life?

Similarly, our rhythm too abstracts from life, and creatively works upon two things, in the main: first, *passage*, which is here to be understood not as path, but as the *act* of passing; and, second, the purely formal[2] character of various sounds. Passage, as we experience it in life, is either reposeful and steady, or just nimble or very fast; merely onward for a while or cyclic; intermittent or pauseless; or wayward or targeted at some goal. Sounds can be just as various. They may be brief, subdued, and crisp; or loud, deep, and resonant. All such features of sheer passage and sound will be found in the

→ right one (दायां) and "the left one" (बायां), because they are put, respectively, to the right and the left of the drummer. But, rather loosely, yet quite freely, the word tablā is also taken to signify the right one alone.

2. Yes, purely formal, not expressive of any verbal meaning or emotion, nor representative of any thing, happening, or situation in the outer world.

rhythmic patterns that have been provided and notated in the chapters that follow.

(b) Second, as in the region of every other art, *form* is important in the case of our rhythm as well; and here too *form* is to be taken not only in the sense of a seeming completeness of shape, but as proper integration and dynamic interplay of the details which go to make a whole.

(c) Thirdly, like all good works in the region of the other arts, a proper rhythmic recital too can give us what has been called disinterested delight, that is, agreeable feeling which is not based on any thought of actual existence or practical usefulness.

Rhythm is indeed as good a source of immediate charm as a sweet *swara*. As I say so, I have in mind the simplest form of rhythm, that is, rhythm as the regular recurrence of beats *at a nimble pace*. But if we consider it in its full artistic compass, rhythm may be said to be, essentially, an ingenious way to organize our sense of passage in ever more various ways; and the basic reason why we relish it is perhaps the fact that even in daily life we tend to prefer orderly variety to sheer plurality or monotonous order. Mechanical devices like clocks and watches also make the *flow* of time appear orderly by means of evenly placed ticks which resemble the *mātrās* of rhythm in respect of temporal evenness. But here, in the actual practice of the art of rhythm, the pace is set, and the intra-beat evenness kept all along, by a living person — by one who plays the drums, *quite without the outer aid of any mechanical instrument*. Nor is the playing here sheer physical exercise. It makes heavy demands on one's mental resources of concentration, self-steadying, and imaginative ability. So it *is* a creative art; and it is not without reason that our cultural tradition has not only put it, but given it a distinct artistic status under the inclusive word *sangeet*.

Indeed, rhythm is not a mere constituent of *sangeet*, but a vital aid to its captivating power. Today, as we know, the overall appeal of a sarod or sitār recital is importantly due to the quality of the rhythmic accompaniment provided to it. If we count the number of occasions when music on a stringed instrument elicits open applause, quite a few of these will be found to be moments when the tablā player marks the advent of the *sama* emphatically by way of climaxing a fluent rhythmic pattern, more or less as a parallel to some melodic passage produced by the main artist. Conversely, when the All India Radio is constrained to 'mourn' the death of an eminent person in terms of music *without* the aid of any drumming, does not the listeners' interest begin to wane very quickly? Therefore, though I cannot presently suggest many better alternatives to it, the word "accompaniment" is not quite adequate to the role of rhythm *in* a music recital. One who does not merely keep, but properly sets the pace for music, and provides a recurring checkpoint (so to say) for the rhythmic accuracy of singing or playing, cannot be fairly regarded as a mere accompanist. The truth rather is that, by virtue of the manifold assistance he provides to the main performer, the tablā or pākhāwaj player, who is said to be an accompanist, is actually an active participant in the evocation of musical beauty; and participation, it is obvious, is no mere accompaniment.

There is one other way to argue for the value of rhythm. Today, of course, rhythm is commonly acclaimed as an art of 'accompaniment.' This is true of the attitude of most of our *rasika*s. But the intrinsic aesthetic potential of rhythm, and its power to cast a spell over those who somehow get drawn to it, have enabled quite a few tablā maestros of the past to create and preserve elaborate compositions — of remarkable variety, beauty and subtlety in respect of syllabic filling (बोल भराव), pace, and design — and so to establish for rhythm a world and artistic status of its own. Further, in so far as this art, like music in general, requires a close and personal supervision (by the teacher) over the practising pupil, these beauteous, winged creations have come down to us in the only way they possibly could, that is, as transmitted from father to son, or from a teacher to his *gandāband shāgird*s (or formally/ceremonically enrolled pupils); and, with the passage of time, in the form of growing mastery over the actual playing and (overt) recitation of the variform syllabic arrangements. Be that as it may, it is unquestionable that a really good tablā player can distinguish himself in the most prestigious music conference. It may surprise the reader of today, but I know it as the evidence of my own past experience that, in respect of winning hearty audience applause, maestros like the late Ahmed Jan Thirakwa or Habeebuddin Khan of Meerut could easily rival the top sarod and sitār players of the country. It is an additional index of the bewitching power of rhythm that even today our best instrumentalists and Kathak dancers vie with each other in enlisting the help of a brilliant tablā accompanist. The practice, however, is also attended with a professional risk *for the drummer*. If *his* 'accompaniment' outshines the work of *the main performer* a bit too freely, though not with any conscious intent to make the latter look inferior, he (the selfsame tablā player) may not be engaged again by the instrumentalist in question! I say so in the light of my own recollections of some of the numberless music conferences that I have participated in as a young tablā artist.

Tablā, however, is only one of the many percussion instruments of India which may be put under two broad categories. The first comprises drums that are used essentially in the region of classical music; and the second covers those that are meant to provide rhythm to folk music. Pakhāwaj and the tablā, the two instruments which are most freely used in classical music for both accompaniment and solo playing, are quite well known to our *rasikas*. In respect of age, pakhāwaj is older than the tablā, which is of comparatively recent origin. But, in so far as my present concern is, and has all along been, essentially with tablā, I propose to focus on this two-piece drum which is very popular today in the field of Hindustani (or North Indian) classical music and Kathak dance.

Here, I may at once add, the tablā player's main function is to pick and establish the basic metric *cycles* in which various types of rhythmic/melodic *compositions* are set. But, under his expert handling, the tablā itself not only produces a wide range of sonorities pleasing to cultivated taste, but provides the performer, the tablā player himself, a great scope to demonstrate his own artistic prowess. In the past, indeed, our country has produced many excellent solo tablā players who not only practised and preserved the rhythmic riches of their mentors, but created a vast repertoire of their own compositions which are remarkable for variety not only in respect of range and syllabic filling, but in that of pace, design, and artistic appeal, and which (I repeat) have been passed on by oral instruction from father to son, or to authentic *shāgirds* (that is, pupils) for more than seven generations.

In the main, indeed, knowledge of the art of tablā playing has been the preserve of families of hereditary professionals. This is why we have gharānās of tablā, quite as naturally as gharānās of Hindustani vocal music; and differences of repertoire and style have been quite as visible in the former as in the latter. One of the more important reasons of variety in the art of tablā playing relates not to how the various patterns are visualized and designed, but to how the different parts of the drum — specially of the right one (*dānyā*) — are (in fact) utilized during the course of performance.

But then, I may add, the tablā itself has to be properly made. Its making is definitely a specialized job, involving workmanship which has been the domain of particular families for centuries, and which has shown continual improvement in respect of regulating the shape and resonant capacity of the drums, as demanded by the varying requirements of both vocalists and instrumentalists.

Our maestros of old would call these artisans "Tablā-*Pāz*" (तबला-पाज़्), which simply means a tablā-maker. Not all these fashioners have been good. Only those who possess a perfect sense of *sur* can produce a sweet-sounding *puḍi* (पुड़ी)[3] which has three distinct parts, namely the *kinār* or *chānt*, (the encircling rim/border), *syāhī* (or the central, inked round), and the part which intervenes these two, which is called *maidān* or *lava*. It is only when all these three parts of it produce the same note or *swara* that the whole *puḍi* can be said to be good.

The Instrument and What it Does

Regarded as a drum set, the tablā comprises two drums which are placed in front of the drummer and played horizontally with the hands. One of these drums, itself often called the tablā and normally played

3. *Puḍi* is the skilfully rounded skin covering of the top of the tablā. Here the reference is to the right hand drum." However, *puḍi* is necessary for both drums, the tablā and the *bānyā*.

with the right hand, is a slightly flared, closed cylindrical drum carved from a solid block of wood, the upper (and narrower) end of which is hollowed and covered with a composite head with the help of a *puḍi* (पुड़ी) made from goat skin. The *bānyā*, played with the left hand, is a modified hemispherical kettle drum the head of which is also covered with a *puḍi* (पुड़ी) at the upper end. When we speak of tablā playing quite generally, what we mean is the proper handling of both the pieces as one, that is, as contributing their proper individual sounds to the evocation of a specific rhythmic cycle or pattern. Both produce identifiable and nameable sounds which are called *bol*s (or tāla mnemonics); and it is the due collocation of these designedly produced sounds which creates full-length patterns or compositions that are numberless in principle. Some *bol*s have to be played on the *bānyā* (the left hand drum), and others on the tablā (the right one). Still others are played by blending the use of both, say, when the two hands are used in producing a single audible stroke. Just as in the use of a language the orderly disposition of words produces a sentence, so when *tāla-akṣara*s (or alphabets of rhythm) are integrated, various types of compositions come into being.

Incidentally, it is interesting to reflect on the tablā alphabets (*akṣara*s) themselves. In India a very elaborate and effective attempt has been made by the tablā wizards of old to identify the different sounds produced by the drums when their different (skin-covered) parts are struck in specific ways. These sounds were given names, so to say, in terms of mnemonic syllables or *bol*s which are but rough vocal analogues of the sounds arising from the drums. It is important to note that the *bol*s are only supposed to resemble, not to describe or explain the character of the sounds produced by the two drums. Thus, whatever is played on the drums can (also) be recited. In fact, the recitation not only of the basic rhythm cycles, but even of the rhythmic patterns that may be woven across (and ultimately within)[4] them, is looked upon as a distinct art in India. Indeed, if it is deprived of its

---

4. I say, "ultimately within" the rhythm cycles, because they (the patterns) are all, as a rule, expected to end, or rather to climax at the *sama* (or the focal beat) of the cycle chosen for playing.

*bol*s — or recitable syllables — our rhythm would at once cease to be what it essentially is in its native character. This is sadly ignored today by those who revel in presenting drum ensembles including both Western drums and the tablā; for in reacting to such concerted numbers, the listeners generally note only the similitude of beats in respect of their number, collocation and emphases, and hardly pay any discriminating attention to the varying *auditory* character of *bol*s, partly because Western rhythm has nothing to do with *bol*s. Some of the *bol*s, such as "धिर धिर" (*dhir; dhir*) have about them a look of repetitive, tremulous fluency. Others appear weighty and elongated, such as धड़न्न (dhaḍ*anna*), in articulating which the italicized portion is required to be elongated a little bit. The semblance of radiation from a common centre is provided by such fragments of a *bol* as त्रै (*trae*) where the *r* follows immediately upon, not loosely after, the *t*. Not each drum is regarded as suitable for producing every kind of *bol*. To illustrate, the right hand drum is expected to contribute sound-syllables which appear crisp and light, and can easily evoke semblances of fineness, fluency and an articulate seamlessness. (Here, to avoid confusion, I may repeat a point that I have already made at the very outset, in a footnote. In our musical parlance the word tablā is used not only to signify both the left and right hand drums as making a single percussion instrument, but also quite freely, to the right one *alone*). The left one, on the other hand, contributes effects of weight, depth, inwardness, continuity and resonance. Perhaps its most likable contribution is the effect of what is called सांस or आस (say, a kind of *breathing depth*). When the two are played properly together, some of the lighter effects of the right one may acquire a shapely roundness within the depth provided by the left one; and then, if what is being duly played is the basic rhythmic cycle (or ठेका), the total playing would appear to be not a mere succession of detached strokes, but a *running, yet articulate* and self-completing whole. Further, not any two *bol*s can be put together; and a proper concatenation of *bol*s depends essentially on the drummer's foreknowledge of the before-after order in which they can be put beautifully *and played without undue effort*. A good player is also helped by his instinctive grasp of such Gestalt laws of perception as those of similarity and contiguity, contrast, figure and ground, and common destiny or coercive design. (What these principles are and how they actually determine the very *creation* of rhythmic patterns will be brought out later, in chapters 7 and 8). I may add that an important mark of one's efficiency *as a player* is the ability to insert such a brief *bol* or *tuft* of *bol*s between two adjacent rhythmic passages as appears to deviate for a moment from the basic, underrunning *laya* (or aesthetic pace) but without at all damaging the shapeliness of the whole pattern. Here, the drummer has, of course, to *try* to keep it all within control; but if he is a seasoned artist, the playing as heard (and seen) would yet appear quite effortless.

Its Making and Keeping

Be it noted, however, that even the making of a tablā set admits of continual improvement. Indeed, between the periods preceding and following the attainment of our political independence, there has been a perceptible change in the ways of constructing the instrument, in accordance with the varying demands made on the tablā player by musicians and dancers. Before 1947, the completed drums presented a somewhat unwieldy appearance. Their मुंह (mouth), height and girth were much bigger than they are today; and they were surely not very good to look at. When they were in vogue, the tablā (or the right hand drum) was tuned with *swara*s in the *mandra* and *madhya saptak*s (or octaves) — with *sa, ma* or *pa,* to be precise — the exact choice of the note depending on the requirements of the main performer. For a *solo* exposition of rhythm, on the other hand, the tablā was normally tuned to the note "black five" or "C sharp" which surely lent an extra measure or resonance to the *bol*s produced. The *bānyā* (or the left drum) was generally allowed to remain at a note in the *mandra* (lower scale) with a view to investing the execution of compositions with a semblance of depth.

With the emergence of khayāl *gāyakī* as the dominant form of our classical vocal music, and the rise and ascendancy of instruments like the sitār and sarod during the Mughal period, the construction of tablā underwent a radical change. It was found necessary to produce tablās of various shapes and sizes, so that they could be tuned to any *swara* in the three octaves. To make it tuneable with the higher notes, the mouth of the tablā (the right hand drum) was narrowed, so that it could produce sharper sounds; and for due accordance with the lower notes, the left hand drums were made with a broad, composite mouth covered at the upper end with a *puḍi* (पुड़ी). In olden days the *bānyā* was made of clay, since no such metal was available as could be easily moulded into a round shape. Nor were any such machines in existence as could enable the maker to prepare a mould. Today, because of the availability of new materials and machines, it is possible to have an instrument of any size and shape; and the tablā player can easily secure drums to suit the precise needs of the occasion. However, it has always been an accepted norm that both pieces — that is, the left and the right hand drums — have to be equal in height so that they may be easily playable. Further, to speak quite generally, no change in the ways of *making* tablās permits any variation in the *execution* of *bols*. It is also noteworthy that whereas the right hand drum can now be attuned to any note of any octave, the *bānyā* must always be pitched at a nondescript low note which the drummer is expected to modulate suitably, by means of proper placement of the wrist and balanced pressure, so as to regulate the overall intonation of the drum winsomely.

Today, for solo performances too, it is easy to secure tablās which go with different *swaras* quite well. But the maestros of old would usually perform on an instrument producing a relatively low note, probably because higher-note tablās were not then available. Or, maybe they felt that the lower-pitch instruments provided better resonance and a measure of depth to the total playing, and so brought it closer to the classical idiom. But where they served as accompanists, tablā players had naturally to go by the requirements of the main artist. My personal opinion is that the size, shape and melodic quality of the drums do not vitally affect the playing ability of the artist, though they are bound to bring about some change in how the total playing *appears* to the listener, in respect of sheer sound, though not in respect of its structural and rhythmic character. The overtopping requirement, in every case, is that the overt reproduction of the *bols* (as mentally visualized) should be lucid and generally pleasing to the ear.

Care is needed also for keeping one's tablā set in proper shape and usable condition. Seasonal changes call for different ways to keep the tablā in shape. This may seem odd to the general reader. But any good tablā player will testify to what I have just said. However, to clarify the point, I may here also make some suggestions of my own. First, one should keep the instrument completely covered when it is not being used. Second, the *bānyā* (or the left hand drum) should always be kept upside down when it is not being used. During winter and summer, when the climate is dry, the left one becomes very tight and may even come to sound as 'high' as the right one. As for *using* the *dānyā* or the right hand drum, if its *sur*[5] has to be lowered, it should never be struck with the palm from above; for if it is so struck, the pitch of the drum will only rise, instead of going down. The right way to deal with such a situation is to rub the skin with one's palm a few times. After this has been done, the pitch of the *dānyā* may be lowered by a *swara* or a half, and then raised as desired. During the rainy season such problems recur quite often, because of moisture in the air. The only way to avoid such emergencies is to keep the drum in question covered and to get the side-strings tightened quite often.

I may, incidentally, make an observation which is bound to surprise the lay reader. Quite a few of the tablā maestros of the past whom I have met were regrettably incapable of *tuning* the tablā properly, *in spite of being fairly good singers themselves*. This has always been a matter of surprise to me, but it has surely not detracted from my immense regard for them. There is hardly any sphere of activity in which we can claim to have attained perfection. We have to be content with what are but mere measures of achievement.

5. *Sur* is how *swara* (meaning musical note) is commonly pronounced in our everyday musical parlance.

2

Alphabets of Rhythm and Ways to Play Them

EVEN like the compositions that make an average tablā recital, the very basic language that this art builds upon is unique. This language is of course a collocation of Hindi alphabets. At places, it even takes the form of individual letters with *guru* or *laghu* (बड़ी or छोटी) *mātrās*, as in the case of ता or ति. But when these very letters are put together to make compound alphabets like *nagtirkiṭtak* (नगतिरकिटतक); or, more importantly, to create whole patterns with varying emphases, pauses, pace and sparseness or closeness of the alphabets which a segment may comprise, they appear utterly different from the way we use everyday language in speech and writing, especially because they neither convey any meaning nor express any feeling in the way of words as commonly used in daily life. So they only tend to amuse those who have no idea of tablā rhythm. Yet the purely formal character of a rhythmic pattern can elicit the interest and attention of one and all, provided it (the pattern) is recited properly; *and* if the same is promptly played out on the tablā with a measure of obvious similarity between the citation and the playing. Indeed, where this similitude is the object of attention, even those who have no idea of the art of rhythm react with a chuckle of delight.

The names of those who first created the language of tablā are not known to me, and I can only guess how the thought of creating this language might have first dawned upon their minds. Maybe someone merely struck a drum variously, and at random, producing different sounds; then gave a little thought of how exactly these sounds are produced; and finally applied his mind to the task of combining them winsomely. Another possible explanation is that it was probably the chirping of some birds — and the louder, more impressive voices of some bigger animals — that first suggested to a creative person the idea of producing rough parallels of these sounds or voices on a drum with a measure of similarity. Be that as it may, the *alphabets* of tablā rhythm surely deserve a little thought.

The alphabets

They have always been an object of controversy. This itself has been due to differences between the syllables used in compositions which make the repertoire of different gharānās. A part reason also is that the maestros of old were not always receptive to views that differed from their own. Anyway, two main views on the matter may here be referred to. According to one view, there are as many as ten basic alphabets of tablā rhythm. According to the other view, they number only seven, like the seven basic notes of music. In my humble but considered opinion, the second view is preferable, in respect of each of the two drums that make a tablā set; and I say so on the basis of the hard evidence of the actual practice of rhythm. I ascribe the following seven alphabets ता, तिं, न, र, ट, ड, त्र = (*tā, tin, na, ra, ṭa, da, tra*) to the *dānyā* (or the right hand drum); and the following seven to the *bānyā* (or the left one): घ, घे, घी, क, के, की, कत (*gha, ghey, ghee, ka, ke, kee, kat*).

It may be noted, in passing, that I have purposely avoided giving diagrams and sketches of the two drums indicating the precise points of the two *puḍis* (top skin coverings) where the basic alphabets have to be produced. The reason for this abstention simply is that the same alphabet can be produced in different ways, at different points of the *puḍis*, partly by changing the fingers used; and that, therefore, illustrative diagrams or sketches are very likely to misguide a student in his initial efforts to produce the alphabets in question. But of course I will take due care, a little later, to explain the technique of *bol* production for the sake of those who wish to learn the art.

Another very important point to note is that there is not even a single alphabet of the tablā (the right one) or of the *bānyā* (the left one) in the production of which two fingers are applied simultaneously, except on the very rare occasions when the player wishes to lend a little extra inflection or weight to a particular *bol*. But a protest is possible here. Is it not a fact that while executing the *bol* धिर-धिर (*dhir-dhir*) all the fingers and the palm too are used collectively? But to this my ready answer is that the *bol* in question is specifically a compound alphabet of pakhāwaj playing. Today, of course, this alphabet is freely played on the tablā by one and all. I personally believe that this particular alphabet was perhaps introduced mainly by maestros of Farrukhabad gharānā, the repertoire and playing idiom of which build heavily upon pakhāwaj mnemonics, specially धिर (*dhir*). I may even venture to suggest that if this particular *bol* is somehow deleted from its repertoire, the gharānā in question will dwindle substantially in its configurational riches. At the same time, I must admit that strict adherence to the norm of keeping the basic *bol*s of different kinds of drums utterly apart is not always possible, or even desirable; and that some relaxation in this respect may be necessary for the sake of smooth execution and greater variety in repertoire. The fact, indeed, is that almost every gharānā of tablā has yielded to this constraint of practice. What is, however, more important is attention to the ways in which the different *bol*s are to be actually produced.

Technique of producing the basic bols

RIGHT-HAND SINGLE ALPHABETS:

1. 'Tā' (ता): When the first phalanx of the first finger of the right hand is struck at the edge (or *kinār*) of the *puḍi*, we get the sound of ता (*tā*).

2. 'Tin' (तिन): It is a resonating alphabet; hence, once again, the first phalanx of the first finger is used, but at the *lava* (लव) or *maidān* (मैदान) location of the *puḍi*, so as to produce the required sound. If, on the other hand, one has to produce *ti* (ती) which is a 'closed' sound, one has to strike the tip of the middle finger at the *lava*-point or edge of *syāhī*.

3. *Na* (न): is played with the tip of the third (or ring) finger striking the edge or *kinār* (किनार); and when the 'open' *Nā* (ना) has to be played, the first finger is to be struck at the inner

edge of the tablā *puḍi* (पुड़ी). *'Nā'* and *'Tā'* are, in fact, both played in the same way and at the same location, with the same finger-point. This is an ambiguity which the creators of alphabets just could not avoid.

4. *Ra* (र) is played with the first finger almost at the centre of the *syāhī* (स्याही) or ink-covered part.

5. The *bol ṭa* (ट) is also played in the same manner as *ra* (र), but exactly at the *centre* of the *syāhī* portion.

6. As for ḍ (ड़), it is played by striking the outer edge or the *kinār* of the *puḍi* with the third or the ring finger.

7. The way of producing the *bol tra* (त्र) is very different. Here, two fingers, the second and the first, are used, and the *ra* is made to follow the *t* immediately, instead of coming loosely after the *ta* (त).

LEFT HAND SINGLE ALPHABETS

1. *Gha* (घ) is executed by bending the middle or second finger inward in a semi-circular way, and by striking the *puḍi* in such a way that the alphabet resonates and is thus heard as an *open* sound.

2. *Ghey* (घे) is played by striking the third or ring finger slightly at the left of the playing space, with just a little pressure, so that the resonance is not wholly subdued.

3. *Ghee* (घी) is produced by striking the *puḍi* with the middle finger with just as much pressure and weight as may invest the alphabet with the requisite measure of resonance.

4. As for the syllable *ka* (क), it is executed by turning all the fingers inward in the shape of an arch and striking the *puḍi* with all the flat nails together at the same time, so that, though many fingers have been used, the actual sound produced may look like the stroke of just a single finger.

5. *Ke* (के) is produced almost in the same way as the alphabet *ka* (क), with just this little difference that it (that is, *ke*) is played

slightly towards the left side of the playing area, and essentially by means of flat nails.

6. In evoking a semblance of the alphabet *Kee* (की), all the flat nails are made use of, but with a slight pressure. I may here add that *Ka, Ke, Kee* (क,के,की) all provide sounds which appear 'closed' in varying degrees.

7. The case of *Kat* (कत) is quite different. It is played with the flat open hand, with some force and in such a way that all the fingers hit the *syāhī* location. But here the palm is not to come in contact with the *puḍi*.

COMPOUND ALPHABETS OF THE TABLĀ (the right one) ONLY

Tā-tā; Tin-tin; Tiṭ-tiṭ; TāsTī; NāsNās; Tir-tir; Tarāsn; Tīn-nā; Din-Din; Tās-Tinnā; Tiṭ-Tin; Nanan-Nanan; Trak-Tinntā

Note: Be it noted that here, as throughout this work, s is to be taken not as a letter, but as signifying a little lapse of time.

ता-ता, तिन-तिन तिट-तिट, ताऽ-ती, नाऽ-नाऽ तिर-तिर, तराऽन्, तिन-ना, दिन-दिन ताऽ-तिंना, तिट-तिन, ननन-ननन, त्रक-तिंता

Note: There are no such *compound* alphabets as may be played *solely* on the *bānyā*.

Some compound alphabets are played by blending the *dānyā* (दायां) with the *bānyā* (बायां):

Dhā-Dhā;	*Dhin-Dhin;*	*Dhiṭ-Dhiṭ;*	*Dhas-Tī*
Ghiḍā-sn;	*Dhir-Dhir;*	*Dhin-Nās;*	*Dhin-Tās*
Ghin-Tas;	*Ghiḍ-Nag;*	*Kiḍ-Nak;*	*Kiṭ-Tak*
Dhin-Gin;	*Tin-Gin;*	*Tin-Kin;*	*Tiṭ-Kat*
Gadi-Gan;	*Gheghe-Tiṭ;*	*Keke-Tiṭ;*	*Kat-TāDhā*
GheGhe-Nānā;	*Keke-Nānā;*	*Ghaḍāsn;*	*Kiḍā-sn*
Tak-Dhin;	*Tak-Tin;*	*Kṛdhi-Tiṭ;*	*Kṛḍhā-Tiṭ*
Dhage-Tiṭ;	*Tāge-Tiṭ;*	*Tiṭakiṭ-Taktā;*	*Takiṭ-Dhin*
Katrak-Dhitiṭ;	*Tiṭ-Ghḍān;*	*Tiṭ-Katān;*	*Dhḍān-Tirkiṭtak*
Kiḍ-Dhās;	*Dhāti-Ghin;*	*Dhāti-Dhāge;*	*Naga-Dhin*
Naka-Tin;	*Tiṭ-Ghin;*	*Ghinag-Dhin;*	*Kinak-Tin*
Ghitak-GhitakDhin;	*Natak-Ghitak;*	*Dhīkḍa-Dhin;*	*Din-Dināgenā*

धा-धा,	धिन-धिन,	धिट-धिट,	धाऽ-ती
घिड़ा-ऽन,	धिर-धिर,	धिन-नाऽ,	धिन-ताऽ
घिन-ताऽ,	घिड़-नग,	किड़-नक,	किट-तक
धिन-गिन,	तिन-गिन,	तिन-किन,	तिट-कत
गदि-गन,	घेघे-तिट,	केके-तिट,	कत-ताधा
घेघे-नाना,	केके-नाना,	घड़ा-ऽन,	किड़ा-ऽन
तक-धिन,	तक-तिन,	कृधी-तिट,	कृधा-तिट
धागे-तिट,	तागे-तिट,	तिटकिट-तकता,	तकिट-धिन
कत्रक-धितिट,	तिट-घ्ड़ान,	तिट-कतान,	ध्ड़ान-तिरकिटतक
किड़-धाऽ,	धाती-घिन,	धाती-धागे,	नग-धिन
नक-तिन,	तिट-घिन,	घिनग-धिन,	किनक-तिन
घितक-घितकधिन,	नतक-घितक,	धीक्ड़-धिन,	दिन-दीनागेना

Note:- The playing of compound alphabets needs no clarification, because they all have to be produced by combining the single alphabets, the way of producing which has been already explained a little earlier.

It is hardly necessary to add that attention to both individual and compound alphabets is alike necessary, because whereas it is actually a set of two, the tablā is in practice taken as just one percussion instrument. The proper coordination of work at the two drums is an important mark of ideal tablā playing. The right one is expected to contribute sound-syllables which are crisp, fluent and sliced; and the left one provides a varying measure of weight, depth, inwardness, continuity and resonance to the total playing. As the maestros of old used to say, दायाँ बोल काटता है, बायाँ बोल बनाता है. (The right one cuts or chisels the *bol*, so to say; and the left one lends wholeness or volume to it).

Yet, there are quite a few *quāyedās* (क़ायदे) and *relās* (रेले) where the prominence of one or the other drum can be easily visualized or heard. Consider the following, for instance:

Dhā Dhā Dhā   Ghin dhā Ghin   Dhā Trak Dhitiṭ
Ghin Tinā Kin   (Tisra jāti)

धा धा धा   घिन धा घिन   घात्रक धितिट
घिन तिंना   किन (तिस्त्र जाति)

Ghitak Ghitak   Tinatiṅ Nākin

घितक घितक   तिनतिं नाकिन

In the first phrase, the right one is prominent; and in the second phrase, the left one dominates.

At this point, I also deem it needful to list a few small phrases from different gharānās to facilitate practice in their individual idioms:

Delhi:	*Dhādhātiṭ;*	*Dādhātiṭkiṭ;*	*Dhāgetiṭ;*
	DhātiṭGhiḍnag;	*DhinGin; Kradhitiṭ*	
Ajrādā:	*Dhāgetrak;*	*GhīnāDhīnāGhīnā; GheGhenag;*	
	Tiṭghiḍnag;	*GhitakGhitak;*	*TakaDhinTakaDhin*
Punjab:	*DhāgeTirkiṭ;*	*DhatDhatDhin;*	*DhereDhereKat;*
	Dhaḍanna Dhaḍanna; GhetakDinnag; DhātīDhātī		
Farrukhabad:	*Takiṭadhātrakdhin; DhātiṭkiṭDhāGhiḍnag;*		
	DhātiṭkiṭDhātiṭkiṭtak; Dhirdhirghiḍnag;		
	Takdhinanatak;	*Trakdhet*	
Lucknow:	*Dhāgetiṭkiṭ;*	*Kradhātiṭ; Dhingin; Ghetiṭkiṭtak;*	
	Ghintarāऽn;	*DhāgenaDhagendhā;*	
Benares:	*Dhīkdhīnā;*	*DhirDhirGhiḍnag;*	*KattaDhikiṭ;*
	Dhātiṭatātiṭ;	*Dhātiṅtāḍa;*	*Gadigan Gadigan*

These may now be put as follows in Hindi, exactly in the same order as has been followed above:

दिल्ली:	धाधातिट, धाधातिटकिट,	धागेतिट,	
	धातिटघिड़नग,	धिनगिन,	क्रधितिट,
अजराड़ा:	धागेत्रक, घीनाधीनाघीना,	घेघेनग,	
	तिटघिड़नग, घितकघितक,	तकधिन	तकधिन,
पंजाब:	धागेतिरकिट, धटधटधिन,	धेरेधेरेकत	
	धड़न्नधड़न्न, घेतकदिननग,	धातीधाती	
फ़र्रुख़ाबाद:	तकिटधात्रकधिन,	धातिटकिटधाघिड़नग,	
	धातिटकिटधातिटकिटतक,	धिरधिरघिड़नग,	
	तकधिननतक,	त्रकधेत	
लखनऊ:	धागेतिटकिट, क्रधातिट,	धिनगिन,	
	घेतिटकिटतक,	घिंताराऽन,	धागेनधागेनधा
बनारस:	धीकधीना, धिरधिरघिड़नग,		

कत्तधिकिट, धातिटतातिट,

धातिंताड़ा, गदिगन गदिगन

I may also here invite attention to the following tufts of *bols* which occur in some old compositions and which tend to hamper, instead of facilitating, smooth playing. In doing so I do not at all wish to underestimate the contribution of our old maestros, but simply to illustrate the truth that where numberless compositions are created, some oddities are bound to occur, because of sheer human limitations. Anyway, the following two examples should prove my point:

1.

Dhātīdhāऽ	*GaddīGhiḍnag*	*Nagtirkiṭatak*	*Nagdhitkḍān*
Dhātirkiṭatak	*TātirKiḍdhā*	*(DiṅgaḍdhāDiṅ*	*GaḍdhāDiṅgad)*
Dhāऽkḍān	*Dhaऽkiḍdhā*	*(DiṅgaḍdhāDiṅ*	*GaḍdhāDiṅgaḍ)*
DhāऽKḍān	*DhāऽKiḍdhā*	*(Diṅgaḍdhādiṅ*	*GaḍdhāDiṅgaḍ)*

धातीधाऽ	गद्दीघिड़नग	नगतिरकिटतक	नगधितक्ड़ान
धातिरकिटतक	तातिरकिड़धा	(दिंगड़धादिं	गड़धादिंगड़)
धाऽक्ड़ान	धाऽकिड़धा	(दिंगड़धादिं	गड़धादिंगड़)
धाऽक्ड़ान	धाऽकिड़धा	(दिंगड़धादिं	गड़धादिंगड़)

2.

1	2	3	4
Kattiṭa	*GheGhetiṭ*	*Kradhātiṭ*	*Dhāgetiṭ*
5	6	7	8
Gadigan	*Nāgetiṭ*	*Kradhātiṭ*	*Dhāgetiṭ*
9	10	11	12
Tāgetiṭ	*Gadigan*	*Nāgetiṭ*	*(DhakiṭtakDhum*
13	14		
Kiṭtak Dhākiṭ	*Tak Dhum Kiṭtak)*[1]		
15	16	17	18
Dhātrak	*Dhitiṭ*	*KatāGa*	*Digan*[2]
19	20	21 22	
DhirDhir Kiṭtak	*Tātir Kiṭtak*	*TakkḍāऽNtā*	

---

1. *Tisra jāti.*
2. *Chatusra jāti*

23	24	25	
DhāऽDhir Dhir	*Kiṭṭak Tātir*	*Kiṭṭak DhirDhir*	
26	27	28	
Kiṭṭak Tātir	*Kiṭṭak GheGhe*	*Nāgheghena*	
29	30	31	32
Dhāऽ GheGhe	*NāGheGhen*	*DhāऽGheGhe*	*NāGheGhen*

1	2	3	4
कततिट	घेघेतिट	क्रधातिट	धागेतिट
5	6	7	8
गदिगन	नागेतिट	क्रधातिट	धागेतिट
9	10	11	12
तागेतिट	गदिगन	नागेतिट	(धकिटतकधुम
13		14	
किटतक धाकिट		तकधुम किटतक)[3]	
15	16	17	18
धात्रक	धितिट	कताग	दिगन[4]
19	20	21 22	23
धिरधिरकिटतक	तातिरकिटतक	तककड़ाऽनता	धाऽधिरधिर
24	25	26	27 28
किटतकतातिर	किटतकधिरधिर	किटतकतातिर	किटतकघेघे नाघेघेन
29	30	31	32
धाऽघेघे	नाघेघेन	धाऽघेघे	नाघे घेन

Explanatory note on the above

Look at the bracketed portions in the first example, and you will find that these groups of (bracketed) *bol*s do not at all fit into the format of the total composition, because of two reasons. First, syllables which have such a sound do not occur in the language of tablā; and second, if I may humbly venture to say so, if such *bol*s are at all produced somehow, they will sound patently odd or just amusing to both learners and players of the art alike.

---

3. *Tisra.*
4. *Chatusra jāti.*

In the second example too, the same type of defect can be easily discerned. Here, again, the bracketed portion seems to be out of place in the smooth running of the other *bol*s which the whole composition comprises. The beauty of the composition could be easily redeemed by replacing the pakhāwaj syllables with tablā alphabets. However, such defects, I believe, are mere aberrations.

But even generally, there are some complexes or tufts of *bols* that prevent easy playing. Here are a few instances:

> *Dhāge Tiṭ Tirkiṭ Dhaḍanna Dhaḍanna Kirghin-Kirkin; Dhākiṭatak-Dhuma-Kiṭatak; Tā Dhī Tiṭa; Dhā-Tiṭ-Dhāgena-Dhā; Tir-Dhir-Tir-Dhir; Dhir-Dhir-Kit-Ghiḍnag; Tiṭkiṭ-Tiṭkiṭ; Dhiṭ-Dhaḍanna; Trak-Tiṭkiṭ; TadiGin-TadiGin; Dhadi-gan; Trang; Trak-Takiṭ; Trak-Tirkiṭ; Trak-Trak*
>
> धागेतिट-तिरकिट, धड़न्न धड़न्न, किरघिन-किरकिन धाकिटतक-धुमकिटतक, ता-धी-तिट, धा-तिट धागेन-धा, तिरधिर-तिरधिर, धिरधिरकिटघिड़नग, तिटकिट-तिटकिट, धिट-धड़न्न, त्रक-तिटकिट, तदिगिन-तदिगिन, धदि-गन, त्रांग, त्रक-तकिट, त्रक-तिरकिट, त्रक-त्रक

Here, in passing, I may also refer to an unhappy feature of the history of tablā teaching. Some great hereditary composers and teachers, who were directly associated with their individual gharānās, had a rather narrow attitude towards those of their pupils who did not directly belong to their gharānā. They would always try to withhold from such 'alien' pupils some secrets relating to the execution of *bol*s and would reveal them only to their own family members. This attitude may be explained as follows:

1. The Ustads always wanted their own family players to excel students from outside, as performers.

2. Those composers who had only a limited number of compositions in their repertoire of *bol*s did not naturally want to be emptied of their artistic riches.

3. It is also possible that the maestros in question simply wanted to prolong the tuition period, so as to extract maximum material gains from 'external' pupils.

4. Nor can we ignore the possibility that the Ustads in question, though excellent as performers themselves, just did not have the skill to teach the deeper subtleties of execution because of lack of analytical ability. After all, performing oneself is not the same thing as teaching others.

As I speak thus, however, my purpose is not to malign the great Ustads or to underestimate their expertise, but simply to help those who are wedded to the art of tablā, by sharing with them reminiscenes of the difficulties I had to face myself as a learner. One has of course to have reverence for one's teacher, but this has to be done with open eyes. I must also add that there have been quite a few such Gharānedār Ustads as well who were quite liberal in teaching their pupils. How, otherwise, could all the gharānās manage to flourish to this day? To take an overall, balanced view of the matter, one could say that, before beginning to impart lessons, these maestros wanted to make sure if the aspiring student was really keen to learn, and also had some real aptitude for the art. If the pupil met such requirements duly, he could be sure of getting almost everything from the teacher. It is indeed this truth which (partly) explains the fact that quite a few tablā artists are playing well today. But, for those who are yet to make a mark, it may be of help to know the following secrets relating to the execution of *bol*s.

1. The difference between Nā, ना and Na, न has never been taught by recitation or by display of actual execution. One has only to mark that Nā (ना) has to be played with the tip of the first right hand finger on the *kinār* (किनार) or the edge of the tablā *puḍi*; and that Na (न) is to be played mainly on the *Kinār*, but with the third (or ring) finger, a little towards the right side. For example, when *Dhinnā-Gīnā* (धिंना-गीना) is to be produced, the first finger must be used at the suggested location; but when *Dhin-Gin* (धिन-गिन) is to be played, the third finger has to be used. Attentive recitation of the two compound alphabets should bring out the point clearly.

2. To turn, now, to (a) *Dhātiṭ* and (b) *dhāgetiṭ*, one can easily see the difference by just reciting the two *bol*s quickly, one after

the other. Ordinarily, when it follows *Dhā, tiṭ* is played by first striking the drum with the second finger, and then with the first one, which is perfectly in order. But when *Tiṭ* (तिट) follows *Dhāge* (धागे), *Ti* (ति) has to be executed by the first finger and *Ṭa* (ट) with the third finger; and the location has to be the *syāhī* portion necessarily, because the alphabet *Tiṭ* (तिट) must provide a 'closed' sound.

3. Another pair of similar *bol*s which deserves attention is *tiṭkatā* (तिटकता) and *ṭiṭkat*, (तिटकत). Mark specially the difference between *Tā* and *Ta*; (ता and त). The compound alphabet तिटकता used to be *taught* as *Ṭiṭkatā,* involving the production of *Tā* at the *kinār*, which blocked easy execution; but this very alphabet was actually *played* by the *gharānedār*s as *Tiṭkat*, तिटकत; that is, the *Ta* (त) was played at the *syāhī* portion, which made the *bol*-production quite easy.

4. The *bol, DhirDhir*, (धिरधिर) too deserves similar attention. Besides being a pakhāwaj *bol* (in the main), it has also come to find a suitable place in the vocabulory of tablā, and is being played quite freely by almost all tablā players. According to the norms of pure theory, both the *Dhir*s have to be played in a similar way, but what is actually played is *Dhir-Tir*, (धिरतिर), not *DhirDhir* (धिरधिर); and so, in the process, the *bānyā* has to be used only once to make the playing run unhampered.

5. Let me now focus attention on another pair of *bols*: *Dhikiṭ* and *Dhitiṭ* (धिकिट, धितिट). When they are *recited,* the *bol*s sound quite different from each other. But during actual *playing* the *bol Dhitiṭ* (धितिट), which was generally *taught as Dhikiṭ* (धिकिट), would always hamper smooth playing, with the result that the player had to use some extra power, wasting a little time and energy; and would yet fail to produce the desired result. The reason is easy to see, and I may put it thus. The *bol Dhikiṭ* (धिकिट) includes three alphabets *Dhi-Ki-Ṭa*. Now, *Dhi* (धि) is executed by striking both right and left hands together at one time, and as a single stroke. *Ki* (कि) is played on the left hand drum (बांया) only. On the other hand, *Ṭa* (ट) is played on

'the right one' — that is, the tablā (तबला), — only. So, when *Dhi* (धि) precedes *'Ki'* (कि); and *Ṭa* (ट) follows *'Ki'* (कि), it is almost impossible for a tablā player to executive the complete *bol*. Comparatively, playing *Dhitiṭ* (धितिट) in place of *Dhikiṭ* (धिकिट) is a very simple matter, and quite convenient for a player.

6. *Tirkiṭ* and *Tiṭkiṭ* (तिरकिट and तिटकिट) are yet another pair of *bol*s which deserves some attention. But before analysing and comparing these two compound alphabets, it is essential to mention here, first, the three single alphabets which are (in my view) never executed on the tablā, and so do not find a place in the language of this drum set. These alphabets are *Ra, Ou* and *Ma* (र, उ, म). Now, the compound alphabet *Tirkiṭ* (तिरकिट) so freely occurs in a number of tablā compositions that it seems to have become indispensable for tablā playing today. Therefore its deletion from the vocabulary of tablā might create problems even for established artists. Yet, at this point, simply for the sake of truth, I have to say the following:

   (1) In olden days, our tablā maestros never recognized the existence of an alphabet like *Tirkiṭ*, (तिरकिट), neither in recitation nor in actual playing. Instead, they would use the *bol Tiṭkiṭ* (तिटकिट) in their compositions whenever required.

   (2) Second, though there is no difference in the technique of producing the two *bol*s — that is, their location on the *puḍi* and the use of fingers are identical in both cases — the sound actually produced resembles only *Tiṭkiṭ* (तिटकिट), rather than *tirkit*. However, simply because of the overwhelming pressure of current practice today, *Tirkiṭ* has to be accepted as a tablā *bol.*

Be that as it may, attention to individual *bol*s is by no means enough. We have also to give some thought to the following:

Norms governing permutation and collocation of *Bols*

The meaning of *permutation* is obvious; but the actual ways of permuting *bols* in tablā rhythm are both intricate and orderly in practice. Mathematical calculation is hardly enough here. To produce effects of beauty one needs a keen insight into, and a profound knowledge of the entire system of rhythm, as also a good deal of mental equilibrium.

Be it noted that the playing of *quāyedās*, (क़ायदे), and *relās* (रेले) remains quite incomplete without improvisation, which means *creative* permutation. A mere shuffling of the points where the alphabets occur in the main format of the composition is never acclaimed by the knowledgeable as an act of aesthetic value. What is really needed is provision of some tuneful *paltās* by manipulating the *interlacement* — not mere *translocation* — of alphabets in the form of beautiful variations. In this context, luckily, some definite principles are available which I may list as follows:

1. No 'alien' alphabet — that is, one which does not figure in the basic composition — should be allowed to enter any *paltā* (or variation/improvisation).

2. Further, the *paltās* provided to the main composition should be playable without much difficulty.

3. No single alphabet should be used too freely, so that the listener may not feel bored.

4. Before introducing permutations in compositions, one has to sub-divide the complete *bol* into shapely bits, strictly in accordance with the sequence in which the alphabets have occurred in the *bol*-pattern; and only then proceed further. The following example of a short and simple *quāyedā* should make my point clear:

(*Tāla-Tritāla*)

1	2	3	4
Dhā	*Dhā*	*Ti*	*Ṭa*
धा	धा	ति	ट

5	6	7	8
Dhā	*Dhā*	*Tin*	*Nā*
धा	धा	तिन	ना
9	10	11	12
Tā	*Tā*	*Ti*	*Ṭa*
ता	ता	ति	ट
13	14	15	16
Dhā	*Dhā*	*Dhin*	*Nā*
धा	धा	धिं	ना

This *quāyedā* has been composed with the help of only three alphabets, namely, *Dhā-Tiṭ* and *Dhinnā* (धा-तिट और धिंना). Hence, the *paltā*s should be provided in the same sequence. First, the *bol*, *Dhā* (धा) should be permuted; then, *Tiṭ* (तिट); and lastly, *Dhinnā* (धिंना). This alone will make for orderly progression and also indicate that the player has received proper *tāleem* (or training).

A more elaborate account of how *paltā*s are to be introduced, but again in a short and simple *quāyedā*, is given below, with a view to dispelling all confusion regarding the matter:

The *quāyedā* proper (as set to *tritāla* of 16 beats)

1	2	3	4	5	6	7	8
Dhā	*Dhā*	*Ti*	*Ṭa*	*Dhā*	*Dhā*	*Tin*	*Nā*
9	10	11	12	13	14	15	16
Tā	*Tā*	*Ti*	*Ṭa*	*Dhā*	*Dhā*	*Dhin*	*Nā*

Now, *paltā*s

I. OF DHA

1.	*Dhā*	*Dhā*	*Dhā*	*Dhā*	*Dhā*	*Dhā*	*Ti*	*Ṭa*
	Dhā	*Dhā*	*Ti*	*Ṭa*	*Dhā*	*Dhā*	*Tin*	*Nā*
	Tā	*Tā*	*Tā*	*Tā*	*Tā*	*Tā*	*Ti*	*Ṭa*
	Dhā	*Dhā*	*Ti*	*Ṭa*	*Dhā*	*Dhā*	*Dhin*	*Nā*
2.	*Dhā*	*Dhā*	ऽ	*Dhā*	*Dhā*	*Dhā*	*Ti*	*Ṭa*
	Dhā	*Dhā*	*Ti*	*Ṭa*	*Dhā*	*Dhā*	*Tin*	*Nā*

	Tā	*Tā*	ऽ	*Tā*	*Tā*	*Tā*	*Ti*	*Ṭ*
	Dhā	*Dhā*	*Ti*	*Ṭa*	*Dhā*	*Dhā*	*Dhin*	*Nā*
	1	2	3	4	5	6	7	8

3.	*Dhā*	ऽ	ऽ	*Dhā*	ऽ	*Dhā*	*Ti*	*Ṭa*
	9	10	11	12	13	14	15	16
	Dhā	*Dhā*	*Ti*	*Ṭa*	*Dhā*	*Dhā*	*Tin*	*Nā*
	Ta	ऽ	ऽ	*Ta*	ऽ	*Ta*	*Ti*	*Ṭa*
	Dhā	*Dhā*	*Ti*	*Ṭa*	*Dhā*	*Dhā*	*Dhin*	*Nā*
	1	2	3	4	5	6	7	8

4.	*Dhā*ऽ	ऽ*Dhā*	*DhāDhā*	*Tiṭ*	*Dhā*ऽ	ऽ*Dhā*	*DhāDhā*	*Tiṭ*
	9	10	11	12	13	14	15	16
	*Dhā*ऽ	ऽ*Dhā*	*DhāDhā*	*Tiṭ*	*DhāDhā*	*Tiṭ*	*DhāDhā*	*Tinnā*
	*Tā*ऽ	ऽ*Tā*	*Tātā*	*Tiṭ*	*Tā*ऽ	ऽ*Tā*	*TāTā*	*Tiṭ*
	*Dhā*ऽ	ऽ*Dhā*	*DhāDhā*	*Tiṭ*	*DhāDhā*	*Tiṭ*	*DhāDhā*	*Dhinnā*
	1	2	3	4	5	6	7	8

5.	*Dhā*ऽ	*DhāDhā*	*TiṭDhā*	*Tiṭ*	*DhāDhā*	*Tiṭ*	*DhāDhā*	*Tinnā*
	9	10	11	12	13	14	15	16
	*Tā*ऽ	*TāTā*	*Tiṭ*ऽ*Tā*	*Tiṭ*	*DhāDhā*	*Tiṭ*	*DhāDhā*	*Dhinnā*
	1	2	3	4	5	6	7	8

6.	*Dhāti*	*Dhā*ऽ*Tiṭ*	*DhāDhā*	*Tiṭ*	*DhāDhā*	*Tiṭ*	*DhāDhā*	*Tinnā*
	9	10	11	12	13	14	15	16
	TāTā	*Tā*ऽ*Tiṭ*	*TāTā*	*Tiṭ*	*DhāDhā*	*Tiṭ*	*DhāDhā*	*Dhinnā*
	1	2	3	4	5	6	7	8

7.	*Dhā*ऽ*Tiṭ*	*Dhā*ऽ	*DhāDhā*	*Tiṭ*	*DhāDhā*	*Tiṭ*	*DhāDhā*	*Tinnā*
	9	10	11	12	13	14	15	16
	*Tā*ऽ*Tiṭ*	*Tā*ऽ	*TāTā*	*Tiṭ*	*DhāDhā*	*Tiṭ*	*DhāDhā*	*Dhinnā*
	1	2	3	4	5	6	7	8

8.	*DhāDhā*	*Tiṭ*	*DhāDhā*	*Tiṭ*	*DhāDhā*	*Tiṭ*	*DhāDhā*	*Tinnā*
	9	10	11	12	13	14	15	16
	Tā Tā	*Tiṭ*	*Tā Tā*	*Tiṭ*	*DhāDhā*	*Tiṭ*	*DhāDhā*	*Dhinnā*
	1	2	3	4	5	6	7	8

9.	*Dhāti*	*Dhāti*	*DhāDhā*	*Tiṭ*	*DhāDhā*	*Tiṭ*	*DhāDhā*	*Tinnā*
	9	10	11	12	13	14	15	16

Tāti	*Tāti*	*TāTā*	*Tiṭ*	*DhāDhā*	*Tiṭ*	*DhāDhā*	*Dhinnā*
1	2	3	4	5	6	7	8

10. *DhāsTiṭ DhāDhā TiṭDhās Dhās Tiṭ DhāDhā Tiṭ DhāDhā Tinnā*

9	10	11	12	13	14	15	16
TāsTiṭ	*TāTā*	*TiṭTās*	*TāsTiṭ*	*DhāDhā*	*Tiṭ*	*DhāDhā*	*Dhinnā*

II. OF TIṬ:

	1	2	3	4
1.	*DhāDhā*	*Tiṭ*	*Tiṭ*	*Tiṭ*
	5	6	7	8
	DhāDhā	*Tiṭ*	*DhāDhā*	*Tinnā*
	9	10	11	12
	Tā Tā	*Tiṭ*	*Tiṭ*	*Tiṭ*
	13	14	15	16
	DhāDhā	*Tiṭ*	*DhāDhā*	*Dhinnā*
2.	*DhāsTiṭ*	*TiṭDhās*	*TiṭDhās*	*Tiṭ*
	DhāDhā	*Tiṭ*	*DhāDhā*	*Tinnā*
	TāsTiṭ	*Tiṭ Tās*	*Tiṭ Dhās*	*Tiṭ*
	DhāDhā	*Tiṭ*	*DhāDhā*	*Dhinnā*
3.	*Dhās Tiṭ*	*DhāsTiṭ*	*TiṭDhās*	*Tiṭ*
	DhāDhā	*Tiṭ*	*DhāDhā*	*Tinnā*
	TāsTiṭ	*TāsTiṭ*	*TiṭsTās*	*Tiṭ*
	DhāDhā	*Tiṭ*	*DhāDhā*	*Dhinnā*
4.	*DhāsTiṭ*	*Dhās Tiṭ*	*Tiṭ Tiṭ*	*DhāsTiṭ*
	DhāDhā	*Tiṭ*	*DhāDhā*	*Tinnā*
	TāsTiṭ	*TāsTiṭ*	*Tiṭ Tiṭ*	*TāsTiṭ*
	DhāDhā	*Tiṭ*	*DhāDhā*	*Dhinnā*
5.	*DhāsTiṭ*	*DhāsTiṭ*	*DhāsTiṭ*	*Tiṭ Dhās*
	DhāDhā	*Tiṭ*	*DhāDhā*	*Tinnā*

	TāsTiṭ	*TāsTiṭ*	*TāsTiṭ*	*Tiṭtās*
	DhāDhā	*Tiṭ*	*DhāDhā*	*Dhinnā*
6.	*DhāsTiṭ*	*Tiṭ Tiṭ*	*Tiṭ Tiṭ*	*Tiṭ Tiṭ*
	DhāDhā	*Tiṭ*	*DhāDhā*	*Tinnā*
	Tās Tiṭ	*Tiṭ Tiṭ*	*Tiṭ Tiṭ*	*Tiṭ Tiṭ*
	DhāDhā	*Tiṭ*	*DhāDhā*	*Dhinnā*
7.	*DhāsDhās*	*Tiṭ Tiṭ*	*Tiṭ Tiṭ*	*Tiṭ Tiṭ*
	DhāDhā	*Tiṭ*	*DhāDhā*	*Tinnā*
	TāsTās	*Tiṭ Tiṭ*	*Tiṭ Tiṭ*	*Tiṭ Tiṭ*
	DhāDhā	*Tiṭ*	*DhāDhā*	*Dhinnā*
8.	*Tiṭ Dhās*	*Tiṭ Tiṭ*	*DhāDhā*	*Tiṭ Tiṭ*
	DhāDhā	*Tiṭ*	*DhāDhā*	*Tinnā*
	Tiṭ Tās	*Tiṭ Tiṭ*	*Tā Tā*	*Tiṭ Tiṭ*
	DhāDhā	*Tiṭ*	*DhāDhā*	*Dhinnā*
9.	*DhāsDhās*	*Tiṭ Tiṭ*	*Tiṭ Dhās*	*Tiṭ Tiṭ*
	DhāDhā	*Tiṭ*	*DhāDhā*	*Tinnā*
	TāsTās	*Tiṭ Tiṭ*	*Tiṭ Dhās*	*Tiṭ Tiṭ*
	DhāDhā	*Tiṭ*	*DhāDhā*	*Dhinnā*
10.	*Tiṭs Dhāti*	*Ta DhāsTiṭ*	*Tiṭ Tiṭ*	*Tiṭ Tiṭ*
	DhāDhā	*Tiṭ*	*DhāDhā*	*Tinnā*
	TiṭsTāti	*Tā Tā sTiṭ*	*Tiṭ Tiṭ*	*Tiṭ Tiṭ*
	DhāDhā	*Tiṭ*	*DhāDhā*	*Dhinnā*

III. OF DHINNA

1.	*DhāDhā*	*Dhinnā*	*Dhinnā*	*Tiṭ*
	DhāDhā	*Tiṭ*	*DhāDhā*	*Tinnā*
	Tā Tā	*Tinnā*	*Tinnā*	*Tiṭ*
	DhāDhā	*Tiṭ*	*DhāDhā*	*Dhinnā*
2.	*DhāsDhin*	*Nādhā*	*Dhinnā*	*Tiṭ*
	DhāDhā	*Tiṭ*	*DhāDhā*	*Tinnā*

	TāSTin	*Nā Tā*	*Tinnā*	*Tiṭ*
	DhāDhā	*Tiṭ*	*DhāDhā*	*Dhinnā*
3.	*Dhin Dhin*	*NāSDhin*	*Dhinnā*	*Tiṭ*
	DhāDhā	*Tiṭ*	*DhāDhā*	*Tinnā*
	Tin Tin	*NāSTin*	*Tinnā*	*Tiṭ*
	DhāDhā	*Tiṭ*	*DhāDhā*	*Dhinnā*
4.	*Tiṭ Dhin*	*NāSTin*	*Dhinnā*	*Tiṭ*
	DhāDhā	*Tiṭ*	*DhāDhā*	*Tinnā*
	Tiṭ Tin	*NāSTin*	*Tinnā*	*Tiṭ*
	DhāDhā	*Tiṭ*	*DhāDhā*	*Dhinnā*
5.	*DhāSDhin*	*NāDhā*	*Dhinnā*	*Dhinnā*
	DhāDhā	*Tiṭ*	*DhāDhā*	*Tinnā*
	TāS Tin	*Nā Tā*	*Tinnā*	*Tinnā*
	DhāDhā	*Tiṭ*	*DhāDhā*	*Dhinnā*
6.	*DhāDhā*	*Dhinnā*	*SDhin*	*NāSTiṭ*
	DhāDhā	*Tiṭ*	*DhāDhā*	*Tinnā*
	Tā Tā	*Tinnā*	*STin*	*NāSTiṭ*
	DhāDhā	*Tiṭ*	*DhāDhā*	*Dhinnā*
7.	*DhāDhā*	*Dhinnā*	*SDhin*	*NāSTiṭ*
	Dhinnā	*Tiṭ*	*DhāDhā*	*Tinnā*
	Tā Tā	*Tinnā*	*STin*	*NāSTiṭ*
	Dhinnā	*Tiṭ*	*DhāDhā*	*Dhinnā*
8.	*DhāSDhin*	*NāSTiṭ*	*DhāDhā*	*Dhinnā*
	DhāDhā	*Tiṭ*	*DhāDhā*	*Tinnā*
	TāSTin	*NāSTiṭ*	*Tā Tā*	*Tinnā*
	DhāDhā	*Tiṭ*	*DhāDhā*	*Dhinnā*
9.	*DhāDhā*	*DhāDhin*	*DhāDhā*	*Dhinnā*
	DhāDhā	*Tiṭ*	*DhāDhā*	*Tinnā*
	Tā Tā	*Tā Tin*	*Tā Tā*	*Tinnā*
	DhāDhā	*Tiṭ*	*DhāDhā*	*Dhinnā*
10.	*Dhin Dhin*	*DhāSTiṭ*	*DhāDhā*	*Dhinnā*
	DhāDhā	*Tiṭ*	*DhāDhā*	*Tinnā*

Tin Tin	*TāSTiṭ*	*Tā Tā*	*Tinnā*
DhāDhā	*Tiṭ*	*DhāDhā*	*Dhinnā*

Ending with the following Tihai

1	2	3	4
DhāDhā	*Tiṭ*	*DhāDhā*	*Dhinnā*
5	6	7	8
DhāS	*DhāDhā*	*Dhinnā*	*DhāS*
9	10	11	
DhāDhā	*Dhinnā*	*DhāS*	

Note:- The above *bol*-pattern comprising (11) beats is to be repeated thrice, so as to convert it into a *Chakradār Tihāi*: (11X3=33).

Hindi script of this *quāyedā* and *paltās* given below:-

कायदा: (मात्रा 16 त्रिताल)

1	2	3	4	5	6	7	8
धा	धा	ति	ट	धा	धा	तिं	ना
9	10	11	12	13	14	15	16
ता	ता	ति	ट	धा	धा	धिं	ना

I. केवल धा के 'पल्टे':

1.	धा	धा	धा	धा	धा	धा	ति	ट
	धा	धा	ति	ट	धा	धा	तिं	ना
	ता	ता	ता	ता	ता	ता	ति	ट
	धा	धा	ति	ट	धा	धा	धिं	ना
2.	धा	धा	S	धा	धा	धा	ति	ट
	धा	धा	ति	ट	धा	धा	तिं	ना
	ता	ता	S	ता	ता	ता	ति	ट
	धा	धा	ति	ट	धा	धा	धिं	ना
3.	धा	S	S	धा	S	धा	ति	ट
	धा	धा	ति	ट	धा	धा	तिं	ना
	ता	S	S	ता	S	ता	ति	ट
	धा	धा	ति	ट	धा	धा	धिं	ना

4.	धाऽ	ऽधा	धाधा	तिट	धाऽ	ऽधा	धाधा	तिट
	धाऽ	ऽधा	धाधा	तिट	धाधा	तिट	धाधा	तिंना
	ताऽ	ऽता	ताता	तिट	ताऽ	ऽता	ताता	तिट
	धाऽ	ऽधा	धाधा	तिट	धाधा	तिट	धाधा	धिंना
5.	धाऽ	धाधा	तिटधा	तिट	धाधा	तिट	धाधा	तिंना
	ताऽ	ताता	तिटऽता	तिट	धाधा	तिट	धाधा	धिंना
6.	धाती	धाऽतिट	धाधा	तिट	धाधा	तिट	धाधा	तिंना
	ताता	ताऽतिट	ताता	तिट	धाधा	तिट	धाधा	धिंना
7.	धाऽतिट	धाऽ	धाधा	तिट	धाधा	तिट	धाधा	तिंना
	ताऽतिट	ताऽ	ताता	तिट	धाधा	तिट	धाधा	धिंना
8.	धाधा	तिट	धाधा	तिट	धाधा	तिट	धाधा	तिंना
	ताता	तिट	ताता	तिट	धाधा	तिट	धाधा	धिंना
9.	धाती	धाती	धाधा	तिट	धाधा	तिट	धाधा	तिंना
	ताती	ताती	ताता	तिट	धाधा	तिट	धाधा	धिंना
10.	धाऽतिट	धाधा	तिटधाऽ	धाऽतिट	धाधा	तिट	धाधा	तिंना
	ताऽतिट	ताता	तिटताऽ	ताऽतिट	धाधा	तिट	धाधा	धिंना

II. केवल तिट के पल्टे:-

1.	धाधा	तिट	तिट	तिट	धाधा	तिट	धाधा	तिंना
	ताता	तिट	तिट	तिट	धाधा	तिट	धाधा	धिंना
2.	धाऽतिट	तिटधाऽ	तिटधाऽ	तिट	धाधा	तिट	धाधा	तिंना
	ताऽतिट	तिटताऽ	तिटधाऽ	तिट	धाधा	तिट	धाधा	धिंना
3.	धाऽतिट	धाऽतिट	तिटधाऽ	तिट	धाधा	तिट	धाधा	तिंना
	ताऽतिट	ताऽतिट	तिटऽताऽ	तिट	धाधा	तिट	धाधा	धिंना
4.	धाऽतिट	धाऽतिट	तिटतिट	धाऽतिट	धाधा	तिट	धाधा	तिंना
	ताऽतिट	ताऽतिट	तिटतिट	ताऽतिट	धाधा	तिट	धाधा	धिंना
5.	धाऽतिट	धाऽतिट	धाऽतिट	तिटधाऽ	धाधा	तिट	धाधा	तिंना
	ताऽतिट	ताऽतिट	ताऽतिट	तिटताऽ	धाधा	तिट	धाधा	धिंना
6.	धाऽतिट	तिटतिट	तिटतिट	तिटतिट	धाधा	तिट	धाधा	तिंना
	ताऽतिट	तिटतिट	तिटतिट	तिटतिट	धाधा	तिट	धाधा	धिंना
7.	धाऽधाऽ	तिटतिट	तिटतिट	तिटतिट	धाधा	तिट	धाधा	तिंना
	ताऽताऽ	तिटतिट	तिटतिट	तिटतिट	धाधा	तिट	धाधा	धिंना

8.	तिटधाऽ	तिटतिट	धाधा	तिटतिट	धाधा	तिट	धाधा	तिंना
	तिटताऽ	तिटतिट	ताता	तिटतिट	धाधा	तिट	धाधा	धिंना
9.	धाऽधाऽ	तिटतिट	तिटधाऽ	तिटतिट	धाधा	तिट	धाधा	तिंना
	ताऽताऽ	तिटतिट	तिटधाऽ	तिटतिट	धाधा	तिट	धाधा	धिंना
10.	तिटऽधाती	ताधाऽतिट	तिटतिट	तिटतिट	धाधा	तिट	धाधा	तिंना
	तिटऽताती	ताताऽतिट	तिटतिट	तिटतिट	धाधा	तिट	धाधा	धिंना

III. केवल धिंना के पल्टे:-

1.	धाधा	धिंना	धिन्ना	तिट	धाधा	तिट	धाधा	तिंना
	ताता	तिंना	तिंना	तिट	धाधा	तिट	धाधा	धिंना
2.	धाऽधिन	नाधा	धिंना	तिट	धाधा	तिट	धाधा	तिंना
	ताऽतिन	नाता	तिंना	तिट	धाधा	तिट	धाधा	धिंना
3.	धिनधिन	नाऽधिन	धिंना	तिट	धाधा	तिट	धाधा	तिंना
	तिनतिन	नाऽतिन	तिंना	तिट	धाधा	तिट	धाधा	धिंना
4.	तिटधिन	नाऽतिन	धिंना	तिट	धाधा	तिट	धाधा	तिंना
	तिटतिन	नाऽतिन	तिंना	तिट	धाधा	तिट	धाधा	धिंना
5.	धाऽधिं	नाधा	धिंना	धिंना	धाधा	तिट	धाधा	तिंना
	ताऽतिं	नाता	तिंना	तिंना	धाधा	तिट	धाधा	धिंना
6.	धाधा	धिंना	ऽधिन	नाऽतिट	धाधा	तिट	धाधा	तिंना
	ताता	तिंना	ऽतिन	नाऽतिट	धाधा	तिट	धाधा	धिंना
7.	धाधा	धिंना	ऽधिन	नाऽतिट	धिन्ना	तिट	धाधा	तिंना
	ताता	तिंना	ऽतिन	नाऽतिट	धिंना	तिट	धाधा	धिंना
8.	धाऽधिंन	नाऽतिट	धाधा	धिंना	धाधा	तिट	धाधा	तिंना
	ताऽतिन	नाऽतिट	ताता	तिंना	धाधा	तिट	धाधा	धिंना
9.	धाधा	धाधिं	धाधा	धिंना	धाधा	तिट	धाधा	तिंना
	ताता	तातिं	ताता	तिंना	धाधा	तिट	धाधा	धिंना
10.	धिंधिं	धाऽतिट	धाधा	धिंना	धाधा	तिट	धाधा	तिंना
	तिंतिं	ताऽतिट	ताता	तिंना	धाधा	तिट	धाधा	धिंना

निम्नलिखित तिहाई द्वारा सम्पन्न:- **(To be concluded with the following *tihāī*)**

1	2	3	4	5	6
धाधा	तिट	धाधा	धिंना	धाऽ	धाधा

7	8	9	10	11
धिंना	धाऽ	धाधा	धिंना	धाऽ

ऊपर लिखी हुई बोलों की श्रृंखला 11 मात्राओं की है; तीन बार बजाने से यह चक्रदार का रूप धारण कर लेगी **(11 X 3 =33).**

(The collocation of the above mentioned mnemonics occupies eleven beats. If it is played thrice, it will come to wear the form of a *chakradār*)

These *paltās* (or orderly variations), however, are not the only ones that our *quāyedās* and *relās* admit of. Their number is (in principle) infinite. But the essential requirement in every case is that the *paltā* resorted to should not merely be an intricate, but a tuneful collocation, involving winsome *layakāri* and revealing a feeling for design. Mere elongation of a *paltā* by just repeating a single alphabet many times will only be a mathematical exercise, though the *sama* may well be reached with split second accuracy. Here is an example of an utterly unaesthetic *paltā* of 32 beats.

DhāDhā Tiṭ Tiṭ Tiṭ Tiṭ Tiṭ Tiṭ Tiṭ Tiṭ Tiṭ
Tiṭ Tiṭ Dhā Dhā Tiṭ Dhā Dhā Tinnā
Tā Tā Tiṭ Tiṭ Tiṭ Tiṭ Tiṭ Tiṭ Tiṭ Tiṭ Tiṭ
Tiṭ Tiṭ DhāDhā Tiṭ DhāDhā Dhinnā
DhāDhā Tiṭ Tiṭ Tiṭ Tiṭ Tiṭ Tiṭ Tiṭ Tiṭ Tiṭ
Tiṭ Tiṭ Dhā Dhā Tiṭ DhāDhā Tinnā
Tā Tā Tiṭ Tiṭ Tiṭ Tiṭ Tiṭ Tiṭ Tiṭ Tiṭ Tiṭ
Tiṭ Tiṭ DhāDhā Tiṭ DhāDhā Dhinnā

धाधा तिट तिट तिट तिट तिट तिट तिट तिट तिट
तिट तिट धा धा तिट धा धा तिन्ना
ताता तिट तिट तिट तिट तिट तिट तिट तिट तिट
तिट तिट धाधा तिट धाधा धिंना

धाधा	तिट	तिट	तिट	तिट	तिट	तिट	तिट	तिट	तिट
तिट	तिट	धा	धा	तिट	धाधा	तिन्ना			
ताता	तिट	तिट	तिट	तिट	तिट	तिट	तिट	तिट	तिट
तिट	तिट	धाधा	तिट	धाधा	धिन्ना				

3

Reyāz or the Discipline of Practice

It is, however, not enough to be told how the basic alphabets of tablā rhythm are to be played. One has to *do* it on one's own, and repeatedly. Practice is, in fact, as important and essential for tablā playing as for any other performing art. To achieve and maintain a good standard the player has to abide by certain technical norms, and to have a positive attitude, along with a professional approach in respect of earnestness. This applies specially to those who wish to take up tablā playing as a career. Those who resort to it as a mere hobby can afford to be irregular in *reyāz;* but then they will not be able to taste the true aesthetic riches of the art.

Norms of Practice

There are mainly two ways to do *reyāz.* The first is that of practising without having any true understanding of the inherent values of the various compositions. The second is to practise with a proper grasp of their intrinsic character and technique of playing.

There is no fixed time limit for practice. It all depends on how much time one can spare for the purpose; but, obviously, the greater the effort one puts in, the richer will be the gains. As a rule, it is desirable to practise at a fixed time and possibly at the same place. This would make for greater regularity and steadfastness, if indirectly. But if during the course of practice one feels exhausted, it would be good to relax and stop for a while and then begin again with renewed vigour and tenacity. I have personally seen many a student practising incessantly in spite of being completely exhausted, simply because their teacher had asked them to just keep going. Such a *guru* and such a slavish obedience to whatever he enjoins are both unhelpful to progress.

Further, select a lonely spot for practice, so as to avoid being disturbed. So regulate conditions that no one else is present where you are practising. Your aim, as you do *reyāz,* is to remove your defects as a player; you have to be self-critical; and the presence of others will tend to inhibit this attitude. You may feel like performing *for them,* instead of minding *your own* defects. It is here noteworthy that the past masters would prefer to practise at night and at lonely places like a cemetery, so as to avoid all disturbance. What is more, one should never practice with a soft touch. On the contrary, it should be done with powerful strokes, because thus alone can one increase the stamina of fingers. Further, a powerful stroke produces a sound that is clearly audible, and so one can easily check whether the desired *bol* is being correctly produced. It would therefore help if, for the purpose of practice, you choose a tablā having a broad 'mouth,' for such a drum naturally produces deep sounds. And if one is able to produce *bol*s at such a tablā winsomely, playing at a tablā which is tuned to some *swara* in the *taar saptak* (upper register) will easily provide sweet sounding syllables.

To begin with, however, one has to pick softer compositions like *peshkār*s and *quāyedā*s. This will enable the tyro to give a shapely look to the hands and nimbleness to fingers as they are being made to work. Every finger will get the exercise it needs exactly as a vocalist has to steady his voice at each individual *swara* before proceeding further.

However, individual *bol*s are not the only objects of *reyāz*. One has to practise phrases and full compositions as well. Here, the best way to achieve clarity, shapeliness and due sonority in playing is to correctly divide a whole composition into shapely segments, practise each one of them intensively, and only then conjoin them to produce the full form of the composition. Couple the first segment with the second, then *both together* with the third segment, and so on. And try to play the whole composition at one go only when you have done the piecemeal work properly. But let me illustrate the point with the help of an example. Take the following *quāyedā*, set in *tritāla*, for instance.

1	2	3	4	5	6	7	8
Dhāti	*Dhāge*	*Nadhā*	*Tiṭkiṭ*	*Dhāti*	*Dhāge*	*Tinnā*	*Kinā*
9	10	11	12	13	14	15	16
Tāti	*Tāke*	*Nadhā*	*Tiṭkiṭ*	*Dhāti*	*Dhāge*	*Dhinnā*	*Ginā*

Now, this is how I would like the learner to proceed:

First practice only *Dhāti* a number of times. Then take up *Dhāge* and play it repeatedly. When the production of this *bol, Dhāge*, begins to satisfy you, go ahead and combine both *Dhāti* and *Dhāge*, and play them repeatedly as one. Next, practise *Nadhā* and *Tiṭkiṭ* with the same gradualness — that is, first, individually and then jointly; and keep following the same manner in practising the remaining *bols*, until you feel empowered to play the whole composition as a singleness. If you regulate your *reyāz* thus, the results will be extremely gratifying.

Fixation of pace

Our old masters have composed thousands of compositions that are to be practised and played at *specific* speeds or gradations of *laya*. Not every *bol* has to be played at one and the same speed. If this detail in respect of specificity is not kept in mind, the results will be frustrating for the player. To take a simple parallel, *yogāsanas* cannot be done as quickly as a wrestler's दंड़ and बैठक. To turn, again, to rhythm, a *peshkār* can never be practised and played at a fast pace, simply because it builds upon such difficult tufts of alphabets that the fingers will never be able to play them very nimbly. The present trend of quite a few players today is to try to play all compositions at top speed, which just cannot be done without caricaturing the form of the compositions and throwing clarity to the winds. Sheer speed, without clear execution and correct sonority of *bols*, is simply a random physical exercise, and not the evocation of articulate rhythmic designs.

The art of tablā playing is a part of *sangeet;* and so the basic norm of agreeableness to the ear has to be followed here too. Feeling for design is also a basic requirement here, as in the case of any other art. And if one has a penchant for fast playing, let him try some such *quāyedās* — and *relās*, of course — which really admit of pacy playing.

Compositions like *Tihāīs*, *Chakkradārs*, *Ṭukḍās*, *Tripallis* and *Fard* can all be played pretty quickly without any loss of design or clarity. But they are not meant for the earlier stages of *reyāz*.

Speed Variation

Basically and essentially, in the initial stages of learning each phrase and composition has to be practised at a very slow speed, taking good care to see that every alphabet or group of *bols* provides a perfect sonority, likeable to the player himself, thus giving hope and encouragement for further practice. The next step should be to increase the speed gradually; and then to try to practise the chosen composition at a manageably fast pace. If a sudden burst of speed is provided to *bols* without feeling at ease even at a lower pace, the results may be disappointing. So the most sensible approach, I repeat, is to be patient and gradual in increasing the pace of practice, and to avoid being too enthusiastic. Prolong the repetition of every phrase, as far as you can, at slow tempo, taking care for every essential aspect of good tablā playing, namely, steadiness of *laya*, neat 'cutting' of *bols* and preservation of shape or design. All this, however, has to be impressed upon the pupil by his personal teacher. An indiscriminate and sweeping command to just go on practising is of no avail here. Adherence to the set principles of practice is absolutely essential.

Reyāz and changes in breathing

It is commonly observed that during practice time, even after a short spell, a tablā player appears completely exhausted and perspires profusely. This is true even of some of the established tablā artists. In my considered view, this is attributable to the following factors:

1. The atmosphere at the place of practice may not be congenial. It may be humid or stuffy.
2. The fearsome thought that one has been asked to "accompany" a very great instrumentalist in near future.
3. Lack of the requisite amount of methodical practice in the way I have already indicated.

4. Inability to stabilize and regulate *laya*, maybe because of temperamental fickleness.

5. Awkwardness of *baithak* or the sitting posture.

Besides the above mentioned factors, the most important reason of easy exhaustion is lack of equilibrium between breathing and movement of hands. During a practice session breathing should just keep steady; it should never follow the changing pace of hand movements. Generally, while doing *reyāz*, a tablā player quickens his breathing too as the playing gathers speed. This is wrong.

I have always been careful in this respect and so have never felt exhausted, neither during practice nor while "accompanying" any artist in long sessions of music. (I mention this fact not by way of self-praise, but simply as an illustration of the point I am trying to make). Generally, when a sitar or sarod player plays the *jhālā* (during the course of *gat*-playing) — which follows a terrific pace (as a rule) — an accompanist, who is not aware of what I have said about the relation of breathing to playing, tends to breathe as hurriedly as the pace of the *jhālā*; so loses control over finger movements; and soon gets exhausted. The important point here is that even during his daily *reyāz* he should try to control breathing properly in *drut* playing. All this, I repeat, has to be impressed upon his mind by his teacher.

Disciplined Living and a Good Health

Allied to what I have just said is the fact that a disciplined life style and good health are at least as essential for a tablā artist as the possession of a rich repertoire of compositions. We may not expect him to become a wrestler, but the very ability to continue *reyāz* in a regular way calls for a reasonably good health. However, *reyāz* too is itself a form of exercise making for greater stamina. At the same time, as has been generally observed, if one goes on practising for long sessions, day in and day out — and say, for ten to twelve hours everyday — without taking care of proper diet, adequate rest, and physical exercise *involving the whole body*, only his hands and fingers will grow stronger, impoverishing general health, and ultimately affecting *reyāz* too, adversely.

Sillā or Chillā

Both these words have the same meaning and significance. In my view, the dominant way of pronouncing the word is as *Chillā*. But players in the neighbourhood of Lucknow (capital of Uttar Pradesh) pronounce the word as *Sillā*. Artists around the national capital (Delhi) pronounce it as *Chillā*. Anyway, the word means those forty days of lent when the religious minded people in India retire to some secluded place, or to a mosque, and engage themselves in fasting and divine worship. For tablā players, however, a *chillā* means a period of forty days reserved for rigorous *reyāz*. The idea is simply to pick some days for very regular practice. What is aimed at is commitment and perseverance. But, I hasten to add, undertaking *chillā*s is not in itself enough. One has to practise with a proper understanding of all the factors that make for good tablā playing which, I repeat, are: equable *laya*, articulateness of playing, proper distribution of emphases and segments, and overall shapeliness of the compositions played. Incidentally, *chillā*s help only the established tablā players who have taken up this art as a profession, and are not meant for, and may even do some harm to beginners.

Selective Practice

Further, not every composition that one knows is to be practised every day. One has to be intelligently selective in this regard. If a player can attain perfect command over a select bunch of compositions, he will find it easier to deal with other compositions. The trouble is that every new entrant in this field aspires to reach the top within a short time. This is perhaps a natural human failing, specially in the case of those who are young, and so full of energy and enthusiasm. But patience is as necessary here as in any other field of human endeavour. What is more, patience is at once an exercise in self-control *without which it is impossible to keep one's laya steady* in actual playing. But I know that life has become a bit too busy for most of us, and that it may be difficult for one to spare long hours for practice. So I may emphasize, once again, the need for a judicious selection of what and how much one can play on different days.

Importance of relaxation

Some periods of relaxation are just as necessary, not only to remedy fatigue, but to counter the possibility of developing aversion for what is done too much. So one must discontinue *reyāz* completely for one day in every fortnight, if not in every week. During such intermissions, forget that you ever played tablā and engage yourself in other interesting activities; and then, on the very next day, re-start your practice with renewed vigour and purposiveness. Be it noted that such days of willed abstention from practice are not a waste of time. The subconscious mind keeps working, and makes for a deeper assimilation of what one has been practising in sessions of *reyāz*. Whatever I have said here, in this para, is entirely based on my personal experience as an active tablā player and teacher for long years.

A Dilemma in reyāz

Finally, let me also point out the possibility of a difficult situation that may arise during the course of *reyāz*. It may be that one's practice is being hampered by some intrinsic defect in what has been taught to him and in what precise way. In such a situation, the pupil is faced with a dilemma. On the one hand, he cannot openly dare to doubt the integrity or efficiency of his *guru*. On the other hand, he cannot abjure his *reyāz*, if he is at all fond of the art. So only two ways are open to him. He may either find out the defect himself through trial and error; or, in case the *guru* is purposely withholding some secret relating to the *nikā*s or execution of some syllables, some extra financial incentive may be given to him.

If, even after undergoing sufficient practice, you feel that your fingers get blocked at some point of execution, take it for granted that you are following the incorrect path of practice. You should immediately check it with your mentor. If his verbal suggestions do not help, just *listen* to your *guru*, as many times as possible, when he is actually *playing* the compositions you already know. There is often some subtle difference between what and how the *guru teaches* and the way he himself *plays* the same composition. So one would do well to listen to the actual playing of the teacher as often and as carefully as possible; and to note, in particular, if he makes any changes in the use of fingers and of touching points at the *puḍi* while raising the playing of the selfsame composition to a quicker pace. Meticulous attention to how exactly the *guru* himself *plays* may indeed be more necessary, at times, than to his *verbal instructions*. After all, rhythm is essentially a performing art, though it also makes heavy demands on one's personal judgement, patience and perseverance, and calls for frequent consultation with the teacher.

4

Vocabulary of Tablā Rhythm

FROM *how to practise* we may now turn to *what to practise*, that is, to the principal compositions that make a standard tablā recital. Collectively, they may well be called the vocabulary of tablā rhythm because they represent the range of its *set* artistic or stylistic forms and techniques, as against those which may be *improvised* on the spur of the moment by a tablā player of exceptional creative ability. The improvised ones are not my concern in the present chapter, partly because they are infinite in principle. I have to confine myself to those regular ones which are common to almost every gharānā (family-school) of tablā playing, if not identically in respect of auditory quality, syllabic filling, and ways of producing the constituent *bol*s.

Peshkār

Generally, this word designates the first or opening composition played in a solo recital. It is a pretty complicated pattern comprising all the tablā *akṣara*s (alphabets), and it is a little longer than the basic structure of an average *quāyedā*. In accordance with our traditional practice of rhythm, a *peshkār* has to be played at a slow pace, so that the fingers may get a little enlivened for the proper execution of the alphabets that make the language of Hindustani rhythm. In other words, it is a kind of artistic warm-up for what is to follow. However, it is not merely physical exercise. The truth rather is that a *peshkār* also serves the purpose of showing (to the player himself and listeners alike) how *laya* admits of controlled variations and so makes for diverse rhythmic designs, though of course with the aid of *bol*s. However, it is only the Delhi and Ajrāḍā gharānās, not the *poorab* (or eastern) ones, that take pains to bring out the full aesthetic potential of a *peshkār*.

The requirement that a *peskhār* has to *open* a solo tablā recital is suggested by its very meaning as a word. Its first segment, *pesh* means 'to present'; and the second one, *kār*, means a maker, as in such better known words as *kalākār, shilpkār*. So the complete word, *peshkār*, may be taken to mean, if a little loosely, that pattern which opens a presentation of tablā playing for an interested audience. To turn to the Hindi idiom, a *peshkār* signals (the beginning of) a प्रस्तुति or presentation. However, another interpretation, a rather amusing one, which is freely bandied about in some circles, can also be put on the word. In the civil law courts of Uttar Pradesh, *peshkār* is the designation that is extended to a person, an employee, who sits outside the courts to collect detailed reports of cases filed by individuals, *as preparatory to* subsequent, expert attention by lawyers. Here, again, the word suggests priority in order. Perhaps *the older name* of what later came to be called *peshkār* — namely, *farshbandi* — is preferable; and I can explain why I say so. The word, *farsh*, means *floor*, or the foundational surface on which a building stands; and in so far as the pattern (now commonly) called *peshkār* enables the player himself to get attuned with the *laya* chosen, *and* also serves as a warm-up of the fingers for the work to follow, it may truly be said to lay the foundation of the whole recital, and so *farshbandi*. It would here be relevant to point out that somewhat similar language is also used in the field of khayāl-singing. Here, we speak of *sthāyi-jamānā*, or *establishing* the first line (of the song) which is, in a way, the anchor of the whole recital. Be that as it may, in olden days a player who did not begin his recital with a *peshkār* was dubbed by the masters, disparagingly, as *koorh* or ill-informed.

Peshkār-quāyedā

Further, according to the gharānās I have specially in mind, a *peshkār* is to be followed immediately by a particular type of *quāyedā* called *peshkār-quāyedā*, which is one of the many kinds of *quāyedā*s that distinguish the art of solo tablā playing. There is a reason why this particular *quāyedā* is called what it is. The point is that it is made to build upon some tufts of alphabets which occur in the format of the *peshkār* itself. It of course admits of quite a few permutations. But, as is the norm in respect of other *quāyedās*, only the basic *bols* of the *quāyedā* are used varyingly. Yet, the other rules which determine *quāyedās* in general do not have to be followed conservatively in playing a *peshkār-quāyedā*. It can, in fact, be more beautifully and profusely permuted (than other *quāyedās*) because the main structure of the *peshkār* includes almost all the alphabets which make the language of tablā. Further, every *peshkār-quāyedā* comprises two lines. The first one starts from *sama* and ends at *khāli* (the offbeat); the second one begins from *khāli* and ends at the *sama*. Therefore, the whole pattern looks segmented in an orderly way. But there is something distinctive too about this *quāyedā*. It admits of pretty pacy playing, quite unlike a *peshkār* which has to wear a reposeful look on the whole. Further, not only in respect of its form and content, but also in its manner of playing, this *quāyedā* differs from to gharānā to gharānā. There are no rigid guidelines to determine its playing.

Quāyedā

As we know, this word directly means rule or system. In the region of solo tablā too, the playing of a *quāyedā* is a very methodical matter. Its structure comprises two lines, roughly in the way of a couplet. The first line or segment starts from the *sama* and ends at *khāli*, while the second one takes off from the *khāli* and terminates at the *sama*. Every *quāyedā* is named after the main alphabet which occurs frequently and prominently in its specific structure. Thus, we have *quāyedās* of तिट, तिरकिट, धिनगिन, धिरधिर and other mnemonics. They all, of course, admit of considerable improvisation, but the *paltās* (or variations) are subject to a clear restriction. No such अक्षर (or alphabet) can be included in the creative variations as is not to be found in the basic composition.

Further, the *paltās* have to follow a particular sequence. The first permutation has to build upon the opening alphabet of the composition; the next variation, on the second *akṣara*; and so on. What is more, the terminal syllables of the two segments have to rhyme, without being identical. Thus, if the last word of the first line is *tinā kinā* (तिना किना), the terminal *bol* of the second line has to be *dhinā ginā* (धिना गिना).

Many different kinds of *quāyedās* have been created by our past masters. Some are set to *chatusra* and *tisra jāti*s and others, to the *misra jāti*. Some are short, but quite a few others are longer in range. It is noteworthy that whereas some *quāyedās* sound good at *madhya laya*, others appear very tuneful at a fast pace, provided they are played with clarity and due regard for accentuation, intervening moments of quiet, and overall design. But whatever be the *quāyedās* which are picked for presentation, if they do not figure at all in the playing, the total recital will be said to be lacking in method and substance by the knowledgeable.

Relā

Structurally, a *relā* (रेला) appears to be similar to a *quāyedā*. The two are also roughly equal in length. But they differ in respect of pace. A *relā* is always played *at a terrific speed*; at a slow pace, it does not sound pleasing to the ear; and it admits of pretty fluent playing because only a *single alphabet* is here repeated freely in the basic composition. In virtue of these two factors, the overall look of a *relā* is that of gently undulating waves. Its playing, I may add, is by no means easy. It calls for perfect mastery in the use of fingers, and agility of both hands; otherwise, the requisite smoothness of the flow of *bol*s may tend to look arrested at places, even before the completion of the pattern. A measure of improvisation is also possible here.

Relā-playing is also an unavoidable part of a solo performance; but besides being used to contribute alacrity to a solo recital, *relās* are freely played also in providing accompaniment to instrumental music. When a sitar or sarod player begins playing what is called *jhālā*, a tablā player can very usefully resort to *relās*; and thereby appear quite fluent in 'accompaniment' *without straining himself overmuch*. This is aided by the fact that the norms of *relā* playing are not rigid.

Ṭukḍā

Speaking quite generally, a *tukḍā* (टुकड़ा) is a segment or piece of a whole. In the region of rhythm, however, the word signifies not *any* piece, but such a segment segregated from some lengthy *paran* of pakhāwaj as has yet been invested with a relative wholeness of its own. Masters of old preferred to pick some simple and soft tuft of alphabets appearing in pakhāwaj *paran*s and then to work creatively on the chosen syllabic complex, producing brief patterns of *bol*s, set in some easily manageable *tāla*-cycles and ending with a *tihāī* (तिहाई). In so far as a *tihāī* in rhythm generally wears a look of self-*completion* (of a complex of three identical segments), what is *called* a *tukḍā* does not *appear* to be a mere fragment, because of the terminal *tihāyī*. In accordance with the way I have just explained, a good number of *ṭukḍā*s, having a measure of wholeness and meant to be played at different *laya*s, were composed; and the total repertoire of compositions was thus substantially enriched. *Ṭukḍā*s, I may add, can be played, with advantage, in providing both accompaniment and solo recitals.

Interestingly, during the days of Nawābs and Mahārājās many musical duels were arranged between tablā and pakhāwaj players, simply to provide entertainment for the royal masters and their courtiers. In most of such duels the tablā players would generally lose, because they were not able to produce adequate parallels of the volley of lengthy, intricate and *high-sounding paran*s played by the *pakhāwajee*s (that is, pakhāwaj players). The patterns of pakhāwaj — generally loud, deep and therefore readily impressive — would utterly eclipse the soft and dainty *quāyedā*s produced out of the *kinār* of the (right) tablā. Hence, the tablā Ustads, unwilling to be easily vanquished, took to a stratagem. They picked the softer alphabets from *paran*s, wove them into some *open-bol ṭukḍā*s, and produced many types of exquisitely beautiful patterns of beady clarity, as a fitting rejoinder to pakhāwaj-players. The tablā Ustads also took extra care to put some power-packed *tihāī* at the end of each *tukḍā*, and thus managed to hold out against the pakhāwaj players, so to say.

Gat

The word *gat* is an abbreviation of *gati* (गति) which means movement. In tablā playing, however, a *gat* is a fixed and generally brief composition of *bol*s, moving at a particular pace, but never ending with *tihāī*. It does not admit of any improvisation. So it differs from both *quāyedās* and *relās*. What is more, a *gat* is always composed of pure tablā *bols*; it eschews the pakhāwaj syllables; and so the *kinār bols* are here seen to dominate. Surprising though it may seem, most of the tablā players of today do not observe, perhaps because they do not know, the difference between a *gat* and *a tukḍā*. A careful look at the traditional repertoire of tablā patterns will easily bear out the difference I am talking of. A *gat* ends quietly, so to say, without a specific *āmad*, that is, without a distinct, self-evolving access to the *sama* which is shorter in range than a *tukḍā*. What is striking about it is rather the grace of its undulating movement. Our rhythm is indeed remarkable not merely for its syllabic filling and variations of pace, but for the ever newer look of the ways it runs, punctuated with due pauses and emphases.

Kinds of gat

Even *gats* differ mutually, in kind. A *tripalli gat* is so called because it repeats an identical bunch of *bols* thrice, in three different *jātis* of *laya* (idioms of aesthetic pace). Similarly, a *chaupalli gat* builds upon similar repetition of the selfsame complex of syllables at four different paces; and a *panchpalli gat* does the same in five *jātis* of *laya*. The suffix *palli* here means one cycle of the basic composition.

Very few tablā players are seen to play a *dupalli gat*. This is so because this *gat* repeats an identical bunch of *bols* only twice, in just two *jātis* of *laya*; and is therefore a very short piece. What is more, it does not provide any impressive climax to the whole pattern. Other *pallis* are more frequently played, just because they end climactically and are designed in a way which is akin to a *tihāī*. *Dupalli gats* are also quite limited in number, and are known to only a few tablā players.

There is yet another kind of *gat* which is called: *do moonh ki gat:* (दो मुंह की गत). Literally, it means a pattern having two similar 'mouths.' It indeed begins and ends with an identical group of *bols*. In all probability, the thought of composing such *gats* arose from observation of a 'she-snake' which does not have a tail at all, but has two similar mouths at both ends. As we know, this type of snake is called 'dumui' (दुमुई).

It is noteworthy that not every *gat* ends exactly *at* the *sama*. Some are made to complete themselves designedly a little before the *sama* proper. Such *gat*s are called *āsama*. They are, by and large, similar to other types of *gat*s. What yet distinguishes them, I repeat, is the device of making them end at the 16th beat, that is, just before the *sama* (focal beat) which is indicated only by a perfectly timed nod — or by just saying *ā* (आ) — at the *sama*-instant. For unknown reasons, very few *gat*s of this kind have been composed by the gharānā-leaders. Anyway, two points about it are noteworthy. First, such a *gat* is played at a very fast pace. This is necessary for minimizing the time interval between the moment where the *gat* is made to end and the proper *sama*-instant. The reason for this is that if the gap betwen the two is *not minimally brief* the listener's imagination may not be able to bridge it easily, and the designed avoidance of the *sama*-instant by the end of the *gat* as played may appear as an involuntary falling-short of the focal beat, and so a lapse. Second, the *gat* has to be so well designed that it may appear to be heading towards the *sama* by virtue of its own inner dynamics. Only then will the *rasika* (or the knowledgeable listener) be able to sense that the actual *sama* has been suggested by the very act of avoiding it designedly, say, because of the operation of the Gestalt law of coercive design or common destiny.

Tihāī

But there are such devices too in our rhythmic system as enable even the average *rasika* to anticipate and identify the advent of *sama* quite easily. One of these is *tihāī*. A simple *tihāī* is a short composition which so repeats a brief pattern *thrice* that the last beat of the third segment falls immaculately at the *sama* (or the focal beat) of the *ṭhekā*. It is of two main kinds : *bedam* (बेदम or non-intervallic, incessant), and *damdār* (दमदार), that is, punctuated with some moments of quiet or breathing space. In the former, no gap is left between any two segments; but in the latter, a measured interval *is* kept between them. In the case of both kinds, however, the pattern's access to the *sama* has to be so designed that the latter (or the *sama*) may appear as the true climax, and not as just a tame ending of the whole passage. There is yet another type of *tihāī*, which is called *chakradār-tihāī*. It is a somewhat complicated arrangement of *bols*, and is longer in range than the ones I have just spoken of. It may even cover quite a few rounds of the tāla being played, their precise number depending on the specific *laya* chosen. The alphabets which go to make a *chakradār tihāī* — variously called *chakradār, chakradār-tukḍā*, and *chakradār gat* or *toḍā* by players from different gharānās — are quite diverse. Simple *tihāī*s serve to lend a little embellishment to 'accompaniment,' while the *chakradār* ones are meant to lend a measure of additional extent and richness to a solo performance. As a rule, the *chakradār*s are played at a fast pace, and they generally provide a climactic finale to a solo recital.

Every gharānā possesses a good number of *chakradār ṭukḍā*s in its repertoire. But, in this one respect, the Farrukhabad gharānā seems to be the richest. Maestros of other gharānās prefer to focus on other types of compositions in their solo recitals.

Mukhḍā/Mohrā

Both these patterns are almost equal in range. They are very small compositions meant only to provide a beautiful and shapely access to the *sama*. Their use in "accompaniment" is sparing. The alphabets used are soft and simple in either case. Yet the two can be distinguished. First, quite unlike a *mohrā*, a *mukhḍā* necessarily ends with a *tihāī*. Second, a *mohrā* is commonly played *before* the actual *ṭhekā*. It rises up from some preceding beat and ends at the first beat or *sama*. The purpose here is simply to draw listeners' attention to the tāla chosen, invitingly. A *mukhḍā* can arise from any beat of (or in) the *ṭhekā* and in the process provide access to the *sama*; but, I repeat, it has to end with a composite *tihāī*. Both, however, can at times be used in providing accompaniment to a vocal recital.

Fard

This is a rare kind of composition, very complicated in both structure and execution. Its actual playing requires an uncanny ability to get mentally adapted to, and to execute variegated tufts of rhythmic syllables, because the *jāti*s of *laya* here change quite abruptly. What is needed in playing this passage of rhythm is not only the ability to mark and follow the *mātrās* accurately, but an intuitive grasp of the idiom (or अन्दाज़) of the various paces and of their reciprocal relationship.

Sometimes, when a composer feels uncertain as to what precise *bols* are to be put in the run of a pattern, he just inserts any syllables that come to his mind, merely on instinct, without of course straying from accuracy in attainment of *sama*. What is thus created without any patient forethought, and without consciously following any set rules that generally determine the disposition of *bols* — except, of course, the cardinal requirement of reaching the *sama* accurately — is called a *fard*.

Normally, a *fard* ends with the compound alphabet '*dhir dhir kiṭ dhā*' (धिरधिरकिटधा). This, however, is not a very binding requirement.

Laggi and Laḍi

These are two smallest compositions in the realm of tablā playing. Both are used mainly in accompanying the lighter forms of vocal music such as *ṭhumrīs*, *ghazals*, and *bhajans*. They have no place in *solo* playing of quality. *Laggi* has been devised on the analogy of a long bamboo which is thick at the root and thin at the end. Its playing indeed begins with a big bang, and gradually tapers in resonance as it moves towards its end. A *laḍi*, when it is played properly, appears to be similar to what it literally means as a word; in other words, it has the look of a chain of similar, shapely beady *bols*, skilfully interwoven. The resonance of *bols* here *does not vary* in intensity in the course of playing which just repeats a very small group of mnemonics.

Misl

In respect of *misl*, however, I cannot make any such definite remark. I can only make a tentative suggestion, say, as follows. The word *misl* seems to be related to *misāl* which means *illustration*; and what is called *misl* in rhythm surely provides *instances* of how the *ṭhekā* itself admits of variations in the manner of playing. The Benares gharānā players seem to attach much importance to this simple display of one's hold over rhythm. But tablā players of other family-schools (gharānās) avoid this artifice for one clear reason. The *ṭhekā* is the very anchor of all subsequent rhythmic work; and if the very foundation is made to change itself, how can it appear to provide a steady ground to the rhythmic patterns to follow? Analogically, if the *lahrā*-player decides to make a similar claim to freedom of variations, and begins to vary the basic melodic line instead of keeping it clear *and steadfast*, will not the tablā player be deprived of the very ground which is expected to sustain him all along?

Anyway, besides the above, fairly popular kinds of compositions, there is a small number of patterns and sound-effects which are oddly named, but which do reveal some individual character to a closer look, and so relieve (in a measure) the seeming oddity of their names. The more important of these patterns are: *chalan* (चलन), *uḍān* (उड़ान), *gumbad* (गुम्बद), *latīfā* (लतीफ़ा), *ishkpechān* (इश्कपेचां), *tatabbo* (ततब्बो), *bulbul-dāstān* (बुलबुल-दास्तान), *quāyedā-lāl-quilā* ('क़ायदा लाल क़िला'), and *gopuchhā* (गौपुच्छा), *gāns* (गाँस), *ghaseeṭ* or *ghissā* (घसीट या घिस्सा), *chābuk mār toḍā* (चाबुक मार तोड़ा), and *gat chārbāgh* (गत चारबाग़).

Let me now quickly explain what all these names signify. *Chalan* is a simple recurring movement of a small *bol*-pattern at a fast pace, and is somewhat similar to a *relā*. The word may also be taken to mean the distinctive style in which an individual tablā player plays a particular pattern. *Uḍān* is a composition which appears to spring quite abruptly from any beat. It also evokes some resonance which lingers for a while. *Gumbad* is a brief composition which appears to be roughly similar to the round shapeliness of a *gumbad* (or dome) of a temple or a mosque. *Latīfā* is nothing but a small part of a long composition; but it can yet be played as a short pattern without appearing to be a mere fragment. To speak quite generally, just as an occasional and unexpected *latīfā* (or joke) in everyday conversation provides some light-hearted animation to our moods, so a *latīfā*, in the region of rhythm, is played with a sudden (but not very loud) burst of speed whereby it lends a little life, so to say, to the total playing.

Even more interesting is what the pattern known as *ishkpechān* (इश्कपेचां) may be taken to mean; and I look on it as a typical index of the culture of our Ustads of old. The word is obviously a compound one : *ishk* means love, and *pechān* seems allied to पेच or the skilful and intentional intertwining of two strings, say, in a bout of kite flying. So the complete word may be taken to mean loving or winsome interlacement. Accordingly, the composition I am talking of also consists of two very small syllabic groups, repeatedly played, producing a very sweet and soft sonority which resembles the intimate and whispered conversation between two lovers.

Even more intriguing is the way in which some Ustads would explain how a particular pattern came to be known as *bulbul dāstān*, or a tale of the bird, *bulbul*. As the story goes, during the Mughal period, an eccentric Nawab had a *bubul* as his favourite pet. Unluckily, this bird somehow fell ill and stopped chirping, which made the Nawab very unhappy. When all sorts of medical treatment had failed, the Nawab, on the suggestion of an intelligent courtier, summoned an old tablā Ustad to do something to revive the bird. The Ustad played a *quāyedā* the tonal quality of which appeared very similar to the chirping of a *bulbul*. The result was positive; the bird responded, regaining its voice; and the Ustad was appointed a court musician.

Quāyedā Lāl Quilā has no such romance about it. It is simply that pattern which, originally, used to be played at the terrace of the Red Fort only by a *naquārā* (नक्क़ारा) player. It was much later that it came to be included in the repertoire of tablā players. There is another pattern which is representational in a different way — I mean *gaupuchhā*. Literally, the word means relating to a cow's tail. Therefore, the pattern which bears this name is similar to the tail of a cow, — that is, it appears thicker at the root (or the beginning) and thinner at the end, of course, by virtue of a specific disposition of some select syllables of rhythm. I may add that *gaupucchā parans* form an important part of the pakhāwaj player's repertoire of rhythmic patterns. Words like *gāns* and *ghissā*, on the other hand, do not signify any *patterns*, but only some distinctive sounds produced by using the drums, specially the left one, in a particular way. Thus, *gāns* (गांस) which is the tablā player's word for *resonance* (गूंज), is produced by withdrawing the fingers of the left hand in a circular motion, and also at the same time, producing a stroke on the *bānyā*. This produces alphabets like *ghā*, *ghey* and *ghin* (घा, घे, घिन).

As for *ghissā* (घिस्सा) or *ghaseeṭ* (घसीट), this sound is produced by supplementing, very promptly, a stroke on *the left one* with an onward rub of the drum with that bodily part which intervenes the wrist and the palm. It may, however, be noted that this artifice does not really accord with the norms of authentic tablā playing, and is rather meant for the one-piece drum, *ḍholak.* To a tablā player it is permitted only where he has to fill the gap between two alphabets and to make a particular alphabet sound a little more tuneful. As an example, when the compound *bol.*

(1)	(2)	(3)	(4)
Ghī	ऽ	ऽnt	Dhā
(घी	ऽ	न्त	धा)

is required to be produced, a *ghissā* becomes unavoidable. But this action has to be done very softly, so that the requisite sweetness of resonance does not suffer. In respect of its heard continuity, and also because of the rub it involves, it may be said to be similar to *meend* ('मींड') on the *sitar*. Some tablā players resort to this device a bit too freely, and in such a vigorous way that it jars on the ear, instead of appealing to it.

To turn, again, to *patterns* in the art of rhythm, as against mere ways of producing *quaint sounds* out of the drums, a *chābuk-mār-toḍā* is so named because its manner of playing resembles the way in which a *chābuk* — that is, a whip — is used to goad a horse to move on. Such parity of verbal meaning and rhythmic character of patterns is also visible in *gat chārbāgh*. This pattern is so called because, unlike an ordinary *gat* which completes itself in just one round of the rhythm cycle, this *gat* repeats a line of rhythmic syllables four times, with but some slight change of alphabets. Every line is beautifully linked with the following one; but, unlike a *quāyedā* or *relā,* this *gat* does not admit of permutations.

To turn now to *rau*, it is a very short composition. It is, in fact, but a segment of a *relā*. It looks like providing a somewhat circular motion to the alphabets used. As distinguished from the playing of a *relā* or *quāyedā*, here the pace is never doubled. But, to make it appear seamless, some extra alphabets are incorporated without, of course, making the run look ruffled. How this incorporation is actually done in the playing of a *rau* may be brought out by taking an example. Suppose the basic *bols*, here, are as follows:

1	2	3	4
Dhati	*Kadhi*	*ऽndhi*	*naka*
Tati	*Kadhi*	*ऽndhi*	*naga*
1	2	3	4
धति	कधि	ऽनधि	नक
तति	कधि	ऽनधि	नग

Now, the making of a *rau* around the above groups of *bols* will proceed thus:

Dhātir	*Kiṭdhin*	*Tirkiṭ*	*DhāTirKiṭtak*
Tātir	*Kiṭdhin*	*Tirkiṭ*	*DhāTirKiṭtak*
धातिर	किटधिन	तिरकिट	धातिरकिटतक
तातिर	किटधिन	तिरकिट	धातिरकिटतक

Here, without the inclusion of the alphabets *Dhin* and *tirkiṭ*, no new composition of *rau* can possibly come into being. In the case of both presenting a solo recital and providing accompaniment, the use of a *rau* can be quite relevant. But it is important to mark that when it is actually played, its last segment has to be made to run at double the basic pace.

Anguṣṭhānā, (अंगुष्ठाना) is yet another pattern which has to be understood in the light of everyday discourse. *Anguṣṭh*, in Urdu language, means a finger; and *anguṣṭhānā* is that thing which covers a finger. The latter is made from a particular type of metal, and it is put over the tip of a key finger, to save it from being pierced by the needle used in stitching clothes. It has a rounded shape. Now, how all this relates to the pattern we are presently concerned with may be brought out as follows:

If, when a *paltā* (or variation) is being attempted, the inclusion of a tuft of alphabets in the composition evokes the look of a rounded movement, the resulting pattern is called *anguṣṭhānā*. Attention to the following should serve to bring out the point I am trying to make:

Dhāऽ	*Kḍedhā*	*Tidhā*	*Genā*
Dhāge	*Dhinnā*	*(Kiḍnak*	*Tiṭkiṭ*
Takat	*Tiṭkiṭ)*	*Dhāऽ*	*Kḍedhā*
Tidhā	*Genā*	*Tinnā*	*Kinā*
धाऽ	क्ड़ेधा	तिधा	गेना
धागे	धिन्ना	(किड़नक	तिटकिट
तकत	तिटकिट)	धाऽ	क्ड़ेधा
तिधा	गेना	तिन्ना	किना

Here, the biggest segment, which I have put within brackets in the above *bol*-pattern, produces the semblance of a rounded movement, and therefore the whole disposition of *bol*s in which the segment in question is included may be called *anguṣṭhānā*.

However, in the region of Hindustani rhythm, patterns are distinguished not only from the viewpoint of how they appear to move, but also from that of how they relate to individual beats within the rhythm cycle. Thus, when a composition begins from the first beat of a *tāla*, which is the *sama*, the *bol*-pattern is said to be of the *sama graha* type. On the other hand, when a composition begins from any other beat than the *sama*, the *bol*-pattern is said to represent the *visham graha* kind. How a pattern relates to the focal beat may also be made a ground for typifying the former. Thus, where the beat which immediately follows the first beat of a *tāla* (as completed) is designedly indicated as being the *sama*, the pattern which does so is said to belong to the *ateet graha* kind — *ateet* (अतीत) because the real *sama* has been *outgone or outstripped*. Correspondingly, when the *sama* is creatively designed to occur at the beat which immediately precedes the original *sama*, (that is, at beat No.16), the total composition is said to be of the *anāgat* (अनागत) kind, because the real *sama* is *yet to come.*

There are two other words, *tatabbo* and *atāi*, which are freely bandied about by those who talk about the playing and players of tablā rhythm. *Tatabbo* signifies not any prefixed composition, but simply the tablā player's ready and spontaneous imitation of the manner in which the melodic passages of the main performer run. What here counts, in the main, is not the accompanist's repertoire of compositions learnt from his teacher, but his own intelligence and alertness. As for the word *atāi,* it simply means one who has taken to tablā playing only light-heartedly, say, as a mere hobby; and has not been initiated into the art by any Gharānedār Ustad. The word, we may note, is in fact merely descriptive, not pejorative in meaning, though because of his sense of self-importance, a well-trained tablā player may well tend to use the word by way of expressing his dislike of mere amateurs.

5

Two Idioms of Tablā Rhythm

Solo and Accompaniment

MOST of the compositions we have discussed in the last chapter are expected to be there in the repertoire of a professional tablā player. But they are not all alike useable on every occasion he may get to perform. It is partly in this context that we have to distinguish the two main idioms of tablā playing: solo and *saṅgati* (or accompaniment).

A properly trained tablā player always welcomes a chance to give a solo recital before a knowledgeable audience, provided he is also given a good *lehrā*-player to provide the needed support of a steadfast melodic line — steadfast in respect of *laya*. A solo recital means that a single drummer is the main performer; and that, out of his personal repertoire, he plays some compositions of his choice in a particular sequence, all conforming (by and large) to the grammatical character and distinctive idiom of the *tāla* chosen for treatment. The repertoire of a solo tablā recital, we may note, comprises some *pre-composed* rhythmic arrangements. These are all fixed forms, fixed in the sense that they build upon phrases which are characteristic of particular types of compositions transmitted as regular lessons to the player in question by the teacher of a particular family-school or gharānā. In respect of temporal extent, such phrases are required (as a rule) to correspond with the structural segments — or with the total range — of the cycle being played. Further, in playing the phrases in question one has to see that *khulā-band* ('open' and 'closed') *bol*s are properly disposed or balanced. In some of the fixed forms the phrase-length not only corresponds with the *vibhāg* (prefixed division or *tāla*-bar) of the rhythm cycle, but takes care to highlight the *band* (or subdued) sonority of the *khāli vibhāg*. In the playing of other kinds of compositions the phrase-lengths overrun the divisions (or the *vibhāg*s), and no extra care is taken to heighten the difference between the *open* and *closed bols*. What the term *pre*-composed means in the context of our rhythm has to be noted with care. It does not signify rhythmic configurations which may have to be improvised by the drummer when, just after he has taken his seat on the stage, the main performer — say, a Sitar player — suddenly announces that he is going to play a composition in a cycle of 11 beats. In such an unforeseen situation, if he does not already know the cycle required, the tablā player has to quickly improvise it in his mind, *immediately before* the recital begins. In the case of a solo tablā recital, on the other hand, the *pre-composed* numbers are already there in his repertoire; they are the settled content of the rhythmic wisdom (or सबक़) of the gharānā which has trained him in the art. Let it not be thought, however, that there is no room here for the individual player's own creative ability. The truth rather is that a little improvisation may well be made even on a pre-fixed form, provided the overall beauty of the composition is not impaired, and the basic *laya* is nowhere flouted wantonly. The manifest preservation of this *laya* is the work of a Sārangi player; and he does this by repeatedly playing a *naghmā* — or a tune duly set in a *rāga-tāla* frame — till the very end of the tablā recital, and with unflagging steadfastness.

This, however, is not everything about a solo tablā recital. A very important aspect of it is the *sequence* observed by the player in executing the various types of patterns. In olden days — say, before the advent of our political independence — this sequence would be fixed from the viewpoint of the individual *laya* (aesthetic pace) demanded by the different compositions, the purpose being twofold: first, facilitation of the neat execution of the rhythmic syllables or *bols* at every pace, by letting the player's hands gain in agility by degrees; and, second, provision of a varying rhythmic fare of method, articulateness and pace, as also the ultimate evocation of a climax of flow and fluency *for the rasika*. Most of our masters of old would stick to this order meticulously. I may put this sequence as follows: (1) *peshkār*, (2) *quāyedās*, (3) *ṭukḍās*, (4) *gats*, (5) *relās*, (6) *chakradār ṭukḍās*; and, lastly, some other types of *bols* meant to be played at a very fast pace. In spite of its overall individual character, however, every one of these compositions was first played at *barābar ki laya*, that is, at the pace of the *ṭhekā*; and only then was the pace increased, and surely not abruptly or jerkily. Very great importance was given to syllabic clarity and compositional design in execution. Sheer hectic pace without neatness of playing was looked down upon, mainly because in resorting to excessive speed the player is likely to lose control over the mutual balancing of the two hands, and so to spoil both the articulateness and original design of the pattern. It is not for nothing that, in olden days, good tablā playing was said to be ख़ुशख़त (neatly written), and that a maestro of tablā was called a *munshi*. Fluency without form and clarity may well be able *to excite a lay audience, but it never satisfies those who know what* tablā *playing as art really is.*

Accompaniment to vocal music:

The term 'accompaniment' here means lending support to the main artist by steadily and incessantly playing the metric cycle (or *ṭhekā*) of the particular *tāla* required by the main performer. Formerly, the tablā accompanist used to provide, in general, a simple *ṭhekā* at the requisite pace. Only occasionally would he exercise his freedom to play some sweet and simple compositions, wherever he possibly could, even during the course of the total recital, but always in such a way that his creative work did nothing to ruffle the main performer's composure (or मिजाज़). *Drut*-singing offered greater scope for the drummer's wizardry than *vilambit* compositions. This is, incidentally, as true today *in respect of vocal music* as it was in the past.

Here, I feel impelled to add that a good *solo* tablā player is not necessarily equally competent in providing 'accompaniment.' I have myself come across quite a few past tablā players who could display wonderful skill in their solo recitals, but would yet fail miserably to provide even a simple steadfast *ṭhekā* to a vocalist. I do not know how this oddity can be explained. I can only venture to say that whereas for the enrichment of one's repertoire one has to depend almost entirely on one's mentor, the ability to provide proper 'accompaniment' is the fruit of one's own alertness, intelligence and self-critical effort.

Accompaniment to instrumental music

As for providing rhythmic accompaniment to instrumental music, be it that of a Sitar or of a Sarod, the idiom is quite different today from what it was in pre-independence days. The *spontaneous* creativity of the tablā accompanist was much better tested, and often vindicated more clearly, in the older way of 'accompaniment' which was called लिपटना (or a friendly, artistic intertwining). But let me explain what this kind of 'accompaniment' really is. Surprising though it may seem to the *rasika*s of today, here (in this kind of *saṅgati*) the main artist and his accompanist would appear to take off, so to say, simultaneously from any point or *mātrā* of the *tāla*, weave some improvised pattern parallelwise, and then arrive at the *sama* immaculately together, highlighting the climactic point of rhythm — that is, the *sama* — not only by virtue of the split second accuracy of advent, but because of the seemingly perfect parallelism of their rhythmic turns and twists, evoking a compelling semblance of लिपटना or intertwining. Accompaniment of this kind — which *I* had to provide, pretty freely, in my younger days[1] — would be not only very joy-giving to the audience, but nerve-racking for the tablā player, since it had to be done on the spur of the moment, quite without prior notice. The listener would here get the feeling that the two artistes were playing a single undivided interlacement. Both had to remain extremely alert, because if any one of them lost the right track, the other too would lose all sense of direction, and the result would be a mere musical jumble, and no proper accompaniment. To be truthful to the evidence of actual practice, however, I must add that rhythmic accompaniment of this kind would not be *strictly* simultaneous everywhere. The fact is that where there was some time-lag in the drummer's taking up the cue, it would be infinitesimal, so that the semblance of strict togetherness would yet be evoked and kept all along. Such moments of adroit artistry would elicit applause for both performers; and, we may note, this fact lends added support to my considered view that the drummer is no mere accompanist, but a co-creator, so to say.

---

1. Say, from 1945 to 1955

Today, however, this is *not* the general way of providing tablā-accompaniment. The present-day accompanist prefers to wait and provide just a simple *ṭhekā* as the main instrumentalist plays a particular melodic pattern, and *then* produces a more or less similar rhythmic parallel on the tablā. Some select instrumentalists and tablā players of today have developed enough understanding of each other's artistic idioms and needs; and the current practice of following, where necessary, a before-after order between the melodic patterns of the main instrumentalist and their rhythmic equivalents on the tablā is certainly providing enjoyable music to the *rasika*s of today.

Let me try to help this cause by making some suggestions, in the light of my own long experience as a teacher and practitioner of the art, about the way to become a good tablā accompanist. What is really needed may be readily put thus:

> first, acquisition of a rich repertoire of compositions set to various *jāti*s of *laya;*
>
> second, cultivation of the ability to interlace *bol*-patterns embedded in different *jāti*s during the very course of performance; and
>
> thirdly, acquisition of the ability to deal with quickening pace effortlessly.

Let me explain the points listed above with the help of an example. Suppose the main instrumentalist sets out to play a melodic passage in *tisra jāti,* and then, in the very course of doing so, suddenly turns to *chatusra jāti,* only to resort anew to a *tisra jāti* phrase or pattern, climaxing it all at the *sama* with a composite *tihāī.* In such a situation if the drummer is not duly able to produce the same variations on the tablā, not only will he feel ill at ease with himself, but the main artist and the listeners too will become dissatisfied. But, of course, it is not easy for the accompanist to interlink the *jāti*-bound *bol*-patterns into a completely new phrase there and then. My own repeated experience has convinced me that to deal with such a performative emergency the tablā player needs a profound knowledge of, and insight into the art of rhythm, and alertness to do the needful promptly. The skill of varying pace without any loss of time, *and yet without seeming abruptness* is not an easy acquisition, but it is surely demanded by consummate tablā accompaniment.

Accompaniment with Kathak dance

Providing rhythmic accompaniment to a Kathak recital is, in fact, a real challenge to the skill of a tablā player. No one who is not fully conversant with the intricacies of Kathak dance should accept such a difficult assignment. As I have personal experience of having played (in my younger days) with almost all the better known Kathaks of the country, beginning with the all-time great Shree Acchan Maharaj, *who would never try to belittle any tablā player on the stage,* I may venture to offer the following suggestions to those tablā players who desire to develop into good accompanists for Kathak dancers:

(a) See as many Kathak performances by dancers of *different* gharānās as you possibly can.

(b) And when you watch a Kathak recital observe very attentively how the accompanist has to vary his manner of playing very promptly to blend with the manner of dance.

(c) Always bear it in mind that not every Kathak dances according to a pre-fixed sequence or format. Our best known Kathak of today, Birju Maharaj, rarely begins with a *thāt*. Indeed, he prefers to open with a few small patterns which, in spite of their brevity, are so subtle in their toying with *laya* that they offer a challenge, so to say, to the drummer at the very outset; and delight the *rasika* (that is, a knowledgeable contemplator) with their adroit playfulness.

(d) Remember also that not all the alphabets or *bol*s that occur in the structure of Kathak *toḍā*s (patterns) can be executed on the tablā identically.

There are only three basic alphabets, namely *Tā, Theyi* and *Tat* — which the entire footwork of the Kathak builds upon. A few great *gurus* felt unhappy with this paucity of alphabets, for it hampered the enrichment of their repertoire with fresh compositions. So they took the prudent step to pick a good number of pakhāwaj and tablā alphabets and incorporated them in creating a very good number of *Kathak toḍās* which nevertheless ended, generally, with *tihāīs* composed of the basic *Kathak bols*, so as to let the pure Kathak idiom appear to dominate. The drummer, I repeat, cannot reproduce *quite* faithfully the *bols* of Kathak; but he can surely produce their approximate sonant analogues on the tablā, say, as follows:

	Kathak Bols		*Tablā Bols*
1.	*Trang-Trang* (त्रांग त्रांग)	-	*Kḍān or Katān* (क्ड़ान या कतान)
2.	*Ta-Thei-Tat* (ता थेई तत)	-	*Dha-Dhin-Tat* (धा धिन तत)
3.	*Drug or Drig* (द्रुग या द्रिग)	-	*Trak or Trik* (त्रक या त्रिक)
4.	*Tadigin* (तदिगिन)	-	*Gadigin* (गदिगिन)
5.	*Tig dhā dig dig* (तिग्धा दिग दिग)	-	*Katdhā-Tiṭ-Tiṭ or Din-Din* (कत्धा तिट तिट या दिन दिन)
6.	*Dig-Dig-Dig-Dig* (दिग दिग दिग दिग)	-	*Kat-Kat-Kat-Kat OR Din-Din-Din-Din* (कत कत कत कत या दिन दिन दिन दिन)
7.	*Tak Dhalāng* (तक धलांग)	-	*Tak Ghiḍān* (तक घिड़ान)
8.	*Thungā* (थुंगा)	-	*DhinTā* (धिनता)
9.	*Thun-Thun* (थुन थुन)	-	*Dhin Dhin* (धिन धिन)
10.	*Kuku Tak* (कुकु तक)	-	*Keke Tak* (केके तक)
11.	*Dim-Tā-Dim* (दिमता दिम)	-	*Dhin-Tā-Dhin* (धिन ता धिन)

This is obviously not an exhaustive list; but it should serve to make my meaning clear and to show the way to one who aspires to be a good accompanist for *Kathak* dancers. It would here be improper to insist that the tablā player should reproduce the Kathak syllables *quite exactly*. Only approximate similarity is achievable here; and the uncovered difference has to be ignored in an attitude of make-believe. Do the Kathak's own basic *bols* — *tā, theyi* — really sound as such when produced by his feet? Certainly not. The plain fact is that the impact of feet on the floor *which does not resonate* can never be exactly similar to the sounds produced by the tablā player. And what is there, I ask, in पदचाप (impact of the Kathak's feet on the floor) or in the finger-work of the tablā player to *truly* replicate the slant (तिरछापन) in the sound of थे in the *bol* थेई ?

'Accompaniment,' however, is not the only function of the art of tablā; and it is important to reflect on what really lends credence to the view that tablā playing is also an autonomous art. It has its own sounds and repertoire; and so I may now give thought to:

Solo playing of different gharānās

The style, compositions, and their disposition that make a solo recital differ from gharānā to gharānā. In each case it naturally comprises the individual gharānā's specific compositions which distinguish it from other schools of tablā playing. Yet a measure of similarity is also visible at some points in the presentation of all gharānās, say, in respect of the content of *ṭukḍās*, *gats*, *chakradārs*, *relās* and *quāyedās*. From the viewpoint of adequacy of sub-forms of rhythm, therefore, every gharānā may be said to be complete in itself. Yet, I hasten to add, an astute listener can surely perceive some differences between the solo recitals of the various gharānās. They differ at least in the production of resonating and non-resonating alphabets.

Solo of Farrukhābad

The Farrukhābad gharānā players begin their solo recital with a *peshkār*, as it is commonly played in some other gharānās. It is followed by a *peshkār-quāyedā* embellished with some apt improvisations. However, the number of *quāyedās* in this gharānā is rather limited, and so they do not here *dominate* a solo recital. Yet, after the *peshkār-quāyedā*, some *quāyedās* are surely presented at times, and they are both beautifully composed and skilfully played, along with a few adroit permutations. But what *distinguishes* this gharānā, and so its solo recitals too, is its huge stock of *gats* and *ṭukḍās*. Here, indeed, the Farrukhābad player revels in displaying admirable virtuosity; and he generally chooses to wind up his solo recital with *chakradār-ṭukḍās* played with great precision and clarity. In respect of *ṭukḍās* and *gats*, I repeat, the repertoire of this gharānā is so rich that each and every player of other gharānās likes to include some of these in his own solo recital.

Solo of Lucknow gharānā

The truth indeed is that, with all their differences of substance and manner, the different gharānās cannot be regarded as being *utterly* dissimilar to one another. Thus, the tablā players of the Lucknow gharānā also begin their solo performances with a *peshkār*, composed in the idiom of their own gharānā; and then turn to a projection of some *quāyedā*s, beautifying them with some variations, all skilfully accomplished. Quite a few *quāyedā*s of this gharānā resemble those of the Delhi school, but they are relatively easier to execute, and so permit the soloist to play even at terrific speed without fumbling. What, however, *distinguishes* the solo recitals of this gharānā is the abounding use of *chalans*, *relā*s, *gat*s and *chakradār*s, all rather weighty in syllabic filling and louder in resonance, and yet all alike played out with remarkable precision and an eye to sweetness of tone. What is equally noteworthy about the *solo* recitals of this gharānā is the fact that they make it a point to avoid presenting Kathak dance *ṭukḍā*s, which (I believe) is only proper, for (as I have already hinted) Kathak dance patterns do not really admit of *literal* presentation on the tablā. The disposition of *bol*s in a Lucknow solo recital is slightly different from that which we find in the solos of other Eastern gharānās. But they share a fair measure of similarity too; and the reason is not far to seek. The doyen of the Farrukhabad gharānā — that is, the late Ustad Haji Vilayat Ali Khan — had himself migrated from Lucknow. Besides, the Ustads from both the gharānās were socially close because of some matrimonial alliances among members of their families. So some sameness is surely visible in their approach to compositional values. At the same time, a slight difference is also noticeable between the *overall* character of the solos of Lucknow and Farrukhabad gharānās essentially because the Lucknow drummers had to accompany Kathak dancers more frequently than the Farrukhabad ones. However, the solo recitals of both gharānās can be quite satisfying — of course, in their own individual ways. The compositions which make their repertoire surely differ, but the *order* of presentation is largely similar.

Solo of Benares

This gharānā has a typical way of presenting a solo performance, though (in some respects) it also has a definite alliance with the other eastern gharānās of tablā playing. Ustad Modhu Khan, the *Khalifā* (doyen) of Lucknow gharānā, taught tablā to Pt. Ram Sahāya, who hailed from Benares, for quite a few decades. After coming back to Benares, Panditji gave an absolutely new turn to the compositions he already knew, and established a new technique of presenting a solo recital. It is indeed noteworthy that, as they stand at present, there is hardly any resemblance between the compositions of the Benares and Lucknow gharānās.

The Benares players begin their solo with a *bol*-pattern named *Uṭhān* (उठान). Most of the alphabets used in this composition clearly belong to the category of pakhāwaj alphabets. This composition is either pre-determined, or composed on the spot as one sets out to play. What follows is a careful playing of the normal *ṭhekā* of *tritāla* and its embellishment with variations of *ṭhekā* alphabets, which is (ordinarily) a very simple exercise. But that which distinguishes the Benares gharānā is, first, its possession of a very rich collection of *parans*, *fards*, *gats*, *kavitā-ṭukḍās* and compositions in the pakhāwaj idiom; and, secondly, the fact that all these compositions are very vigorously presented, producing an extremely loud resonance.

The solo format of this gharānā is totally different from that of the other eastern gharānās. Indeed, the overall impression of a Benares solo tablā recital is quite singular.

Solo of Punjab

To turn now to the western parts of North India, a solo tablā presentation of the Punjab gharānā is quite different from that of the other (western) gharānās, such as the Delhi and Ajrāḍā ones. Here, more emphasis is put on the mathematical than on a winsome collocation of *tāla* mnemonics. The players of this gharānā do begin a solo recital with an innovative *peshkār*, the overall look of which may tend to remind a knowledgeable listener of its Delhi parallel. This is followed by some *quāyedās* of a distinct kind. These are also embellished with some improvisations in the *kaharwā* idiom which are a treat for the listening ear. But the number of *quāyedā*s in this gharānā is rather limited; so they do not dominate a solo recital here. Instead, what the Punjab drummers revel in is the playing of *relā*s which they do with great efficiency and technical skill. As most of the leading drummers of the Punjab gharānā have been pakhāwaj players basically, their compositions too are executed with a markedly loud resonance. Yet, as they appear in *solo* recitals, these compositions often appear very tuneful to the listener. Adroit manipulation of *jāti*s of *laya* is also a unique feature of the solos of this gharānā, especially when they build upon intricately composed *bol*-patterns. What is more, the Punjab tablā players seem to love playing some difficult pakhāwaj tālas; and, in the process, successfully present pakhāwaj *parans* in such a way that their original, excessively loud resonance appears duly tempered.

Solo of Delhi

The Delhi gharānā is the oldest gharānā of tablā playing. The players of this school observe a set order in their solo recitals. They tend to be rather conservative in their way of presentation and execution of compositions. This, indeed, is why they find it very difficult to approve of a player who tries to deviate from the fixed norms of the gharānā during a performance. Their set order of presenting compositions may be put thus: *peskhār*; *peshkār-quāyedā* (with a small number of *bols*); *quāyedā*s of different designs; *chāla*s or *chalan*s, *relā*s, some *ṭukḍā*s of smaller range; and finally, a few beautifully executed *chakradār*s.

The opening *peshkār*, composed in the typical idiom of the gharānā, and the following *peshkār-quāyedā* are both embellished with some intricately designed *paltā*s or variations. Next, quite a few *quāyedā*s, with beautifully inwoven permutations are played with absolute technical accuracy. In so far as only some select fingers are allowed to be used, the players cannot here provide a very fast pace to compositions. The total playing indeed proceeds at *madhya laya*, with sustained emphasis on clarity and crispness; and so it sounds very tuneful and, what is more, fairly true to the phonetic character of *bols* as *recited*. Very winsomely executed *ṭukḍā*s of smaller compass are here a listener's delight. Some *chāla*s or *chalan*s, which are very intricately designed, are also a feature of the recital. I have always looked on them as eloquent evidence of the creative prowess and aesthetic sense of the Ustads, quite a few of whom were quite unlettered. The close of an authentic Delhi solo recital is provided by an artistic display of some such *chakradār ṭukḍā*s as do not at all resemble the pakhāwaj *ṭukḍā*s or *paran*s.

If method, intricacy, clarity and sweetness of tone are all taken into account as a composite criterion of good drumming, no gharānā of tablā playing can be ranked higher than the Delhi one.

Solo of Ajrāḍā

The Ajrāḍā gharānā of tablā is commonly regarded as an off-shoot of the Delhi gharānā. But it is also widely agreed in the circle of established and reputed tablā players that, because of the structural intricacy of the compositions it comprises and projects, an Ajrāḍā solo recital is meant to be presented only in the setting of a *baiṭhak* (or in camera), that is, to a select audience of connoisseurs of the art, and not to lay listeners. I may add that where the audience is knowledgeable, the rhythmic fare that an authentic Ajrāḍā solo presents, specially in the form of a patient and methodical unfoldment of *quāyedā*s, is often found to cast a spell on the listeners, instead of merely dazzling them with loud and fluent playing. At this point, I may add, I am reminded of the distinction that Bharata drew, long ago, between two kinds of aesthetic response: one that occurs overtly — and even audibly — at the end of every segment of a work of art's presentation; and the other which so steeps the *rasika*s with deep, rom inner relish that they just do not feel like disturbing it with too open applause.

Be that as it may, my present task should rather be to outline the format of an Ajrāḍā solo. Now, the beginning is here provided by a *peshkār* — embellished with some astutely knit variations — which is followed by a *peshkār-quāyedā* in *chatusra jāti*. The introduction of *paltā*s (or winsome variations) into this *quāyedā* depends on the virtuosity of the individual performer. Thereafter, the players of this school prefer to play some *quāyedās*, set to *āḍi laya*, which are smaller in range. A few longer *quāyedās* of thirtytwo or even sixtyfour beats, composed by blending *chatusra, tisra* and *chatusra jāti* (this *jāti* again, but now at double speed) are presented with an uncanny sense of hold over changes in *laya*. What this gharānā is known for, however, is its repertoire of *āḍi-laya quāyedās*; and this is why it is commonly regarded also as an *āḍi-laya* gharānā.

However, this is not the only feature that distinguishes this school of tablā playing. The solo recital of this gharānā is bound by a fixed sequence of compositions, and the performer who claims to represent this gharānā has to abide by its norms of presentation religiously. The playing of *quāyedās* is here followed by a few *relās* and *raus* which are quite different from other gharānās' compositions of the same categories. Another noteworthy point about the art of this gharānā is that its players are permitted to use three fingers of the right hand and three of the left, for the purpose of executing some alphabets of special subtlety. This co-ordinated use of six fingers enables the Ajrāḍā artist to invest some *quāyedās* and *relās* with such fluency as can hardly be attained by the use of only four fingers.

The Delhi and Ajrāḍā gharānās differ perceptibly in their ways of presenting a solo. The first impresses us with its calculative ordering of *bols*; and the second, with its aesthetic arrangement which pleases us at times by virtue of its adroit and intentional waywardness. Yet both gharānās are alike capable of providing exquisitely beautiful solos in their own individual manner. Their compositions surely differ in content and structure, but the order of presentation is quite similar.

6

Gharānās of Tablā

Introduction

THE way is now paved to a more detailed discussion of the gharānās (traditional family-schools) of tablā playing. They made their first appearance about seven centuries back. We may define a gharānā as a musical lineage, more or less similar to real blood relationships, through which musical techniques, compositions and even approaches to music are transmitted — in the main, orally — from one generation of musicians to the next. The initiators of gharānās were so particular about keeping their art confined within their own families that they freely encouraged inter-marriages between their own members. Therefore, it should not surprise us that even today it is not at all easy for an 'outsider' to gain free access to the distinctive repertoire of a gharānā, or to receive the benefit of personal training under one of its leading maestros. Luckily, however, there have always been some liberal gharānā-Ustads as well who could be persuaded to impart their treasured knowledge to common people, if only in lieu of absolute loyalty to the teacher and commitment to the art. Otherwise, tablā as an art would have become a thing of mere memory.

Anyway, the noteworthy point here is that every gharānā has its own conception of the right way to compose and play rhythmic motifs and forms. In spite of being uneducated in the formal sense, the founding fathers of these gharānās were so thoroughly conversant with the grammar of rhythm — and had acquired, by virtue of sheer commitment to the art, such profound insight into its aesthetics — that they could compose thousands of brilliant patterns which remain unsurpassed to this day, lending credence to the hypothesis that love of rhythm is perhaps a more basic feature of human nature than the desire to cultivate reading and writing skills. I realize that some tablā players of today would disagree with me at this point, and may like to contend that since the art of tablā playing depends entirely on the individual artist's own creative talent and commitment to rigorous practice, *anybody* can compose and play rhythmic patterns pretty well, and quite in accordance with his own aesthetic taste. But to all such sceptics, my rejoinder would run roughly as under:

First, we are of course all justified in trying to create something new, provided (I must add) we have the ability to do so. But in such creative ventures, is it wise and possible to ignore all that has been done in the past in connection with the activity we are presently concerned with? To look at the history of our *sangeet*, though Khayāl-*gāyakī* is surely a new and creative emergence of musical form after *dhruvapada*, did not even our earliest composers in the field of Khayāl, who are revered to this day, borrow and build upon some basic features of *dhruvapada*-singing? Were not our earliest *vilambit* khayāls clearly *dhruvapadāngi* in idiom?

Second, all artistic creation is an exercise of freedom within certain limits or according to some rules. There is indeed admirable sense in what an eminent aesthetician, C.J. Ducasse, declared long ago:

> Art . . . actually begins only when . . . [some] limitations are not only understood and accepted, but are perceived as definite and positive opportunities for free spontaneous self-expression."[1]

Therefore, if any tablā player of today decides to compose some *new* rhythmic patterns, would it not be prudent for him to acquaint himself with the principles of composition which our maestros of old have used in their creative work, perhaps unknowingly and only under the plastic stress of sheer aesthetic relish?[2]

Thirdly, with all due respects to them, I would like to put a simple question to the young luminaries of today. Have they been able to

---

1. C.J. Ducasse: *The Philosophy of Art*, New York: Dover Publications, Inc., 1966, pp. 38-39.
2. I have tried to seize some of these principles, and to explain them briefly in chapter 7.

discover even a single new tablā alphabet, or a new musical sound which has not been identified and built upon by the gharānā maestros? I am not suggesting that our traditional Ustads have *exhausted* the creative possibilities which tablā rhythm offers, but only that new, technically sound, and winsome compositions can be created only by those who have already acquired a very thorough knowledge of the art from some maestro of an authentic gharānā. I speak here on the solid basis of my own experience. Luckily, as is evidenced by the eighth chapter of this work, I have myself been able to do substantial creative work in the region of tablā rhythm; but I see it clearly that this work would have been impossible without the creative impulse and guidelines provided by a variety of factors which all alike make me feel beholden to the wisdom of gharānedār Ustads. I think it proper to list these factors quickly, not with a view to exaggerating the richness of my own concern with the art of tablā rhythm, but simply for the sake of indicating how much and how varied learning is required before one can set out to do *original* and *authentic* composing in the region of rhythm.

The outstanding factors have been the following three: first, my training, as a regular, *gandāband shāgird*, under Ustad Habeebuddin Khan of Meerut for years on end; second, my fifty-five years' experience as a teacher of tablā rhythm, including many a talk and article on the subject; and, thirdly, the privilege of getting numberless occasions to provide, in my younger days, tablā accompaniment to almost every top musician and Kathak dancer of the country. In addition to all this, I had the wonderful opportunity of being enlightened, through intimate discussions, on the art with such acknowledged maestros as the following: Masit Khan, Ahmad Jan Thirakwa and Amir Hussain Khan of Farrukhabad gharānā; Abid Hussain Khan, Wajid Khan and Afaq Hussain Khan of Lucknow gharānā; Feroze Khan, Malang Khan and Faquir Bux of Punjab gharānā; Vasudev Sahay, Biru Mishra and Kanthe Maharaj of Benares gharānā; Gami Khan, Munnu Khan and Nanhe Khan of Delhi gharānā; and Kale Khan, Shamoo Khan and Habeebuddin Khan of Ajrāḍā gharānā.

The gharānās I have just referred to can all be divided into two groups: 'eastern style' (*poorab*-baaj) and the 'western style' (or *paschim-*

baaj). The first group may be taken to cover the Lucknow, Farrukhabad and Benares gharānās. The baaj (or playing idiom) of the eastern region is खुला बाज, which means that the tonal resonance of compositions is noticeably open and striking to the ear. It may be said to proclaim itself, so to say. The impact on the average listener is here undoubtedly impressive. The Western baaj, on the other hand, is distinguished by a gently bridled and mellow quality of tonal resonance, and a pervasive crispness of playing which is all quite winsome to the *rasika*. The difference between the two styles arises essentially from a use of hands in executing not only the basic alphabets, but whole compositions. The *open style* uses the whole hand very freely; the *closed* — or, as I would prefer to call it, सिमटा हुआ (or controlled, gathered, not sprawling) style — relies mainly on the deft and liberal use of fingers. The one almost compels us to listen. The other quietly unfolds itself, and gently elicits sympathetic following. Such a way of distinguishing the two style is, however, a bit too general. Some sharper differences are needed. But before they are brought out, a common feature may also be noted.

There are quite a few alphabets which are frequently used by all gharānās in their compositions. It is indeed impossible to create any composition without such alphabets as *dhā* (धा), *"Tā"* (ता) *Dhin-Tin* (धिन-तिन), *"Tiṭ-Ghiḍ"* (तिट-घिड़). But the differences are just as clear; and it is to these that I now turn:

Eastern Gharānās

(a) Manifest affinity with the art of pakhāwaj playing.

(b) So, a liberal use of 'open' *bol*s in compositions which therefore sound loud and impressive.

(c) A marked preference for *ṭukḍās*, *chakradārs*, *fard*, *chalans*, *gats* and *tripallis* or *chaupallis*.

(d) Comparatively meagre attention to the playing of *quāyedās*.

(e) Because of points listed as a.b.c., the 'eastern' style is specially suited to provide accompaniment to Kathak dance and *dhruvapada* style of our vocal music.

Western Gharānās

(a) The style of playing, here, is quite removed from the pakhāwaj idiom.

(b) Liberal use of 'closed' *bol*s in compositions which therefore appear soft and mellow to the listening ear.

(c) Penchant for playing *peshkārs*, *quāyedās*, *relās*, *gat*s using 'closed' *bols*, *ṭukḍās* (smaller in range than those which figure in *poorab-*baaj), and *rau*s.

(d) A comparative deficiency of long *chakradārs*.

(Because of the four points listed above (a-d), the solo recital of a Western gharānā is quite different from that of an Eastern one).

(e) In virtue of the greater clarity of constituent *bol*s and (hence) articulateness of whole rhythmic passages, the *Western* baaj is more suited to provide accompaniment to sitar and sarod than the *Eastern* baaj which, because of its sheer loudness, can easily swamp the individual clarity of *swara*s produced by a plectrum. But, I hasten to add, however great be the differences between the repertoires and playing styles of the two regional gharānās, any artist belonging to any one of them can provide good solos and accompaniment in case he has the ability to do so. Indeed, a great deal depends on the prowess of the individual artist. I know that controversies have been raging for long between some of the orthodox gharānā Ustads as to which gharānā is supreme. But no mere argument can put an end to such debates. The answer is to be had only in the performance of a particular drummer on a particular occasion. Anyone who plays well in a specific concert gets and deserves acclaim. And to speak quite generally, all gharānās must be said to have contributed substantially to the preservation and promotion of the art of tablā rhythm. One has to acknowledge this with an open mind. Nor would it be proper to underestimate the work of the Ustads just because most of them had not received formal education. The devoted practice of an art is itself a kind of education. Knowing *how to do* a thing is as much knowing as the understanding of what *a word means.*[3] Practice opens up ever newer ways *to think about* better ways of *doing* an activity; and it is practical insight into the art and understanding of tablā rhythm which has enabled our Ustads of old not only to preserve, but to enrich the art in respect of both form and content.

GHARĀNĀS OF EASTERN STYLE

(Farrukhabad, Lucknow, Benares)

Farrukhābād Gharānā

The Farrukhābād gharānā of tablā was established by Ustad Haji Wilayat Ali Khan, who migrated from Lucknow to Farrukhabad after learning the art from Ustad Bakshu Khan; and, in the process, also marrying the latter's daughter. Wilayat Ali Khan was a player and composer of *very* great merit. By virtue of his sheer creativity he produced innumerable compositions, giving a wholly new turn to the Lucknow ones. The main features of this gharānā may be put as follows:

1. Quite without any trace of Kathak influence, this style is neither so ostentatious as the Benares or Punjab baaj nor so soft and dainty as the *kinār* baaj of Delhi and Ajrāḍā.

2. The repertoire of this gharānā includes many more *gats*, *relā*s and *chalans* than *peshkār*s and *quāyedā*s. Patterns known as समेट or चलन (composed by Salāri Khan) are very popular, and pleasing to the ear. Liberal use of *bol*s like *dhir-dhir* (धिर-धिर) and *tak-tak* (तक-तक) is a peculiarity of this gharānā.

3. Aptness for both solo playing and accompaniment.

4. Utter freedom from admixture with the alphabets of *naqqārā* and *dhol* rhythm.

---

3. Here, the reference is to Gilbert Ryle's well-known distinction between *knowing how* and *knowing that.*

As I have already said, Ustad Haji Wilayat Ali Khan learnt tablā at Lucknow for a pretty long time before migrating to Farrukhabad, to become the pioneer of this gharānā. Hence his compositions surely bear some influence of the Lucknow style of tablā playing. But this influence, I repeat, is quite limited; and Wilayat Khan is rightly credited with having produced innumerable compositions which bear the stamp of his own genius. His *chakradār ṭukḍā*s, in particular, are just brilliant and speak volumes for his creative prowess. The repeated use of the alphabet धिर-धिर (*dhir-dhir*) in such a way that instead of boring the listener, it only throws a spell over him, is simply remarkable. In compositions of other gharānās of the east, this alphabet occurs only sparingly. The composers of Farrukhabad gharānā indeed seem to be specially fond of this particular *bol*. In most of their compositions one finds its occurrence either in the beginning, or in the middle, or towards the close of the pattern; but wherever it appears, it looks very correctly placed.

So far as I know, the Farrukhabad gharānā seems to have the richest stock of *gat*s and *chakradār ṭukḍā*s. I may add that these compositions appear also in the recitals of most of the other gharānā players. I may also strike a personal note here. Whenever I heard these compositions, I recall, I always wondered whether such a variety of exquisite compositions, which reveal a remarkable capacity for intricate, yet musical grouping of alphabets, could ever be produced by any one who had not received practical guidance from some Ustad of the gharānā in question. Some actual specimens of the compositions I have been talking about are given at the end of this chapter; and a careful look at them may be expected to delight the knowledgeable reader. In quite a few of these compositions the blending of difficult tufts of alphabets like *natak-ghitak, takiṭ-takiṭ tak* has been done with exemplary skill. Further, the *āmads* — that is, the closing *tihāī*s — of some of these patterns are so beautifully structured, and therefore so project themselves that the listener cannot help feeling fascinated. I here feel impelled to make a special mention of the adroit way in which Ustad Salāri Khan, in his typical compositions, manages the passages of *samet* (or gathering) in *relā*s of exceptional difficulty, so that, in spite of their structural subtlety, they yet end immaculately at the *sama* without any seeming oddity in the management of *laya* or execution of *bols*. The *quāyedās* of this gharānā bear a clear resemblance to those of the Delhi school. The former gain distinction only by putting the alphabets in a different order. But this gharānā has surely produced some of the best known tablā players of the country, like Chudia Imambux and Munir Khan. It is noteworthy that such masters of yesteryear as Ahmad Jan Thirakwa, Habeebuddin Khan, and Amir Hussain Khan, all learnt the baaj of this gharānā from Ustad Munir Khan who lived in a small village, Laliyānā, in the Meerut district of Uttar Pradesh.

Ustad Munir Khan himself had learnt this baaj from Ustad Haji Vilayat Khan for a long time, and had thus accumulated a huge repertoire of compositions, which he freely passed on to his disciples. They propagated the baaj in question further; and this is why this gharānā still flourishes. Today, there is no player of repute who does not possess the compositions of this gharānā in his repertoire or never presents at least a few of its *bols* in his solo recitals. So I take pleasure in presenting the notated structure of some compositions of this gharānā.

The illustrative patterns that follow are all to be taken in the light of the following points:

1. All compositions are set to *tritāla.*
2. A big line signifies one beat; a smaller one, half a beat; and an even smaller one, one fourth of a beat. To follow *these* distinctions, however, the reader has to look at the notations *as given in Hindi.*
3. Sign ऽ shows a gap or an off-beat.
4. Sign of a cross (X) points to *Sama;* and a circle (O), to the *khāli* beat. These two beats, the *sama* and the *khāli*, may also be called *accented* and *unaccented.*
5. Notations have been done according to the *laya-jātis* of compositions.

Gharānā-Eastern style (Farrukhābad)

1. ***Peshkār*** **- Tāla-Tritālā** (16 beats)

(*Chatuśra-Jāti*)

The composition:

1 x	2	3	4	5	6	7	8
9 O	10	11	12	13	14	15	16

**Dhikḍa*	*Dhintā*	*ऽ dhā*	*Dhintā*
Dhātiṭ	*Dhāti*	*Dhādhā*	*Dhintā*
Tiṭ Dhāऽ	*ऽgadhā*	*Dhintā*	*Dhātiṭ*
Dhāऽkḍa	*Dhātiṭ*	*Dhādhā*	*Dhintā*
Kiḍnag	*Tīऽn*	*Tin Nā*	*Kiḍnag*
Tintinā	*Kintāke*	*Trakatin*	*Tinākinā*
Tiṭdhā	*ऽGadhā*	*Dhintā*	*Dhātiṭ*
Dhaऽkḍa	*Dhāti*	*Dhādhā*	*Dhintā*

*Note: The whole composition covers 32 beats. In so far as it is a *peshkār*, not a *quāyedā*, it cannot be provided a distinct second line, beginning (say) with *tikḍa tintā*. Nor can it be permuted in its full form because the *bol kiḍnag* provides the *khāli* or the off-beat.

धीकड़	धिन्ता	ऽधा	धिन्ता
धातिट	धाति	धाधा	धिन्ता
तिटधाऽ	ऽगधा	धिन्ता	धातिट
धाऽकड़	धातिट	धाधा	धिन्ता
किड़नग	तीऽन	तीना	किड़नग
तिनतिना	किनताके	त्रकतिन	तिनाकिना
तिटधा	ऽगधा	धिन्ता	धातिट
धाऽकड़	धाती	धाधा	धिन्ता

2. Peshkār-Quāyedā

The composition is set to *ādi laya* and in *Tishra-jāti*

Dhīnāऽ	*Dhāgenā*	*Dhātrka*	*Dhāgenā*
Dhātrka	*Dhātīdhā*	*Ghinādhi*	*Nāgenā*

Tirkiṭtak	*Tātirkiṭ*	*Dhināऽ*	*Dhāgena*
Dhātrak	*Dhātīdhā*	*Ghīnatī*	*Nākinā*
Tīngati	*Nāginā*	*Tāgeti*	*Rakiṭ*
Tāgeti	*Ṭatāge*	*Trakti*	*Nākiḍnag*
Tirkiṭtak	*Tātirkiṭ*	*Dhīnnāऽ*	*Dhāgena*
Dhātrak	*Dhātidhā*	*Ghinādhi*	*Nāgīnā*

धीनाऽ	धागेना	धात्रक	धागेना
धात्रक	धातीधा	घीनाधि	नागेना
तिरकिटतक	तातिरकिट	धीनाऽ	धागेन
धात्रक	धातीधा	घीनती	नाकीना
तींगति	नागीना	तागेति	रकिट
तागेति	टतागे	त्रकति	नाकिड़नग
तिरकिटतक	तातिरकिट	धींनाऽ	धागेन
धात्रक	धातिधा	घिनाधि	नागीना

3. Quāyedā : *Chatushra-Jāti*

Ghintā	*Ghintiṭ*	*Ghindhāge*	*Dhināginā*
Tiṭghin	*Dhāghin*	*Tiṭghin*	*Tīnākinā*
Kintā	*Kintiṭ*	*Kintāke*	*Tīnākinā*
Tiṭghin	*Dhāghin*	*Tiṭghin*	*Dhināginā*

घिनता	घिनतिट	घिनधागे	धिनागिना
तिटघिन	धाघिन	तिटघिन	तीनाकिना
किनता	किनतिट	किनताके	तीनाकिना
तिटघिन	धाघिन	तिटघिन	धिनागिना

4. Quāyedā : Mishra-Jāti

Dhāgen	*Dhāgedhin*	*Dhāgen*	*Dhinākḍdhā*
Tiṭakḍa	*Dhādhātiṭa*	*Dhāgen*	*Tīnākinā*
Tāken	*Tāketin*	*Tāken*	*Tīnākḍdhā*
Tiṭkḍa	*Dhādhātiṭa*	*Dhāgen*	*Dhināgīnā*

धागेन	धागेधिन	धागेन	धीनाक्ड़धा
तिटक्ड़	धाधातिट	धागेन	तीनाकीना
ताकेन	ताकेतिन	ताकेन	तीनाक्ड़धा
तिटक्ड़	धाधातिट	धागेन	धीनागीना

5. Relā : Chatushra-Jāti

Dhātir	*Ghiḍnag*	*Dhirdhir*	*Ghiḍnag*
Dhātir	*Ghiḍnag*	*Tīnnā*	*Kiḍnag*
Tātir	*Kiḍnag*	*Tirtir*	*Kiḍnag*
Dhātir	*Ghiḍnag*	*Dhinnā*	*Ghiḍnag*

धातिर	घिड़नग	धिरधिर	घिड़नग
धातिर	घिड़नग	तींना	किड़नग
तातिर	किड़नग	तिरतिर	किड़नग
धातिर	घिड़नग	धिन्ना	घिड़नग

6. Relā : Mishra-Jāti

*Dhā*ऽ	*tirkiṭ*	*Dhātir*	*Ghiḍnag*
*Dhā*ऽ	*tiṭkiṭ*	*Dhirdhir*	*Ghiḍnag*
*Dhā*ऽ	*tirkiṭ*	*Dhātir*	*Ghiḍnag*
*Dhā*ऽ	*tiṭkiṭ*	*Tinnā*	*Kiḍnag*
*Tā*ऽ	*tirkiṭ*	*Tatir*	*Kiḍnag*
*Tā*ऽ	*tiṭkiṭ*	*Tirtir*	*Kiḍnag*
*Dhā*ऽ	*tirkiṭ*	*Dhātir*	*Ghiḍnag*
*Dhā*ऽ	*tiṭkiṭ*	*Dhinnā*	*Ghiḍnag*

धाऽ	तिरकिट	धातिर	घिड़नग
धाऽ	तिटकिट	धिरधिर	घिड़नग
धाऽ	तिरकिट	धातिर	घिड़नग
धाऽ	तिटकिट	तिन्ना	किड़नग
ताऽ	तिरकिट	तातिर	किड़नग
ताऽ	तिटकिट	तिरतिर	किड़नग
धाऽ	तिरकिट	धातिर	घिड़नग
धाऽ	तिटकिट	धिन्ना	घिड़नग

7. Gat (Chatushra-Jāti)

Dhagnag	*Tiṭdhāge*	*Trakdhin*	*Ghiḍnag*
Dhingin	*Dhāgetrak*	*Tinākinā*	*Dha*ऽ
Dhādhāgege	*Nakdhin*	*Dha*ऽ	*Dhādhāgege*
Nakdhin	*Dha*ऽ	*Dhāgetiṭ*	*Tāgetiṭ*
Gadigin	*Dha*ऽ	*Dhāgetiṭ*	*Tagetiṭ*
Takiṭdhā	*Trakdhin*	*Dha*ऽ	*Dhāgenadhā*

Trakdhin	*Dhaऽ*	*dhaऽ*	*Dhāgenadhā*
Trakdhin	*Dhaऽ*	*Dhāgendhā*	*Trakdhin*

धगनग	तिटधागे	त्रकधिन	घिड़नग
धिनगिन	धागेत्रक	तिनाकिना	धाऽ
धाधागेगे	नकधिन	धाऽ	धाधागेगे
नकधिन	धाऽ	धागेतिट	तागेतिट
गदिगिन	धाऽ	धागेतिट	तागेतिट
तकिटधा	त्रकधिन	धाऽ	धागेनधा
त्रकधिन	धाऽ	धाऽ	धागेनधा
त्रकधिन	धाऽ	धागेनधा	त्रकधिन

8. Gat (Mishra-Jāti)

Dhagatt	*Tiṭkat*	*Dhiṭdhā*	*Dhiṭkat*
Dhiṭdhā	*Dhiṭdhāge*	*Nānāge*	*Tiṭkatā*
Kiḍnagtak	*Taktirkiṭtak*	*Tirkiṭtak*	*Kiṭkatā*
Gheऽnt	*Dhāghiḍnag*	*DhāghiḍnagDhir*	*DhirdhirGhiḍnag*

धगत्त	तिटकत	धिटधा	धिटकत
धिटधा	धिटधागे	नानागे	तिटकता
किड़नगतक	तकतिरकिटतक	तिरकिटतक	किटकता
घेऽन्त	धाघिड़नग	धाघिड़नगधिर	धिरधिरघिड़नग

9. Ṭukḍā (Chatushra-Jāti)

Takdhin	*ऽDhāge*	*Tirkiṭ*	*Ghintarā*
ऽNadhā	*Dhinnā*	*Tiṭ*	*Tiṭ*
Tā tiṭ	*Tiṭ tā*	*Kḍeऽdhātiṭ*	*Dhākḍeऽdhā*
Tiṭghin	*Tarān*	*Diganadi*	*Ginnag*
Nanagena	*Dhinnā*	*Dhīndhīn*	*Nātin*
Nādhīṅ	*Dhīnnā*	*Dhīnnā*	*Dhīndhīn*
Nātīn	*Nādhīn*	*Dhīnnā*	*Dhīnnā*
Dhīndhīn	*Nātīn*	*Nādhīn*	*Dhīnnā*

तकधीं	ऽधागे	तिरकिट	घिंतरा
ऽनधा	धींना	तिट	तिट
तातिट	तिटता	क्ड़ेऽधातिट	धाक्ड़ेऽधा
तिटघिन	तरान	दिगनदि	गिननग

ननगेन	धींना	धींधीं	नातीं
नाधीं	धींना	धींना	धींधीं
नातीं	नाधीं	धींना	धींना
धींधीं	नातीं	नाधीं	धींना

10. Tukḍā (Tishra-Jāti)

Dhinghiḍnag	*Tiṭakatān*	*Dhinghiḍnag*	*Tiṭakatān*
Tiṭakatān	*Dhāghiḍnag*	*Dhirdhirghiḍ*	*Nagdintak*
Tiṭakatān	*Dhādhādhā*	*Trakdhetdhirdhir*	*Kiṭṭaktātirkiṭṭak*
Trakdhet	*Dhirdhir*	*Kiṭṭak*	*Tātirkiṭṭak*
Trakdhet	*Dhirdhir*	*Kiṭṭak*	*Tātirkiṭṭak*

धिनघिड़नग	तिटकतान्	धिनघिड़नग	तिटकतान
तिटकतान	धाधिड़नग	धिरधिरघिड़	नगदिनतक
तिटकतान	धाधाधा	त्रकधेत्धिरधिर	किटतकतातिरकिटतक
त्रकधेत्	धिरधिर	किटतक	तातिरकिटतक
त्रकधेत्	धिरधिर	किटतक	तातिरकिटतक

11. Samet (Chatushra-Jāti)

Tiṭaghin	*Dhātrakdhi*	*Tiṭaghin*	*Kaऽt*
Katghin	*Dhātrakdhi*	*Tiṭaghin*	*Tiṭ*
Gheऽnt	*Dhāऽ*	*Dhirdhirkiṭṭak*	*Tātirkiṭṭak*
Dhirdhirkiṭṭak	*Tātirkiṭṭak*	*Dhirdhirkiṭṭak*	*Tātirkiṭṭak*

तिटघिन	धात्रकधि	तिटघिन	कऽत
कतघिन	धात्रकधि	तिटघिन	तिट
घेंऽनत	धाऽ	धिरधिरकिटतक	तातिरकिटतक
धिरधिरकिटतक	तातिरकिटतक	धिरधिरकिटतक	तातिरकिटतक

12. Samet (Kaherwā Ang)

Dhātrakdhi	*Nakdhin*	*Katakghi*	*Nagtak*
Dhātrakdhi	*Nakdhin*	*Dhirdhirkiṭṭak*	*Tātirkiṭṭak*
Takḍāऽntā	*Dhādhirdhir*	*Kiṭṭaktātir*	*Kiṭṭaktakḍā*
ऽntadhā	*Dhirdhirkiṭṭak*	*Tātirkiṭṭak*	*Takḍāऽnta Dhā*

धात्रकधि	नकधिन	कतकघि	नगतक
धात्रकधि	नकधिन	धिरधिरकिटतक	तातिरकिटतक

तक्डाऽनता	धाधिरधिर	किटतकतातिर	किटतकतक्डा
ऽनत्धा	धिरधिरकिटतक	तातिरकिटतक	तक्डाऽनत् धा

13. Chakradār-Tripalli, at three different *layas*: Tishra, Chatushra and double of Tishra

Note: Given below is just one *palla* (or segment) of 27 beats. It is to be repeated thrice, so as to make for a *chakradār* pattern of 81 beats.

Din	*Din*	*Takiṭ*	*Takiṭ*
Dhātrak	*Dhitiṭ*	*Kataga*	*Digin*
Dhātrakdhi	*Tiṭkat*	*Gaऽdi*	*Giऽna*
Dindin	*Takiṭtakiṭ*	*Dhātrakdhitiṭ*	*Katgadigin*
Dhāऽ	*Dindin*	*Takiṭtakiṭ*	*Dhātrakdhitiṭ*
Katgadigin	*Dhaऽ*	*Dindin*	*Takiṭtakiṭ*
Dhātrakdhitiṭ	*Katgadigin*	*Dhaऽ*	

दिन	दिन	तकिट	तकिट
धात्रक	धितिट	कतग	दिगिन
धात्रकधि	तिटकत	गऽदि	गिऽन
दिनदिन	तकिटतकिट	धात्रकधितिट	कतगदिगिन
धाऽ	दिनदिन	तकिटतकिट	धात्रकधितिट
कतगदिगिन	धाऽ	दिनदिन	तकिटतकिट
धात्रकधितिट	कतगदिगिन	धाऽ	

14. Simple Chakradār-Chatushra-Jāti

Dhirdhirkiṭtak	*Takiṭdhāऽ*	ऽ*Dhā*	ऽ*Takiṭ*
Dhāऽ	*Dhāgendhā*	*Gadigin*	*Dhāgetrak*
Dhināginā	*Dhagaऽt*	*Kiḍnag*	*Tiṭkata*
Kiḍnag	*Takdhīntir*	*Kiṭtaktakdhīn*	ऽ*tirkiṭtak*
Tātirkiṭtak	*Taऽ*	ऽ*Dhirdhir*	*Kiṭtaktakit*
Dhaऽ	ऽ*Dhirdhir*	*Kiṭtaktakiṭ*	*Dhāऽ*
ऽ*Dhirdhir*	*Kiṭtaktakit*	*Dhāऽ*	

धिरधिरकिटतक	तकिटधाऽ	ऽधा	ऽतकिट
धाऽ	धागेनधा	गदिगिन	धागेत्रक
धीनागीना	धगऽत	किड़नग	तिटकत
किड़नग	तकधींतिर	किटतकतकधीं	ऽतिरकिटतक
तातिरकिटतक	ताऽ	ऽधिरधिर	किटतकतकिट

धाऽ	ऽधिरधिर	किटतकतकिट	धाऽ
ऽधिरधिर	किटतकतकिट	धाऽ	

15. Chalan (Chatushra-Jāti)

Dhātidhāऽ	*Dhātighin*	*Dhināgīnā*	*Dhātīdhāऽ*
Kḍedhetdhi	*Tiṭaghin*	*Dhātighin*	*Dhinākiḍnag*
Taऽkiṭtak	*Tāऽkiḍnag*	*Tātirkiṭtak*	*Tātirkiṭtak*
Tirkiṭtaktā	*Tirkiṭdhātī*	*Dhāgendhā*	*Tidhāgena*
धातीधाऽ	धातीघिन	धीनागीना	धातीधाऽ
कड्धेत्धि	तिटघिन	धातीघिन	धीनाकिड्नग
ताऽकिटतक	ताऽकिड्नग	तातिरकिटतक	तातिरकिटतक
तिरकिटतकता	तिरकिटधाती	धागेनधा	तिधागेन

16. Another Chalan (Chatushra-Jāti)

Dhingin	*Taktak*	*Dhingin*	*Dhātīgin*
Takdhin	*Gintak*	*Dhingin*	*Dhātīgin*
Tinkin	*Taktak*	*Tinkin*	*Tātīkin*
Takdhin	*Gintak*	*Dhingin*	*Dhātīgin*
धिनगिन	तकतक	धिनगिन	धातीगिन
तकधिन	गिनतक	धिनगिन	धातीगिन
तिनकिन	तकतक	तिनकिन	तातीकिन
तकधिन	गिनतक	धिनगिन	धातीगिन

Lucknow Gharānā

This gharānā was established by Ustads Modhu Khan and Bakshu Khan, two talented brothers who had migrated to Lucknow from Delhi. They were naturally quite conversant with the basic principles and niceties of the Delhi gharānā baaj (or idiom of playing). But, because of the different cultural climate of Lucknow, where Kathak dance was very popular, they had to introduce some changes in the pure Delhi style, say, by incorporating in their repertoire some pakhāwaj compositions and patterns appropriate for the dance form referred to. Some of the more important features of Lucknow baaj may be put thus:

1. Instead of a liberal use of *Kinār* or *Chānti* alphabets which distinguish the Delhi baaj, they (that is, the *Khalifās* of Lucknow) introduced some open strokes to be played at the *lau* (*maidān*) point, that is, at the place *between* the *syāhī* (स्याही) and *kinār* (किनार) and also at a part of the *syāhī* area itself.

2. Again, in place of two fingers, all the five fingers were freely put to use by the Lucknow maestros while playing at the right drum; and on the left one, the thumb began to be used primarily for the sake of producing a typical resonance which, in the technical language of tablā, was (and is still) called *ghissā*, *ghaseeṭ*, or *meend* (घिस्सा, घसीट or मींड). In producing this particular sound, we may note, a slight pressure has to be put on the wrist to evoke the requisite look of an insistent rub.

3. The *quāyedā*s too of the Lucknow gharānā are different from those of the Delhi and Ajrāḍā schools, essentially in respect of being larger in extent. What is more, in this school *quāyedās* are not played so liberally as other kinds of patterns such as *ṭukḍās*, *nauhakkā*s (नौहक्का), *parans*, *gat-parans*, *chakradār*s and *fard*s.

4. Further, as I have already hinted, the Lucknow style of tablā playing has been much influenced by the requirement of having to 'accompany' Kathak dance recitals. As is widely known, during the regime of the Lucknow *nawāb*s, good Kathak dancers were freely invited to perform at royal courts; and most of the better tablā players were commissioned to 'accompany' the dancers. This is indeed why the Lucknow baaj is often spoken of as the *naach-karan*-baaj (नाचकरनबाज).

5. But there is a good deal more which makes the Lucknow baaj distinctive. Besides using the basic alphabets which are used by the composers of other eastern gharānās, the masters of Lucknow gharānā used their creative genius in liberally punctuating their compositions with alphabets like "*Dhiṭ-Dhiṭ*" (धिट-धिट), "*Kḍedhi-Tiṭ*" (क्ड़ेधि-तिट), "*Dhin-Ghiḍnag*" (धिन-घिड़नग), "*Katān-Ghiḍān*" (कतान-घिड़ान), "*Tiṭakat-Gadigin*" (तिटकत-गदिगिन)

and some others at such points of the compositions as made for added beauty. Here, indeed, they may be said to reveal an uncanny insight into some structural principles, say, as those of contrast and similarity. All this has served to lend a quite distinct identity to the tablā baaj of Lucknow.

6. This should not, however, blind us to the fact that some of the *quāyedās* of Lucknow gharānā are not quite independent of the influence of the Delhi gharānā, and that they resemble the *chalan* (or manner of *movement*) of the Delhi style, barring some intelligent changes in the *disposition* of alphabets. dhin

7. What, however, I wish to emphasize is the individuality of the Lucknow school. Some of its *gats*, *ṭukḍās*, *relās* and *chalans* have been brilliantly composed. What is more, besides their being able to provide excellent support to Kathak dancers, the Lucknow Ustads were adept at playing *laggis* and *laḍis* with *ghazal* and *ṭhumrī* singers with equal competence and brilliance.

8. Finally, (to turn to a matter of technical detail) in the Lucknow gharānā, execution of the alphabet *Dhā* (धा) is done somewhat differently from the way it is done in the other gharānās. Quite often, if not always, they produce *dhā* at the *maidān* or *lau* location of the tablā *puḍi*, and they designate it as *swara-kā-dhā*. Now, both technically and theoretically, there is nothing like a *swara-kā-dhā*. *Dhā* is generally played at the "*kinār*" or "*chānt*." So there must be some other reason, which I am not able to guess with certainty, behind this singularity of execution. At the same time, I cannot help offering a tentative explanation here. Barring a few *quāyedās*, most of the Lucknow gharānā compositions are produced out of the middle portion of the *puḍi*; hence it is bound to be quite tough for a player to quickly draw his forefinger back to the *kinār* every time he may have to play the *dhā*. This is perhaps why, for the sake of sheer convenience, the Lucknow drummers preferred to play the syllable in question close to *syāhī* adjoining the *maidān* portion. What is, however, likely to interest the lovers of tablā rhythm is not

such matters of detail as some specimens of compositions of the Lucknow gharānā; and it is to this aspect of the matter that I now turn:

Lucknow

1. Illustrative Patterns-Peshkār

Dhīkḍa	*Dhinnā*	*ऽDhā*	*Dhinnā*
Dhātiṭ	*Dhātiṭ*	*Dhādhā*	*Tinnā*
Tiṭ Dhā	*Tādhā*	*Dhinnā*	*Dhātiṭ*
Dhākḍa	*Dhātiṭ*	*Dhādhā*	*Tinnā*
Tīkḍa	*Tinnā*	*ऽTā*	*Tinnā*
Tātiṭ	*Tātiṭ*	*Tātā*	*Tinnā*
Tiṭ dhā	*Tādhā*	*Dhinnā*	*Dhātiṭ*
Dhākḍa	*Dhātiṭ*	*Dhādhā*	*Dhinnā*

धीकड़	धिन्ना	ऽधा	धिन्ना
धातिट	धातिट	धाधा	तिन्ना
तिटधा	ताधा	धिन्ना	धातिट
धाकड़	धातिट	धाधा	तिन्ना
तीकड़	तिन्ना	ऽता	तिन्ना
तातिट	तातिट	ताता	तिन्ना
तिटधा	ताधा	धिन्ना	धातिट
धाकड़	धातिट	धाधा	धिन्ना

2. Peshkār-Quāyedā (Chatushra-Jāti)

Dhātiṭ	*Dhādhā*	*Dhinnā*	*Dhātiṭ*
Dhākḍa	*Dhāti*	*Dhādhā*	*Tinnā*
Tātiṭ	*Tātā*	*Tinnā*	*Dhātiṭ*
Dhākḍa	*Dhātī*	*Dhādhā*	*Dhinnā*

धातिट	धाधा	धिन्ना	धातिट
धाकड़	धाती	धाधा	तिन्ना
तातिट	ताता	तिन्ना	धातिट
धाकड़	धाती	धाधा	धिन्ना

3. Quāyedā

Dhāgetiṭ	*Dhīnāgīnā*	*Dhāgetiṭ*	*Dhīnāgīnā*
Dhāgetiṭ	*Dhāgetiṭ*	*Dhāgetiṭ*	*Tīnākīnā*
Dhāgetiṭ	*Dhāgetiṭ*	*Dhīnāgīnā*	*Dhāgetiṭ*
Dhāgendhā	*Tiṭdhiṭ*	*Dhāgetiṭ*	*Tīnākīnā*
Tāketiṭ	*Tīnākīnā*	*Tāketiṭ*	*Tīnākīnā*
Tāketiṭ	*Tāketiṭ*	*Tāketiṭ*	*Tīnākīnā*
Dhāgetiṭ	*Dhāgetiṭ*	*Dhīnāgīnā*	*Dhāgetiṭ*
Dhāgendhā	*Tiṭdhiṭ*	*Dhāgetiṭ*	*Dhīnāgīnā*

धागेतिट	धीनागीना	धागेतिट	धीनागीना
धागेतिट	धागेतिट	धागेतिट	तीनाकीना
धागेतिट	धागेतिट	धीनागीना	धागेतिट
धागेनधा	तिटधिट	धागेतिट	तीनाकीना
ताकेतिट	तीनाकीना	ताकेतिट	तीनाकीना
ताकेतिट	ताकेतिट	ताकेतिट	तीनाकीना
धागेतिट	धागेतिट	धीनागीना	धागेतिट
धागेनधा	तिटधिट	धागेतिट	धीनागीना

4. Quāyedā (Chatushra-Jāti)

Dhāti	*Ṭadhi*	*Tiṭa*	*Ghīnā*
Dhāti	*Ghīnā*	*Dhīnā*	*Gīnā*
Dhāti	*Ṭati*	*Tiṭa*	*Ghīnā*
Dhāti	*Ghīnā*	*Tīnā*	*Kīnā*
Tāti	*Ṭati*	*Tiṭa*	*Kīnā*
Tāti	*Kīnā*	*Tīnnā*	*Kīnā*
Dhāti	*Ṭadhi*	*Tiṭa*	*Ghīnā*
Dhāti	*Ghīnā*	*Dhīnā*	*Gīnā*

धाति	टधि	तिट	घीना
धाति	घीना	धीना	गीना
धाति	टति	तिट	घीना
धाति	घीना	तीना	कीना
ताति	टति	तिट	कीना
ताति	कीना	तींना	कीना
धाति	टधि	तिट	घीना
धाति	घीना	धीना	गीना

5. Relā ādi-laya (Tishra-Jāti); Āḍi laya

Dhātiṭdhā	*Dhīnnādhīn*	*Dhātiṭdhā*	*Tiṭghiḍnag*
Dhādhīṅtiṭ	*Ghiḍnagdhīn*	*Nagnagdhā*	*Tiṭghiḍnag*
Tātiṭatā	*Tīnnātīn*	*Tātiṭtā*	*Tiṭkiḍnag*
Dhādhīṅtiṭ	*Ghiḍnagdhīn*	*Nagnagdhā*	*Tiṭghiḍnag*
धातिटधा	धींनाधीं	धातटिधा	तिटघिड़नग
धाधींतिट	घिड़नगधीं	नगनगधा	तिटघिड़नग
तातिटता	तींनातीं	तातिटता	तिटकिड़नग
धाधींतिट	घिड़नगधीं	नगनगधा	तिटघिड़नग

6. Relā (Chatushra-Jāti)

Dhingin	*Dhātir*	*Ghiḍnag*	*Dhātir*
Ghiḍnag	*Dhingin*	*Dhātir*	*Kiḍnag*
Tinkin	*Tātir*	*Kiḍnag*	*Dhātir*
Ghiḍnag	*Dhingin*	*Dhātir*	*Ghiḍnag*
धिनगिन	धातिर	घिड़नग	धातिर
घिड़नग	धिनगिन	धातिर	किड़नग
तिनकिन	तातिर	किड़नग	धातिर
घिड़नग	धिनगिन	धातिर	घिड़नग

7. "Gat" Tishra-Jāti

Dhinghiḍnag	*Tiṭghiḍāsn*	*Dhirdhirghiḍ*	*Nagdintak*
Takiṭ takiṭ	*Takghiḍnag*	*Dhirdhirghiḍ*	*Nagdintak*
Kḍedhintā	*Dhādhintā*	*Dhirdhirghiḍ*	*Nagdintak*
Takiṭdhāsḍ	*Dhādhintā*	*Dhirdhirghiḍ*	*Nagdintak*
धिनघिड़नग	तिटघिड़ाऽन	धिरधिरघिड़	नगदिनतक
तकिटतकिट	तकघिड़नग	धिरधिरघिड़	नगदिनतक
क्ड़ेधिन्ता	धाधिन्ता	धिरधिरघिड़	नगदिनतक
तकिटधाऽड़	धाधिन्ता	धिरधिरघिड़	नगदिनतक

8. Gat (Tishra-Jāti)

Dhinghiḍnag	*Tiṭghiḍāsn*	*Dhirdhirghiḍ*	*Nagdintak*
Takiṭdhikiṭ	*Ghintarāsn*	*Dhirdhirghiḍ*	*Nagdintak*

Ghintarāऽn	*Dhādintā*	*Dhirdhirghiḍ*	*Nagdintak*
Takiṭdhāऽḍ	*Dhadintā*	*Dhirdhirghiḍ*	*Nagdintak*

धिनधिड़नग	तिटघिड़ाऽन	धिरधिरघिड़	नगदिनतक
तकिटधिकिट	घिंतराऽन	धिरधिरघिड़	नगदिनतक
घिंतराऽन	धादिंता	धिरधिरघिड़	नगदिनतक
तकिटधाऽड़	धादिंता	धिरधिरघिड़	नगदिनतक

9. Ṭukḍā (Chatushra-Jāti)

Dhiṭdhiṭ	*Tāgetiṭ*	*Kḍedhātiṭ*	*Tāgetiṭ*
Kḍedhātiṭ	*Kḍedhātiṭ*	*Kḍedhātiṭ*	*Tāgetiṭ*
Dhāgetiṭ	*Tāgetiṭ*	*Kḍedhātiṭ*	*Tāgetiṭ*
Kaऽtadhi	*Tiṭakatā*	*Kaऽऽt*	*Tirkiṭ*
Ghintarāऽ	*ऽnadhā*	*Diऽ*	*Kaऽऽt*
Dhāऽ	*Tirkiṭ*	*Ghintarā*	*ऽnadhā*
Diऽ	*kaऽt*	*Dhāऽ*	*tirkiṭ*
Ghintarā	*ऽnadhā*	*Diऽ*	*Kaऽऽt*

धिटधिट	तागेतिट	क्ड़ेधातिट	तागेतिट
क्ड़ेधातिट	क्ड़ेधातिट	क्ड़ेधातिट	तागेतिट
धागेतिट	तागेतिट	क्ड़ेधातिट	तागेतिट
कऽतधि	तिटकता	कऽऽत	तिरकिट
घिंतराऽ	ऽनधा	दिऽ	कऽऽत
धाऽ	तिरकिट	घिंतरा	ऽनधा
दिऽ	कऽत	धाऽ	तिरकिट
घिंतरा	ऽनधा	दिऽ	कऽऽत

10. Ṭukḍā

Dhīkḍadhīkḍadhīn	*Tāgheghenakdhīn*	*Katakghetakdhin*
Dhāgetrakdhināgin	*Kiḍnagtinkin*	*Tāketraktīnākīnā*
Ghetakghetakdhin	*Dhāgetrakdhināgina*	*Taktaktaktak*
Dhagattakiṭdhātrakdhitiṭ	*Katagadigandhā*	*ऽTāऽghenऽnt*
Dhā dhā	*Tāऽghenऽnt Dhā dhā*	*Taऽghenऽnt*

धीक्ड़धीक्ड़धीं	ताघेघेनकधीं	कतकघेतकधिन	धागेत्रकधिनागिन
किड़नगतिनकिन	ताकेत्रकतीनाकीना	घेतकघेतकधिन	धागेत्रकधिनागिन
तकतकतकतक	धगततकिटधात्रकधितिट	कतगदिगनधा	ऽताऽघेंऽन्त
धा धा	ताऽघेंऽन्त	धा, धा	ताऽघेंऽन्त

11. Given below is just one *pallā* (or segment) containing 27 beats. It has to be repeated thrice. 27 x 3 = 81, which will make the whole pattern appear *chakradār*.

Chakradār Tishra-Jāti

Dhāऽn	*Dhitiṭ*	*Dhātiṭ*	*Dhitiṭ*
Kaऽt	*Dhitiṭ*	*Katag*	*Digan*
Nagan	*Nagan*	*Tirkiṭ*	*Tādhin*
Dhātiṭ	*Dhitiṭ*	*Katag*	*Digan*
Dhāऽ	*Dhātiṭ*	*Dhitiṭ*	*Katag*
Digan	*Dhaऽ*	*Dhātiṭ*	*Dhitiṭ*
Katag	*Digan*	*Dhāऽ*	

धाऽन	धितिट	धातिट	धितिट
कऽत	धितिट	कतग	दिगन
नगन	नगन	तिरकिट	ताधिन
धातिट	धितिट	कतग	दिगन
धाऽ	धातिट	धितिट	कतग
दिगन	धाऽ	धातिट	धितिट
कतग	दिगन	धाऽ	

12. **Chakradār-Tishra-Jāti**

Dhaऽn	*Dhikiṭ*	*Kaऽt*	*Dhikiṭ*
Dhātrak	*Dhikiṭ*	*Ghinak*	*Tīऽn*
Nagan	*Nagan*	*Tiṭti*	*Tātiṭ*
Dhātrak	*Dhikiṭ*	*Ghinak*	*Tīऽn*
Dhāऽ	*Dhātrak*	*Dhikiṭ*	*Ghinak*
Tīऽn	*Dhāऽ*	*Dhātrak*	*Dhikiṭ*
Ghinak	*Tīऽn*	*Dhāऽ*	

धाऽन	धिकिट	कऽत	धिकिट
धात्रक	धिकिट	घिनक	तीऽन
नगन	नगन	तिटति	तातिट
धात्रक	धिकिट	घिनक	तीऽन
धाऽ	धात्रक	धिकिट	घिनक
तीऽन	धाऽ	धात्रक	धिकिट
घिनक	तीऽन	धाऽ	

13. Chalan (Chatushra-Jāti)

Dhaऽ	*ऽDha*	*Tiṭa*	*Genā*
Dhātī	*Dhāge*	*Dhīnā*	*Gīnā*
Dhāऽ	*ऽTā*	*Dhāऽ*	*Tiṭa*
Dhā	*Dhā*	*Dhin*	*Nā*

धाऽ	ऽधा	तिट	गेना
धाती	धागे	धीना	गीना
धाऽ	ऽता	धाऽ	तिट
धा	धा	धिन	ना

14. Chalan-Chatushra-Jāti

Dhin	*Gin*	*Tak*	*Tak*
Dhin	*Gin*	*Dhāge*	*Tiṭ*
Dhāge	*Tiṭ*	*Kiṭ*	*Dhin*
Tak	*Tak*	*Tin*	*Kin*

धिन	गिन	तक	तक
धिन	गिन	धागे	तिट
धागे	तिट	किट	धिन
तक	तक	तिन	किन

Benares Gharānā

The Benares gharānā owes its emergence and identity to Pandit Ram Sahayji, who learned the art of tablā playing under the expert guidance of Ustad Modhu Khan of Lucknow gharānā. After migrating to Benares, Ram Sahayji gave a new turn to the art and innovated a distinct (Benares) style, the special features of which may be listed as follows:

1. It is a completely open baaj. In other words, whole hands are used here, as against mere fingers; and therefore the sounds produced are, at times, a bit too loud, tending (incidentally) to detract from articulateness of playing. However, one must also acknowledge the striking quality of this baaj.

2. A solo recital here begins not with a *peshkār,* but with the playing of a big *bol*-pattern, technically called *uthān*. The repertoire also comprises *toḍās*, *ṭukḍās*, *parans*, *fards*, *kavitā-toḍās* and *chakradārs*.

3. Further, strange though it may seem, this gharānā draws a distinction between *masculine* and *feminine gats*. The former are, as a rule, emphatic in character and emit loud sounds; and the latter are comparatively gentle in their impact. I wonder if this distinction owes its origin to the one that is freely drawn between *tāṇḍava* and *lāsya* in our dances.

4. What is more, the compositions of this gharānā are influenced much more by pakhāwaj than by *naqqārd, tāśā* or *dhol*; and the permutations are here called *bol-bāṅṭ*.

The Benares gharānā compositions are indeed replete with alphabets that relate to pakhāwaj. Syllables like *dhumkiṭ* (धुमकिट), *takiṭṭakā,* (तकिटतका), *gadigan,*(गदिगन), *ghiḍān-kiḍān,*(घिड़ान-किड़ान) here dominate. This can easily lend an impressive look to the total recital, specially if the audience is of a kind that does not look for subtleties, and is struck by mere loudness. But one cannot help putting a sceptical question here. If the tablā has to be played exactly in the way of *pakhāwaj,* what is the point in having a distinct instrument like the tablā at all? And if the tablā has in fact flourished as a separate instrument of rhythm, the way it is played, and the sounds it emits, must also be kept maximally apart from those of the pakhāwaj. In spite of all that it has owed to *dhruvapada*-singing, is not the idiom of khayāl *gāyakī* kept quite distinct, on the whole, from that of its venerable forerunner?

But, I hasten to add, the open (खुला) manner of Benares tablā is an artistic asset too. It enables the drummer to provide good accompaniment to Kathak dance and the *dhruvapada* style of vocal music. There are quite a few Kathaks who prefer to have a voluminous type of accompaniment with their performances. In such cases the Benares players can easily score over tablā players from other gharānās. I do not, however, wish to suggest that a mellow kind of 'accompaniment' to Kathak dance is not possible or necessary. Luckily, there *are* some Kathaks — I mean, the maturer ones — who prefer controlled 'accompaniment,' specially when they have to perform before an audience of authentic *rasikas*.

To turn, now, to solo playing in the fold of Benares gharānā, it is quite different from the way it is done in other schools. Here, the player opens his solo recital with an *uthān*, (उठान) which is an "open" type of rhythmic phrase, so called because it is played with an open hand, and is expected to herald (so to say), and not merely to usher us in, the beginning of a recital. Some *uthān*s are pre-composed; others, not very many, are composed on the spot, in case the player is intelligent enough to do so. *Uthān*s are followed by some *quāyedā*s which are typical of the gharānā. Thereafter, richer filling is provided to the recital by a playing of *ṭukḍā*s, *fards*, *kavitā toḍā*s, *parans* and *chakradār*s etc.

1. Illustrative patterns

Uthān (In place of *peshkār*)

Dhiṭdhiṭ	*Kḍedhātiṭ*	*Dhāgediṅ*	*Nagnag*
Tiṭakatā	*Gadigan*	*Katākatā*	*Kiṭdhā*ऽ
*Nadhā*ऽ*n*	*Dhā*ऽ*katā*	*Katākiṭ*	*Dhā*ऽ*nadhā*
ऽ*nadhā*	*Katākatā*	*Kiṭadhā*ऽ	*Nadhā*ऽ*n*
धिटधिट	कड़ेधातिट	धागेदिं	नगनग
तिटकता	गदिगन	कताकता	किटधाऽ
नधाऽन	धाऽकता	कताकिट	धाऽनधा
ऽनधा	कताकता	किटधाऽ	ऽनधाऽन

2. Quāyedā-(Tishra-Jāti)

Dhāgdhā	*Tiṭat*	*Dhāgdhā*	*Dhinak*
Tiṭdhā	*Tiṭat*	*Dhāgen*	*Tinak*
Tāktā	*Tiṭat*	*Tāktā*	*Tinak*
Tiṭdhā	*Tiṭat*	*Dhāgen*	*Dhinak*
धागधा	तिटत	धागधा	धिनक
तिटधा	तिटत	धागेन	तिनक
ताकता	तिटत	ताकता	तिनक
तिटधा	तिटत	धागेन	धिनक

3. Quāyedā - (Chatushra-jāti)

Dhik	*Dhīnā*	*Trak*	*Dhīnā*

Dhāge	*Nati*	*Kati*	*Nāḍā*
Tik	*Tīnā*	*Trak*	*Tīnā*
Dhāge	*Nati*	*Kati*	*Nāḍā*

धिक	धीना	त्रक	धीना
धागे	नति	कति	नाड़ा
तिक	तीना	त्रक	तीना
धागे	नति	कति	नाड़ा

4. Fard (Chatushra-Jāti)

Tiṭghiḍā	*ऽndhāऽ*	*Ghiḍnag*	*Dhīnākat*
Kiṭdhin	*Ghiḍnag*	*Dhiṭdhāge*	*Tiṭtāke*
Dhaḍaऽn	*Gaऽddi*	*Katghin*	*Dhāgendhā*
Genadhāge	*Dignāge*	*Tirkiṭ taktāऽ*	*ऽDhirdhirkiṭ*

तिटघिड़ा	ऽनधाऽ	घिड़नग	धीनाकत्
किटधिन	घिड़नग	धिटधागे	तिटताके
धड़ऽन्	गऽद्दी	कतघिं	धागेनधा
गेनधागे	दिगनागे	तिरकिटतकताऽ	ऽधिरधिरकिट

5. Another Fard (Chatushra-jāti)

Tiṭtiṭ	*Dhiṭdhiṭ*	*Dhāgendhā*	*Gendhāऽ*
Taktin	*Kiḍnag*	*Traktin*	*Kiḍnag*
Kḍedhikḍa	*Dhiṅdhet*	*Tagaऽna*	*DhāऽDhāऽ*
Dhettag	*ऽNadhā*	*Tirkiṭtaktāऽ*	*Dhirdhirkiṭ*

तिटतिट	धिटधिट	धागेनधा	गेनधा
तकतिन	किड़नग	त्रकतिन	किड़नग
क्ड़ेधिक्ड़	धिंधेत	तगऽन	धाऽधाऽ
धेततग	ऽनधा	तिरकिटतकताऽ	धिरधिरकिट

6. Jhoolanā Gat, Drut Laya

(*Mishra-Jāti*) 24x2 = 48 (or 3 rounds of Tritāla)

Dhātrak	*Dhiṭdhiṭ*	*Takiṭ*	*Taktak*
Dhiṭdhā	*Gadigan*	*Dhāgadi*	*Gandhāऽ*
Tirkiṭtak	*Tāऽtiṭ*	*Dhiṭdhā*	*Gadigan*
Nātiṭ	*Tāgetiṭ*	*Dhiṭdhā*	*Gadigan*

Tirkiṭtak	*Tāऽtiṭ*	*Dhiṭdhā*	*Gadigan*
Dhāऽt	*Gadigan*	*Dhāऽt*	*Gadigan*

धात्रक	धिटधिट	तकिट	तकतक
धिटधा	गदिगन	धागदि	गनधाऽ
तिरकिटतक	ताऽतिट	धिटधा	गदिगन
नातिट	तागेतिट	धिटधा	गदिगन
तिरकिटतक	ताऽतिट	धिटधा	गदिगन
धाऽत	गदिगन	धाऽत	गदिगन

7. Gat Chatushra-Jāti

Kattak	*Tiṭtiṭ*	*Kattirkiṭtak*	*Tirkiṭghiḍāऽn*
Tirkiṭtaktir	*Kiṭtakghiḍāऽn*	*Tirkiṭghiḍāऽn*	*Tirkiṭghiḍāऽn*
Takghḍāऽntak	*Takghḍāऽntak*	*Dhatirkiṭtak*	*Takghḍāऽntak*
Takghḍāऽntak	*Dhatirkiṭtak*	*Takghḍāऽntak*	*Takghḍāऽntak*

कततक	तिटतिट	कततिरकिटतक	तिरकिटघिड़ाऽन
तिरकिटतकतिर	किटतकघिड़ाऽन	तिरकिटघिड़ाऽन	तिरकिटघिड़ाऽन
तकध्ड़ाऽनतक	तकध्ड़ाऽनतक	धातिरकिटतक	तकध्ड़ाऽनतक
तकध्ड़ाऽनतक	धातिरकिटतक	तकध्ड़ाऽनतक	तकध्ड़ाऽनतक

8. Ṭukḍā Chatushra-jāti

Dhāgetiṭ	*Tāgetiṭ*	*Kḍedhāऽkḍ*	*Dhāऽkat*
Dinऽdinऽ	*Nānānānā*	*Katiṭadhā*	*ऽKaऽt*
Dhāऽkat	*Dhāऽkati*	*Ṭadhāऽk*	*ऽTadhā*
Katdhāऽ	*Katiṭdhā*	*ऽKऽt*	*Dhāऽkat*

धागेतिट	तागेतिट	क्ड़ेधाऽक्ड़	धाऽकत
दिंऽदिंऽ	नानानाना	कतिटधा	ऽकऽत
धाऽकत	धाऽकति	टधाऽक	ऽतधाऽ
कतधाऽ	कतिटधा	ऽकऽत	धाऽकत

9. Ṭukḍā (Tishra-jāti)

Kaऽt	*Dhikiṭ*	*Katag*	*Digan*
Dhātrak	*Dhikiṭ*	*Katag*	*Digan*
Nagan	*Ganag*	*Tiṭati*	*Tātiṭ*
Dhātrak	*Dhikiṭ*	*Katag*	*Digan*

कऽत	धिकिट	कतग	दिगन
धात्रक	धिकिट	कतग	दिगन
नगन	गनग	तिटति	टातिट
धात्रक	धिकिट	कतग	दिगन

10. Chakradār (Chatushra-jāti)

Note: Below is given just one *pallā* (segment), containing 11 beats, of two *chakradār* patterns (Nos. 10 & 11). The full range of the patterns is to be unfolded by repeating the segment thrice: 11x3. Here are the *bol*s of the patterns (10 & 11):

Dhirdhirkat	*ऽDhirdhir*	*Katऽ*	*Dhirdhirkat*
ऽDhirdhir	*Kiṭtaktāऽn*	*Dhādhirdhir*	*Kiṭtaktāऽn*
Dhādhirdhir	*Kiṭtaktāऽn*	*Dhāऽ*	

धिरधिरकत	ऽधिरधिर	कतऽ	धिरधिरकत
ऽधिरधिर	किटतकताऽन	धाधिरधिर	किटतकताऽन
धाधिरधिर	किटतकताऽन	धाऽ	

11. Chakradār (Tishra-jāti)

Dhādhādhā	*Dindindin*	*Nānānā*	*Katrakdhikiṭ*
Katāgadigan	*Dhā katrak*	*Dhikiṭkatāg*	*Digandhā*
Katrakdhikiṭ	*Katāgadigan*	*Dhā*	

धाधाधा	दिंदिंदिं	नानाना	कत्रकधिकिट
कतागदिगन	धाकत्रक	धिकिटकताग	दिगनधा
कत्रकधिकिट	कतागदिगन	धा	

12. Relā (Chatushra-jāti)

Dhāऽghiḍ	*Nagdhir*	*Dhirdhir*	*Ghiḍnag*
Dhirdhir	*Ghiḍnag*	*Tīnnā*	*Kiḍnag*
Taऽkiḍ	*Nagtir*	*Tirtir*	*Kiḍnag*
Dhirdhir	*Ghiḍnag*	*Dhīnnā*	*Ghiḍnag*

धाऽघिड़	नगधिर	धिरधिर	घिड़नग
धिरधिर	घिड़नग	तींना	किड़नग
ताऽकिड़	नगतिर	तिरतिर	किड़नग
धिरधिर	घिड़नग	धींना	घिड़नग

13. Another Relā, in Chatushra-Jāti

Dhin	*Gin*	*Tak*	*Tak*
Dhin	*Gin*	*Tāke*	*Trak*
Tin	*Kin*	*Tak*	*Tak*
Dhin	*Gin*	*Dhāge*	*Trak*
धिन	गिन	तक	तक
धिन	गिन	ताके	त्रक
तिन	किन	तक	तक
धिन	गिन	धागे	त्रक

Punjab Gharānā

The Punjab gharānā was originated by Lala Bhawani Das, who was essentially a pakhāwaj player. The following features distinguish the new style of tablā playing that he brought into being:

1. Power and 'openness' of playing, akin to the Pakhāwaj idiom, and a liberal use of the open *Thāp* (थाप).

2. A predominantly mathematical, rather than configurational approach to the making of compositions; and a clear tinge of Punjabi accent in the recitation of *bol*s, so that the syllables which are normally recited as *"dhātī"* (धाती) and *"dhir-dhir-kat"* (धिरधिर कत) become *"dhat"* (धत्) and *"dhere-dhere kiṭ"* (धेरे-धेरे किट) in the *parhant* (syllabic recitation) of this gharānā.

3. Noticeable ease and efficiency in the playing of *tālā*s comprising an odd number of beats, possibly because of the knowledge of *pakhāwaj* repertoire.

4. Infrequent use of *quāyedā*s which are, however, longer here than in the other gharānās.

How exactly the Punjab gharānā of tablā came into being has for long been a matter of controversy. But this is unquestionable that it is very much there, and is flourishing today, like any other gharānā. Some tablā players of Punjab claim that because — quite in the way of *pakhāwaj* playing — flour-dough is applied to the left drum (बायां) by the players of their gharānā, theirs is the oldest and most authentic school of tablā playing and is quite unlike the other gharānās. Now, I may not challenge its being *distinctive* in many ways; but I find it very difficult to regard it as the *oldest* gharānā. I have had personal discussions with some of the most famous tablā players of Punjab — like Baba Malang; his son, Ustad Faiyaz (working as staff artist, Delhi, A.I.R.; in the thirties), Ustad Fakir Mohammad (father of Roshan Kumari, one of our best known Kathak dancers of the recent past); Ustads Feroze Khan and Tūfell Ahmed (who worked with me at the Calcutta Radio in 1945); Laxman Singh, Bahadur Singh (of Ludhiana), and quite a few others — about the age of the Punjab gharānā. They all agreed, I remember, that the main source of all tablā rhythm was the Delhi gharānā. Yet this is undeniable that the baaj of this gharānā shows very clear traces of affinity with pakhāwaj which is admittedly older that the tablā. It surely strikes the listening ear as vigorous and loud. What is more, *ṭukḍās* and *chakkradārs* of this gharānā show some very clever variations of *laya*. Above all, its players excel in presenting *gāts* and *relās*. Another noteworthy excellence of this gharānā is the ability to play the *open bols* of pakhāwaj baaj in a (more or less) 'gathered' and mellow way. I may also add that the players, here, seem to have a special liking for the alphabet *tirkit*, which they use very freely in their *relā* compositions, — so freely indeed that at times it tends to cloy our relish of the total playing. Yet in respect of the skill, as against the frequency, with which this syllable is played, this gharānā is praiseworthy.

On the whole, however, the way in which quite difficult compositions are played by representatives of this gharānā appears more as a mathematical and physical exercise than as an essay in such a disposition of *bols* as works through changes of emphases and *laya* and through variations in the extent or phonetic character of syllabic phrases. Their main guiding principle seems to be sheer fluency, and power, and skill in presenting rhythm cycles that comprise an *odd* number of beats. Yet one should not belittle the distinguishing features of this gharānā; and it pains me to say that, because it no longer boasts of having any real maestro, it has now become virtually impossible to come across recitals of pure Panjab tablā. The fact indeed is that what is being presented today under the guise of Panjab gharānā tablā lacks the purity of its originally distinctive baaj and is merely a motley exposition of compositions of diverse kinds.

I may end this brief account of the Punjab gharānā with the remark that, in so far as its representatives excelled in presenting difficult *tāla*s and also because the playing of *elaborate* compositions in such cycles requires calculative accuracy in a special measure, the art of this gharānā has been freely called the *ginatkāri* (गिनतकारी) baaj or the calculative style of playing.

GHARĀNĀ-WESTERN STYLE

PUNJAB GHARĀNĀ

ILLUSTRATIVE COMPOSITIONS

1. Peshkār; Tritāla (Chatushra-Jāti)

Dhāऽkḍa	*Dhātīṅ*	*Nādhā*	ऽ*Dhā*
Tīnnā	*Genā*	*Dhādhā*	*Tīnnā*
Tāऽkḍa	*Tātīṅ*	*Nādhā*	ऽ*Dhā*
Tīnnā	*Genā*	*Dhādhā*	*Dhīnnā*

धाऽक्ड़	धातीं	नाधा	ऽधा
तींना	गेना	धाधा	तींना
ताऽक्ड़	तातीं	नाधा	ऽधा
तींना	गेना	धाधा	धींना

2. Peshkār-Quāyedā (Chatushra-Jāti)

Dhītā	*Kḍedhī*	*Tākḍa*	*Dhīdhī*
Dhāg	*Dhādhā*	*Tūnnā*	*Kiṭṭak*
Tintā	*Kḍedhī*	*Tākḍa*	*Tītī*
Dhāg	*Dhādhā*	*Tūnnā*	*Kiṭṭak*

धीता	कड़ेधी	ताक्ड़	धीधी
धाग	धाधा	तूंना	किटतक
तिनता	कड़ेधी	ताक्ड़	तीती
धाग	धाधा	तूंना	किटतक

3. Quāyedā (Chatushra-Jāti)

Dhādhāऽdhā	*Tiṭṭādhā*	*Gendhāge*	*Dhīnāgīnā*
Dhiṭ dhiṭ	*Dhāgendhā*	*Tīdhāgenā*	*Tīnākīnā*
Tātāऽtā	*Teṭṭeṭ*	*Kentāke*	*Tīnākīnā*
Dhiṭ dhiṭ	*Dhāgendhā*	*Tīdhāgenā*	*Dhīnāgīnā*

धाधाऽधा	तिटताधा	गेनधागे	धीनागीना
धिटधिट	धागेनधा	तीधागेना	तीनाकीना
ताताऽता	तेटतेट	केनताके	तीनाकीना
धिटधिट	धागेनधा	तीधागेना	धीनागीना

4. Quāyedā (Chatushra-Jāti)

Dhātir	*Kiṭṭak*	*Tirkiṭ*	*Dhātir*
Kiṭṭak	*Tirkiṭ*	*Dhīnnā*	*Gīnā*
Dhātī	*Dhāge*	*Tīnna*	*Kīnā*
Dhātī	*Dhāge*	*Tīnnā*	*Kīnā*
Tātir	*Kiṭṭak*	*Tirkiṭ*	*Tātir*
Kiṭṭak	*Tirkiṭ*	*Dhīnnā*	*Gīnā*
Dhātī	*Dhāge*	*Dhīnnā*	*Gīnā*
Dhātī	*Dhāge*	*Dhīnnā*	*Gīnā*

धातिर	किटतक	तिरकिट	धातिर
किटतक	तिरकिट	धींना	गीना
धाती	धागे	तींना	कीना
धाती	धागे	तींना	कीना
तातिर	किटतक	तिरकिट	तातिर
किटतक	तिरकिट	धींना	गीना
धाती	धागे	धींना	गीना
धाती	धागे	धींना	गीना

5. Relā (Chatushra-Jāti)

Dhāge	*Dhīnnā*	*Kedhā*	*Teṭa*
Kiṭ	*Tak*	*Tiṭ*	*Kiṭ*
Tāke	*Tīnnā*	*Ketā*	*Teṭa*
Kiṭ	*Tak*	*Tiṭ*	*Kiṭ*

धागे	धींना	केधा	तेट

किट	तक	तिट	किट
ताके	तींना	केता	तेट
किट	तक	तिट	किट

6. Another Relā (Chatushra-Jāti)

Dhāge	*Nadhā*	*Teṭe*	*Kiṭ*
Teṭe	*Kiṭ*	*Tin*	*Kin*
Tāke	*Natā*	*Teṭe*	*Kiṭ*
Teṭe	*Kiṭ*	*Dhin*	*Gin*

धागे	नधा	तेटे	किट
तेटे	किट	तिन	किन
ताके	नता	तेटे	किट
तेटे	किट	धिन	गिन

7. Gat (Tishra-Jāti)

Dhīndhāऽḍ	*Dhagnagdhin*	*Dhingindhin*	*Gindhagnag*
Takiṭdhāऽḍ	*Takdhingin*	*Takdhintak*	*Dhintakdhin*
Kintāऽḍ	*Taknaktin*	*Tinkintin*	*Kintaknak*
Takiṭdhāऽḍ	*Takdhingin*	*Takdhintak*	*Dhintakdhin*

धींधाऽड़	धगनगधिन	धिनगिनधिन	गिनधगनग
तकिटधाऽड़	तकधिनगिन	तकधिनतक	धिनतकधिन
किन्ताऽड़	तकनकतिन	तिनकिनतिन	किनतकनक
तकिटधाऽड़	तकधिनगिन	तकधिनतक	धिनतकधिन

8. Another Gat (Chatushra-Jāti)

Takiṭat	*Kiṭdhin*	*Nagdhin*	*Takiṭat*
Kiṭdhin	*Nagdhin*	*Dhaऽtak*	*Tiṭkiṭ*
Dhātakdhi	*Kiṭkat*	*Gadigan*	*Dhāऽghin*
Gadigan	*Dhātakdhi*	*Kiṭkat*	*Gadigan*

तकिटत	किटधिन	नगधिन	तकिटत
किटधिन	नगधिन	धाऽतक	तिटकिट
धातकधि	किटकत	गदिगन	धाऽघिन
गदिगन	धातकधि	किटकत	गदिगन

9. Ṭukḍā (Up to beat No. 8 in Chatushra Jāti; Tihāi in Tishra Jāti)

Dintak	*Dintak*	*Taktak*	*Dintak*
Takdin	*Taktak*	*Dintak*	*Dintak*
Dintaktak	*Takdintak*	*Dhāऽ*	*Dintaktak*
Takdintak	*Dhāऽ*	*Dintaktak*	*Takdintak*

दिनतक	दिनतक	तकतक	दिनतक
तकदिन	तकतक	दिनतक	दिनतक
दिनतकतक	तकदिनतक	धाऽ	दिनतकतक
तकदिनतक	धाऽ	दिनतकतक	तकदिनतक

10. Another ṭukḍā (Chatushra-Jāti)

Ghetak	*Dintak*	*Tiṭkatā*	*Kiṭtak*
Tiṭkatā	*Kiṭdhāge*	*Tiṭghiḍā*	*ऽnadhin*
Dhindhinā	*Gindhāge*	*Traktinā*	*Kiḍnag*
Dhirdhirkiṭtak	*Dhādhirdhir*	*Kiṭtakdhā*	*Dhirdhirkiṭtak*

घेतक	दिनतक	तिटकता	किटतक
तिटकता	किटधागे	तिटघिड़ा	ऽनधिन
धिनधिना	गिनधागे	त्रकतिना	किड़नग
धिरधिरकिटतक	धाधिरधिर	किटतकधा	धिरधिरकिटतक

11. Chakradār

Ghetak	*Dhintak*	*Tiṭakatā*	*Kiṭtak*
Tiṭkatā	*Kiṭdhāge*	*Tiṭghiḍa*	*ऽNadhin*
Dhindhinā	*Gindhāge*	*Traktinā*	*Kiḍnag*
(*Dhirdhirkiṭtak*	*Dhādhirdhir*	*Kiṭtakdhā*	*Dhirdhirkiṭtak Dhā*)

घेतक	धिनतक	किटकता	किटतक
तिटकता	किटधागे	तिटघिड़ा	ऽनधिन
धिनधिना	गिनधागे	त्रकतिना	किड़नग
(धिरधिरकिटतक	धाधिरधिर	किटतकधा	धिरधिरकिटतक धा)

Note: The bracketed *tihāī bol*s are to be repeated thrice, to make them cover 27 beats; and the whole composition is to be repeated thrice to make it appear an elaborate *chakradār*; 27x3 = 81 beats.

12. Another Chakradār (Tishra-Jāti)

Dhāऽn	*Dhikiṭ*	*Dhātrak*	*Dhetiṭ*
Tiṭkḍa	*Dhetiṭ*	*Katag*	*Digan*
Dhātrak	*Dhetiṭ*	*Katag*	*Digan*
Dhāऽn	*Dhikiṭ*	*Dhātrak*	*Dhetiṭ*
Tiṭkḍa	*Dhetiṭ*	*Katag*	*Digan*
Dhāऽ	*Katag*	*Digan*	*Dhāऽ*
Katag	*Digan*	*Dhāऽ*	

धाऽन	धिकिट	धात्रक	धेतिट
तिटक्ड	धेतिट	कतग	दिगन
धात्रक	धेतिट	कतग	दिगन
धाऽन	धिकिट	धात्रक	धेतिट
तिटक्ड	धेतिट	कतग	दिगन
धाऽ	कतग	दिगन	धाऽ
कतग	दिगन	धाऽ	

The whole composition is to be repeated thrice, to make it a *chakradār* - 27x3 = 81.

Delhi Gharānā

The whole credit for initiating and establishing the Delhi gharānā as a distinct school of tablā playing goes to Ustad Sidhār Khan Dhadi; and I want this to be taken as a very great compliment to the maestro, because so far as tablā rhythm is concerned the signal importance of this gharānā is unquestionable. I say so on the basis of some definite reasons. First, even today perhaps it is the only gharānā the baaj (or idiom of playing) of which can be said to be utterly free from the influence of pakhāwaj. Second, almost all the great Ustāds of other gharānās had actually migrated from Delhi to other cities of India, and so always had the art of Delhi gharānā in mind, if only for the purpose of expressly deviating from it. In other words, probably every other gharānā is in some way indebted to the Delhi school of tablā playing. The distinctive features of this gharānā are perhaps more widely known than those of the other gharānās. Still, for the sake of those who may not be quite conversant with the art of tablā, I think it is necessary to list the more important artistic excellences of this school, say, as follows:

1. A manifestly sweet and soft look of the compositions, so that they may well be said to be winsome even from the viewpoint of sheer musical quality, without of course becoming music in the strict sense of the term. It is therefore admirably capable of drawing and holding attention entirely because of its intrinsic excellences, that is, in the form of solo recitals.

2. Very liberal use of *the first two fingers of both hands* which lends crispness, accuracy and sonority to the *bols*. Also, a very free use of *kinār* (किनार) because of which this style of playing is called *kinār* baaj.

3. The repertoire, here, abounds in *quāyedās*, *peshkārs*, *relās*, *mukhḍās* and *mohrās* which are not too long in range, and therefore do not strain listeners' attention.

4. *Chatusra-jāti* as the dominant rhythmic idiom of most of the compositions of this gharānā.

5. A duly controlled, and never sprawling, resonance of *bols* as played, because of which this style is called *closed* baaj (बन्द बाज).

6. Finally, and this is a remarkable feature of the art of this gharānā, once the player's hands have been put on the tablā for beginning a recital, they are not allowed to retract before the entire playing is over.

7. Avoidance of a very fast pace. This negative demand is set by the very inner structure of the compositions of this gharānā, as also by the requirement that one has to use *only two fingers of the right hand and two of the left*, in executing the various *bol*-patterns.

At this point, however, I would like to make a slightly critical remark and also a remedial suggestion. The stipulation in respect of the use of fingers can be fully met only by very long sessions of regular practice. Today, people cannot spare so much time for the purpose; and this is likely to check the progress of new entrants in the fold of this gharānā. What is more, whereas the first finger of the right hand is stronger than the other four, the parallel finger of the left hand is the weakest of all in this hand. Therefore, whereas the prescribed use of right hand fingers is not likely to pose any problem, if repeated pressure is put on the first finger of the left hand — say, for the sake of eliciting louder sound from 'the left one' — the exertion entailed is likely to be very damaging for the overall working of fingers of this hand. The player may even come to develop a feeling of permanent pain and discomfort in the left hand, which may ultimately mar his capacity for smooth and effortless playing. I would therefore suggest that young players of today may circumvent this difficulty by innovating some convenient deviation from the orthodox prescription in respect of the use of fingers. A rhythmic recital should be a joy, not an arduous task for the player all along.

The suggestion I have made is specially relevant to occasions where the tablā player has to provide proper accompaniment to some very fluent instrumental music. In a solo recital *more* importance has to be given to the clarity, neatness, tonal quality — and to correct execution of *bol*-patterns — than to variations of pace. So, here, it may not be too difficult to follow the prescribed way of using fingers.

The Delhi gharānā repertoire is replete with *quāyedā*s that sound quite tuneful to the ear when properly played; and they also provide ample room for improvisation, that is, for a display of the player's own creative prowess. The alphabets that are most commonly used in these *quāyedā*s are *"tiṭa* (तिट) *"tirkiṭ"* (तिरकिट) and some other soft syllables. The surprising thing is that whereas these *quāyedā*s appear very simple and easily playable when *recited*, their *actual execution* on the tablā is pretty tough going, because the collocation of *bol*s is so intricately designed that intense concentration during a concert performance and a lot of prior practice are required.

Delhi Gharānā

LLUSTRATIVE COMPOSITIONS

1. Peshkār Tāla Tritāla (Chatushra-Jāti)

Dhikḍa	*Dhiṅdhā*	*Tiṭadhā*	*Kḍedhiṅ*
Dhātiṭa	*Dhādhā*	*Tiṭakiṭ*	*Dhīnnā*
Dhiṅdhā	*ऽKḍedhiṅ*	*Dhādhiṅ*	*Dhātiṭa*
Dhākḍa	*Dhiṅdhā*	*Dhādhā*	*Tīnnā*
Tīkḍa	*Tiṅtā*	*Tiṭatā*	*Kḍetiṅ*
Tātiṭa	*Tātā*	*Tiṭakiṭ*	*Tīṅtā*
Dhiṅdhā	*Kḍedhiṅ*	*Dhādhiṅ*	*Dhātiṭa*
Dhākḍa	*Dhiṅdhā*	*Dhādhā*	*Dhīnnā*

धीक्ड़	धिंधा	तिटधा	क्ड़ेधिं
धातिट	धाधा	तिटकिट	धींना
धिंधा	ऽक्ड़ेधिं	धाधिं	धातिट
धाक्ड़	धिंधा	धाधा	तींना
तीक्ड़	तिंता	तिटता	क्ड़ेतिं
तातिट	ताता	तिटकिट	तींता
धिंधा	क्ड़ेधिं	धाधिं	धातिट
धाक्ड़	धिंधा	धाधा	धींना

2. Peshkār-Quāyedā (Chatushra-Jāti)

Dhākḍa	*Dhātiṭa*	*Kiṭadhā*	*Dhinnā*
Dhātī	*Dhādhā*	*Tīdhā*	*Tinnā*
Tākḍa	*Tātiṭa*	*Kiṭatā*	*Tinnā*
Dhātī	*Dhādhā*	*Tīdhā*	*Dhinnā*

धाक्ड़	धातिट	किटधा	धिन्ना
धाती	धाधा	तीधा	तिन्ना
ताक्ड़	तातिट	किटता	तिन्ना
धाती	धाधा	तीधा	धिन्ना

3. Quāyedā (Chatushra-Jāti)

Dhāgenadhā	*Takadhin*	*Dhinkadhi*	*Ṭadhāgenā*
Dhātidhātir	*Kiṭadhāgena*	*Dhātidhāge*	*Tīnnākinā*

Tākenatā	*Takatin*	*Tinkati*	*Ṭadhāgenā*
Dhātidhātir	*Kiṭadhāgena*	*Dhātīdhāge*	*Dhinnāginā*

धागेनधा	तकधिन	धिनकधि	टधागेना
धातिधातिर	किटधागेन	धातिधागे	तींनाकिना
ताकेनता	तकतिन	तिनकति	टधागेना
धातिधातिर	किटधागेन	धातीधागे	धींनागिना

4. Quāyedā (Tishra-Jāti)

Dhātiṭadhā	*Gendhā*	*Tiṭakiṭdhīṅ*	*Nāgin*
Dhātiṭadhā	*Gedhātiṭa*	*Dhāgetiṅ*	*Nākīnā*
Tātiṭatā	*Kentā*	*Tiṭkiṭtīṅ*	*Nākin*
Dhatiṭadhā	*Gedhātiṭa*	*Dhāgedhīṅ*	*Nāgīnā*

धातिटधा	गेनधा	तिटकिटधीं	नागिन
धातिटधा	गेधातिट	धागेतिं	नाकीना
तातिटता	केनता	तिटकिटतीं	नाकिन
धातिटता	गेधातिट	धागेधीं	नागीना

5. Relā (Chatushra-Jāti)

Ghiḍnag	*Tiṭakiṭa*	*Dhāऽtiṭa*	*Ghiḍnag*
Dhāऽtiṭa	*Ghiḍnag*	*Tiṭakiṭa*	*Tāketiṭa*
Kiḍnag	*Tiṭakiṭa*	*Taऽtiṭa*	*Kiḍnag*
Dhāऽtiṭa	*Ghiḍnag*	*Tiṭakiṭa*	*Dhāgetiṭa*

घिड़नग	तिटकिट	धाऽतिट	घिड़नग
धाऽतिट	घिड़नग	तिटकिट	ताकेतिट
किड़नग	तिटकिट	ताऽतिट	किड़नग
धाऽतिट	घिड़नग	तिटकिट	धागेतिट

6. Another Relā (Chatushra-Jāti)

Dhāऽtiṭ	*Ghiḍnag*	*Dhāऽtiṭ*	*Ghiḍnag*
Dhāऽtiṭ	*Ghiḍnag*	*Tīṅtīṅ*	*Kiḍnag*
Tāऽtiṭ	*Kiḍnag*	*Tāऽtiṭ*	*Kiḍnag*
Dhāऽtiṭ	*Ghiḍnag*	*Dhīṅdhīṅ*	*Ghiḍnag*

धाऽतिट	घिड़नग	धाऽतिट	घिड़नग
धाऽतिट	घिड़नग	तींतीं	किड़नग

ताऽतिट	किड़नग	ताऽतिट	किड़नग
धाऽतिट	घिड़नग	धींधीं	घिड़नग

7. Gāt (Chatushra-Jāti)

Dhāgetiṭ	*Ghiḍāऽn*	*Dhingin*	*Dhāgetrak*
Dhināgin	*Tiṭakiṭ*	*Ghenkatā*	*Tiṭghin*
Takiṭadhā	*Trakadhin*	*Ghiḍnag*	*Dhāgetiṭ*
Ghiḍāऽn	*Dhingin*	*Dhāgetrak*	*Dhināginā*

धागेतिट	घिड़ाऽन	धिनगिन	धागेत्रक
धिनागिन	तिटकिट	घेनकता	तिटघिन
तकिटधा	त्रकधिन	घिड़नग	धागेतिट
घिड़ाऽन	धिनगिन	धागेत्रक	धिनागिना

8. Another Gāt or Chāl

Dhinnak	*Dhinnak*	*Takdhin*	*Taktiṭa*
Ghiḍnag	*Dhinnag*	*Tiṭakatā*	*Kiḍnag*
Dhingin	*Dhāgetrak*	*Dhingin*	*Dhāgetiṭ*
Ghiḍāऽn	*Dhagnag*	*Dhindhag*	*Nagdhin*

धिननक	धिननक	तकधिन	तकतिट
घिड़नग	धिननग	तिटकता	किड़नग
धिनगिन	धागेत्रक	धिनगिन	धागेतिट
घिड़ाऽन	धगनग	धिनधग	नगधिन

9. Ṭukḍā (Chatushra-Jāti)

Dhitdhit	*Trakadhit*	*Dhiṭdhiṭ*	*Gheghetiṭ*
Kḍedhitiṭ	*Nāgetiṭ*	*Gadigan*	*Nāgetiṭ*
Kḍedhitiṭ	*Tāgetiṭ*	*Nāgetiṭ*	*Gadigan*
Nāgetiṭ	*Ghintarāऽ*	*ऽNadhā*	*Gaऽdi*
Gheऽna	*Dhāऽ*	*ऽ*	*Katiṭat*
Gandhin	*Tagandhi*	*Natagan*	*Dhākati*
Taṭagan	*Dhintag*	*Nadhin*	*Tagandhā*
Katiṭat	*Gandhin*	*Tagandhi*	*Natagan*

धित्धित्	त्रकधित	धिटधिट	घेघेतिट
क्ड़ेधितिट	नागेतिट	गदिगन	नागेतिट

क्ड़ेधितिट	नागेतिट	नागेतिट	गदिगन
नागेतिट	घिंतराऽ	ऽनधा	गऽदी
घेऽन	धाऽ	ऽ	कतिटत
गनधिन	तगनधि	नतगन	धाकति
तटगन	धिनतग	नधिन	तगनधा
कतिटत	गनधिन	तगनधि	नतगन

10. Another Ṭukḍā (Chatushra-Jāti)

Dhiṭdhiṭ	*Tiṭatiṭa*	*Tiṭatiṭa*	*Kattiṭa*
Katiṭadhā	*ऽNadhā*	*Tiṭkat*	*Gadigan*
Dhāऽ	*Kiṭadhāऽ*	*Nadhāऽn*	*Dhāऽkiṭa*
Dhāऽnadhā	*ऽNadhā*	*Kiṭadhāऽ*	*Nadhāऽn*
Dhāऽ	*Kiṭadhāऽ*	*Nadhāऽn*	*Dhāऽkiṭa*
Dhāऽnadhā	*ऽNadhā*	*Kiṭadhāऽ*	*Nadhāऽn*
Dhāऽ	*Kiṭadhāऽ*	*Nadhāऽn*	*Dhāऽkiṭa*
Dhāऽnadhā	*ऽNadhā*	*Kiṭadhāऽ*	*Nadhāऽn*

धिटधिट	तिटतिट	तिटतिट	कततिट
कतिटधा	ऽनधा	तिटकत	गदिगन
धाऽ	किटधाऽ	नधाऽन	धाऽकिट
धाऽनधा	ऽनधा	किटधाऽ	नधाऽन
धाऽ	किटधाऽ	नधाऽन	धाऽकिट
धाऽनधा	ऽनधा	किटधाऽ	नधाऽन
धाऽ	किटधाऽ	नधाऽन	धाऽकिट
धाऽनधा	ऽनधा	किटधाऽ	नधाऽन

11. Chakradār (Mishra-Jāti)

Dhāऽghi	*Nāऽtiṭa*	*Tiṭaghi*	*Nāऽtraka*
Dhiṭghi	*Nāऽghin*	*Dindi*	*Nāऽghinā*
Kaऽta	*Tiṭakiṭa*	*Tāgena*	*Tāgetiṭa*
Kḍedhinऽn	*Nānānānā*	*Tirkiṭtak*	*Dhirdhirkiṭtak*
Dhāऽ	*Kḍedhinऽn*	*Nānānānā*	*Tirkiṭtak*
Dhirdhirkiṭtak	*Dhāऽ*	*Kḍedhinऽn*	*Nānānānā*
Tirkiṭtak	*Dhirdhirkiṭtak*	*Dhāऽ*	

धाऽघि	नाऽतिट	तिटघि	नाऽत्रक
धिटघि	नाऽघिन	दिनदि	नाऽघिना

कऽत	तिटकिट	तागेन	तागेतिट
क्ड़ेधिंऽन	नानानाना	तिरकिटतक	धिरधिरकिटतक
धाऽ	क्ड़ेधिंऽन	नानानाना	तिरकिटतक
धिरधिरकिटतक	धाऽ	क्ड़ेधिंऽन	नानानाना
तिरकिटतक	धिधिरकिटतक	धाऽ	

The above composition is to be repeated thrice, to make it a *Chakradār* - 27 x 3 = 81.

12. Another Chakradār Tishra-Jāti

Dindi	*Nāgin*	*Dindi*	*Nāgin*
Takiṭa	*Dhātrak*	*Dindi*	*Nāgin*
Dhḍāsn	*Dhḍāsn*	*Dhātir*	*Kiṭtak*
Dhirdhirkiṭtak	*Dhātirkiṭtak*	*Dhātirkiṭtak*	*Takḍāsn*
Dhās	*Dhirdhirkiṭtak*	*Dhātirkiṭtak*	*Dhātirkiṭtak*
Takḍāsn Dhās	*Dhirdhirkiṭtak*	*Dhātirkiṭtak*	*Dhātirkiṭtak*
Takḍāsn	*Dhās*		

दिनदि	नागिन	दिनदि	नागिन
तकिट	धात्रक	दिनदि	नागिन
ध्ड़ाऽन	ध्ड़ाऽन	धातिर	किटतक
धिरधिरकिटतक	धातिरकिटतक	धातिरकिटतक	तक्ड़ाऽन
धाऽ	धिरधिरकिटतक	धातिरकिटतक	धातिरकिटतक
तक्ड़ाऽन धाऽ	धिरधिरकिटतक	धातिरकिटतक	धातिरकिटतक
तक्ड़ाऽन	धाऽ		

Ajrāḍā Gharānā

This gharānā is commonly regarded as an offshoot of the Delhi gharānā because its founding brothers, Ustads Kallū Khan and Mīrū Khan, had learnt tablā under the guidance of the Delhi maestros. However, on returning to their birthplace, Ajrāḍā, the two brothers, both thoroughly conversant with the riches of the Delhi baaj, composed numberless new patterns of *bols*; and their creations soon won them recognition as the progenitors of a quite new gharānā. Most of their compositions were set in *tisra jāti* and would appear to evoke, when properly played, the semblance of an undulating flow. However, there are quite a few other artistic features too, mainly the following, which distinguish the structural idiom of the baaj of this gharānā:

1. Occasional punctuation of a whole composition with moments of intentional deviation from the basic *laya* without letting the run of the pattern go haywire, — a structural subtlety to which one could well apply Milton's characterization of some good music as marked by "wanton heed and giddy cunning."

2. In actual playing a co-ordinated use, all along, of the two drums, the left and the right ones, so as to work up (in the playing of the *ṭhekā*) the delightful semblance of a seamless, breathing sound — *clear and articulate, yet not without depth.*

3. Further, in respect of the technique of actual playing, it is noteworthy that, as against the maestros of the Delhi style, the Ajrāḍā Ustāds use the first three fingers of *both* hands to facilitate proper executions of the very intricate *quāyedā*s for which this gharānā is rightly famous. It is precisely because of this intrinsic subtlety of conception and dexterity in execution that most of the fair-minded tablā maestros openly declare that the Ajrāḍā idiom is essentially meant for those who are fairly competent players themselves, and not for lay listeners who can only respond to fluency and accordant bodily jerks. This style is indeed so rich in its inner filling and so intricate in the collocation of its *bol*s that one needs a sense of both design and skill of execution to play and follow the *quāyedā*s of this gharānā discriminatingly.

4. A sprinkling of *gat* compositions of exquisite beauty which are noteworthy for the way they make use of दाब-गांस — that is, regulated pressure and a certain breathing depth — in conjoining the *dānyā-bānyā* mnemonics, so that the total playing acquires what Susanne Langer has spoken of as the semblance of 'livingness,' and in the absence of which the presentation, with all its fidelity to *laya* and attainment of *sama*, appears cold and lifeless, or ठंडा and बेजान, as we would say in our everyday parlance.

Basically, I may add, all gharānās use more or less similar alphabets in their compositions, for the most part. What they differ in is only in respect of intergrating the *bols*, and in the choice of fingers and extent (or parts) of hands to be used. I may now turn to some details of structure, execution and effect that distinguish the gharānā I am presently dealing with.

Perhaps the most distinctive thing about the repertoire, as distinguished from the playing technique, of this gharānā is its possession of quite a few exquisitely composed *quāyedās* which are quite distinct from their rhythmic parallels in other gharānās. In a good number of the more elaborate ones of these, covering as many as thirtytwo beats or even more, the *khāli* section of the *quāyedā* is deftly made to occur as an implict segment in the very basic format of the *quāyedā*. The attentive reader should not find it difficult to notice this feature when he goes through the notated examples provided later in this chapter.

Another striking detail of Ajrāḍā *quāyedās*, which often catches the eye of knowledgeable tablā players, is the aesthetic interplay (loosely called, *laḍanta* or लड़न्त by our *rasikās*) of syllables that sound similar, without being identical — such as *ghinā, tinā, ghinā* (घिना, तिना, घिना) — which gives the player a chance to use 'the left one' impressively, yet not fuzzily; and also to lend a depth of impact, and so some classical dignity, to the total playing. It is this artistic device which enables the Ajrāḍā tablā player to steer clear of *the two undesirable extremes of merely skimming the surface of the bānyā or just thumping it to produce a loud, but indistinct sound.*

Yet another distinguishing feature of the baaj (style of playing) of this gharānā may be mentioned here, piecemeal. First, the drummer plays, only once, the whole *quāyedā* comprising two phrases in *chatusra jāti;* thereafter, the composition is repeated upto the 12th beat; then, from the 13th beat the playing suddenly swerves to the idiom of *tisra jāti,* surpassing the *sama* a little daintily and designedly; and then, as a crowning finale, from the *sama* anew, it takes up the run of *chatusra jāti,* and plays the original *quāyedā* at double speed, followed by as many permutations as the player's creative ability may permit. As for the *syllables* used in the compositions of this gharānā, the ones that abound are: *ghitak* (घितक), *ghey ghey tak* (घेघेतक), *dhin dhīnā ginā* (धिन धीना गिना), and *dhin-gin-tinkin* (धिन-गिन-तिनकिन).

In respect of *gat*s of this gharānā, one is struck by the skill or the way they have been composed, not only in respect of technical subtlety, but also in that of their pleasing impact on the listening ear. To turn again to *quāyedā*s of this school of tablā, there are some in which a span of 17 beats has been adroitly accommodated in the format of a 16-beat *tāla*, without the slightest suggestion of forced adjustment. This is a very clear index of the immaculate hold over *laya* possessed by the pioneers of this gharānā. What is more, the use of fingers is here so varyingly, yet aptly adapted to the run of rhythm that it cannot be captured for use by mere attentive listening. *The technique of bol-production has to be learnt practically under the watchful eye of a maestro.* One's own independent effort cannot here produce the desired musical effects. Finally, what further distinguishes the Ajrāḍā baaj, I may add, is the proper employment of three fingers of the right hand *and* three of the left one.

Now, let me reveal some of the representative compositions of this gharānā:

Illustrative Compositions

1. Peshkar (Kaherwā Ang-Chatushra-Jāti)

Dhigandhā	*Trakdhin*	*Dhāgendhiṅ*	ऽ*Dhinak*
Dhāgendhiṅ	ऽ*dhādhātī*	*Dhāgentiṅ*	ऽ*Tinak*
Tigantā	*Traktin*	*Tākentiṅ*	ऽ*Tinak*
Dhāgendhiṅ	ऽ*dhādhātī*	*Dhāgendhiṅ*	ऽ*Dhinak*

धिगनधा	त्रकधिन	धागेनधिं	ऽधिनक
धागेनधिं	ऽधाधाती	धागेनतिं	ऽतिनक
तिगनता	त्रकतिन	ताकेनतिं	ऽतिनक
धागेनधिं	ऽधाधाती	धागेनधिं	ऽधिनक

2. Peshkar-Quāyedā

Dhāऽkḍadhā	*Tidhāgena*	*Dhāgedhinnā*	*Dhāgedhinnā*
Ghinadhātiṭ	*Kiṭdhātidhā*	*Gendhāge*	*Tinākinā*
Tāऽkḍtā	*Tiṭāken*	*Tāketinnā*	*Dhāgedhinnā*
Ghinādhātir	*Kiṭdhātidhā*	*Gendhāge*	*Dhināginā*

धाऽक्ड़धा	तिधागेन	धागेधिंना	धागेधिंना
घिनधातिट	किटधातिधा	गेनधागे	तिनाकिना
ताऽक्ड़ता	तिटाकेन	ताकेतिंना	धागेधिंना
घिनाधातिर	किटधातिधा	गेनधागे	धिनागिना

3. Quāyedā of 17 beats artistically disposed within a range of only 16 beats:

Dhāgenti	*Ṭadhāgena*	*Dhināginā*	*Dhiṭdhāge*	
Nadhināgi	*Nadhāgena*	*Dhiṭdhāge*	*Nadhināgi*	17 Beats
Nātāken	*Tiṭtāke*	*Nātināki*	*Nadhiṭdhā*	
Gendhinā	*Ginādhāge*	*Nadhiṭdhā*	*Genadhinā Ginā*ऽ	

Dhāgenti	*Ṭadhāgena*	*Dhināginā*	*Dhiṭdhāgenā*	
Dhināginā	*Dhāgendhi*	*Ṭadhāgen*	*Tinākinā*	16 Beats
Tākenti	*Ṭatākena*	*Tinākinā*	*Dhiṭdha genā*	
Dhināginā	*Dhāgendhi*	*Ṭadhāgen*	*Dhināginā*	

धागेनति	टधागेन	धिनागिना	धिटधागे	
नधिनागि	नधागेन	धिटधागे	नधिनागि	(17 मात्रा)
नाताकेन	तिटताके	नातिनाकि	नधिटधा	
गेनधिना	गिनाधागे	नधिटधा	गेनधिना गिनाऽ	

धागेनति	टधागेन	धिनागिना	धिटधा गेना	
धिनागिना	धागेनधि	टधागेन	तिनाकिना	(16 मात्रा)
ताकेनति	टताकेन	तिनाकिना	धिटधागेना	
धिनागिना	धागेनधि	टधागेन	धिनागिना	

4. Quāyedā of 32 beats in Chatushra-Jāti

1	2	3	4
*Dhā*ऽ *kḍedhi*	*Tiṭtiṭ*	*Kḍedhitiṭ*	*Dhāgetiṭ*
5	6	7	8
Kḍedhitiṭ	*Dhāgetiṭ*	*Dhāgetrak*	*Dhināginā*

9	10	11	12
Dindinā	*Ghintiṭ*	*Kḍedhitiṭ*	*Dhāgetiṭ*
13	14	15	16
Kḍedhitiṭ	*Dhāgetiṭ*	*Dhāgetrak*	*Tīnākinā*
1	2	3	4
TāSkḍeti	*Tiṭtiṭ*	*Kḍetitiṭ*	*Tāketiṭ*
5	6	7	8
Kḍetitiṭ	*Tāketiṭ*	*Tāketrak*	*Tīnākinā*
9	10	11	12
Dindinā	*Ghintiṭ*	*Kḍedhitiṭ*	*Dhāgetiṭ*
13	14	15	16
Kḍedhitiṭ	*Dhāgetiṭ*	*Dhāgetrak*	*Dhināginā*

(X)

धाSक्ड़ेधि	तिटतिट	क्ड़ेधितिट	धागेतिट
क्ड़ेधितिट	धागेतिट	धागेत्रक	धिनागिना
दिनदिना	घिनतिट	क्ड़ेधितिट	धागेतिट
क्ड़ेधितिट	धागेतिट	धागेत्रक	(तीनाकिना)
ताSक्ड़ेति	तिटतिट	क्ड़ेतितिट	ताकेतिट
क्ड़ेतितिट	ताकेतिट	ताकेत्रक	(तीनाकिना)
दिनदिना	घिनतिट	क्ड़ेधितिट	धागेतिट
क्ड़ेधितिट	धागेतिट	धागेत्रक	धिनागिना

(X)

Note: Here, in the above, from the thirteenth beat (of the second part of the composition) — the part which has been marked thus (X), one is required to read/play the *following* 4-beat *bols* (that pave the way to the *sama*) in *tisra jāti*:

नोटः- यहां, बन्दिश के दूसरे भाग की तेरहवीं मात्रा से, जहाँ (X) चिन्ह लगाया गया है, सम तक पहुंचने के लिये, नीचे लिखे हुए चार मात्राओं के बोल तिस्त्र जाति में पढ़ने/बजाने हैं:

	1	2	
Dindinānghin	*Tiṭkḍedhitiṭ*	*Dhāgetiṭ Dhāge*	*trakDhināgina*
	3	4	
Dhā Skḍedhitiṭ	*Tiṭkḍedhitiṭ*	*DhāgetiṭDhāge*	*trakDhināgina*

1		2	
दिनदिनाधिन	तिटक्ड़ेधितिट	धागेतिटधागे	त्रकधिनागिन
	3	4	
धा ऽक्ड़ेधितिट	तिटक्ड़ेधितिट	धागेतिटधागे	त्रकधिनागिन

Note: Further, after playing the *Tisra-Jāti* segment, one has to play the main *quāyedā* at double speed, followed by *paltā*s (or variations).

नोट:- तिश्र जाति के बोल बजाने के पश्चात, मुख्य क़ायदे को दुगुने लय में बजाकर, फिर पल्टे बजाइये!

5. Rela, Chatsura-Jāti

Dhāgetiṭ	*Kiṭgheghe*	*Tiṭkiṭ*	*Dhingin*
Dhāgetiṭ	*Kiṭgheghe*	*Nānāgin*	*Tinkin*
Tāketiṭ	*Kiṭkeke*	*Tiṭkiṭ*	*Tinkin*
Dhāgetiṭ	*Kiṭgheghe*	*Nānāgin*	*Dhingin*

धागेतिट	किटघेघे	तिटकिट	धिनगिन
धागेतिट	किटघेघे	नानागिन	तिनकिन
ताकेतिट	किटकेके	तिटकिट	तिनकिन
धागेतिट	किटघेघे	नानागिन	धिनगिन

6. Rela, Chatusra-Jāti

Ghiḍnag	*Dhingin*	*Dhāgetrak*	*Dhingin*
Dhāgetrak	*Dhinghiḍ*	*Nagtin*	*Tinkin*
Kiḍnag	*Tinkin*	*Tāketrak*	*Tinkin*
Dhāgetrak	*Dhinghiḍ*	*Nagdhin*	*Dhingin*

घिड़नग	धिनगिन	धागेत्रक	धिनगिन
धागेत्रक	धिनघिड़	नगतिन	तिनकिन
किड़नग	तिनकिन	ताकेत्रक	तिनकिन
धागेत्रक	धिनघिड़	नगधिन	धिनगिन

7. "Gat," Chatusra-Jāti

Ghiḍnag	*Dhindhāge*	*Trakdhin*	*Ghiḍnag*
Dhindhag	*Dhagdhin*	*Dhāgetrak*	*Dhinghiḍ*
Nagdhin	*Dīnāginā*	*Tāऽ Ghiḍ*	*Nagdhin*
Dhāgetrak	*Dhinghiḍ*	*Nagdhin*	*Dhināginā*

घिड़नग	धिनधागे	त्रकधिन	घिड़नग
धिनधग	धगधिन	धागेत्रक	धिनघिड़
नगधिन	दीनागिना	ताऽघिड़	नगधिन
धागेत्रक	धिनघिड़	नगधिन	धीनागिना

8. "Gat," Tisra-Jāti

Dhagat takiṭ	*Takdintak*	*Tiṭkatāऽn*	*Dhiṭkatāऽn*
Dhagnagdhin	*Dhagnagdhin*	*Dhingheghenak*	*Dindināginā*
TakanTiṅऽn	*Tāketiṭkiṭ*	*Tāketiṭṭāke*	*Traktinākina*
Dhāgdhādhāgheghe	*Nagdhinnā*	*Dhingheghenak*	*Dindināginā*

धगततकिट	तकदिनतक	तिटकताऽन	धिटकताऽन
धगनगधिन	धगनगधिन	धिनघेघेनक	दिनदिनागिना
तकनतिंऽन	ताकेतिटकिट	ताकेतिटताके	त्रकतिनाकिन
धागधाधाघेघे	नगधिंना	धिनघेघेनक	दिनदिनागिना

9. Ṭukḍā : Chatusra and Tisra Jātis

Kat	*Din*	*Din*	*Din*
Dhāgheghe	*Nagdhin*	*Dhāgetrak*	*Dhināginā*
Ghinā	*Kati*	*Ṭak*	*Tiṭ*
Tākey	*Tākey*	*Tākey*	*Tākey*
Dhaऽn	*Dhitiṭ*	*Dhātrak*	*Dhitiṭ*
Kḍedhet	*Dhitiṭ*	*Dinan*	*Nāऽ*
Kaऽt	*Dhāऽ*	*Tirkiṭṭak*	*Tāऽ*
Dhirdhirkiṭṭak	*Dhādin*	*ऽGhin*	*ऽNāt*
ऽGhin	*ऽNat*	*Dhāऽ*	*Dhirdhirkiṭṭak*
Dhādin	*ऽGhin*	*ऽNat*	*ऽGhin*
ऽNat	*Dhāऽ*	*Dhirdhirkiṭṭak*	*Dhādin*
ऽGhin	*ऽNat*	*ऽGhin*	*ऽNat*

कत्	दिन	दिन	दिन
धाघेघे	नगधिन	धागेत्रक	धिनागिना
घिना	कति	टक	तिट
ताके	ताके	ताके	ताके
धाऽन	धितिट	धात्रक	धितिट
कड्धेत	धितिट	दिनन	नाऽ
कऽत	धाऽ	तिरकिटतक	ताऽ

धिरधिरकिटतक	धादिन	ऽघिन	ऽनत
ऽघिन	ऽनत	धाऽ	धिरधिरकिटतक
धादिन	ऽघिन	ऽनत	ऽघिन
ऽनत	धाऽ	धिरधिरकिटतक	धादिन
ऽघिन	ऽनत	ऽघिन	ऽनत

10. Ṭukḍā : Chatusra and Tisra Jātis

Dhādhā	*Dhātrak*	*Diṅdiṅ*	*Dhagetiṭ*
Dhagaऽta	*Kiṭadhin*	*Nagtāge*	*Tiṭkatā*
ऽNdhā	*Dhirdhirkiṭṭak*	*Dhirdhirkiṭṭak*	*Takḍdhā*
Nagdhe	*ऽTā*	*Dhāऽ*	*Ghiḍnag*
Dhādhā	*ऽDhā*	*Dhādiṅtā*	*Takiṭdhitiṭ*
Dhākatān	*Dhāऽ*	*Diṅdiṅ*	*Dhāऽdhirdhir*
Kiṭṭak takiṭ	*Dhādiṅ*	*Diṅdhā*	*Dhirdhirkiṭṭak*
Takiṭdhā	*Diṅdiṅ*	*Dhāऽdhirdhir*	*Kiṭṭaktakiṭ*

धाधा	धात्रक	दिंदिं	धागेतिट
धगऽत	किटधिन	नगतागे	तिटकता
ऽनधा	धिरधिरकिटतक	धिरधिरकिटतक	तक्ड़धा
नगधे	ऽता	धाऽ	घिड़नग
धाधा	ऽधा	धादिंता	तकिटधितिट
धाकतान	धाऽ	दिंदिं	धाऽधिरधिर
किटतकतकिट	धादिं	दिंधा	धिरधिरकिटतक
तकिटधा	दिंदिं	धाऽधिरधिर	किटतकतकिट

11. Chakradār : Tisra and Chatusra Jātis

Dindi	*Nadin*	*Nagan*	*Nagan*
Takiṭ	*Dhitiṭ*	*Gheṅऽnta*	*Rāऽn*
Takiṭdhi	*Tiṭkat*	*Ghiऽntarā*	*ऽnkat*
Dindindin	*Nagannagan*	*Takiṭdhitiṭ*	*Ghinऽntarāऽn*
Dhāऽ	*Dindindin*	*Nagannagan*	*Takiṭdhitiṭ*
Ghiऽntarāऽn	*Dhāऽ*	*Dindindin*	*Nagan nagan*
Takiṭdhitiṭ	*Ghiऽntarāऽn*	*Dhāऽ*	

दिनदि	नदिन	नगन	नगन
तकिट	धितिट	घेंऽनत	राऽन

तकिटधि	तिटकत	घिऽनृतरा	ऽनकत
दिनदिनदिन	नगननगन	तकिटधितिट	घिऽनतराऽन
धाऽ	दिनदिनदिन	नगननगन	तकिटधितिट
घिऽनतराऽन	धाऽ	दिनदिनदिन	नगननगन
तकिटधितिट	घिऽनृतराऽन	धाऽ	

12. Chakradār

Dinnag	*Dinnag*	*Taktak*	*Dinnag*
Tiṭghiḍ	*Nagtak*	*Dinnag*	*Dinnag*
Taktaktak	*Takghiḍnag*	*Dinnagdin*	*Nagdinnag*
*Tiṭghiḍā*ऽ*n*	*Dinnagtak*	*Dhā*ऽ	*Ghe*ऽ*nt*
*Dhā*ऽ	*Tiṭaghiḍā*ऽ*n*	*Dinnagtak*	*Dhā*ऽ
*Gheṅ*ऽ*nt*	*Dhā*ऽ	*Tiṭaghiḍā*ऽ*n*	*Dinnagtak*
*Dhā*ऽ	*Gheṅ*ऽ*nt*	*Dhā*ऽ	

दिननग	दिननग	तकतक	दिननग
तिटघिड़	नगतक	दिननग	दिननग
तकतकतक	तकघिड़नग	दिननगदिन	नगदिननग
तिटघिड़ाऽन	दिननगतक	धाऽ	घेऽनत
धाऽ	तिटघिड़ाऽन	दिननगतक	धाऽ
घेंऽनत	धाऽ	तिटघिड़ाऽन	दिननगतक
धाऽ	घेंऽनत	धाऽ	

Practical examples of the patterns signifed by the following terms: *"Tihāī, Fard, Mukhḍā, Mohrā, Laggī & Laḍi."*

Tīntāla-16 Beats

13. Tihāī (तिहाई)

Tiṭ	*Kata*	*Gadi*	*Gan*
Dhā	ऽ	*Tiṭ*	*Kata*
Gadi	*Gan*	*Dhā*	ऽ
Tiṭ	*Kata*	*Gadi*	*Gan*

तीनताल-16 मात्रा

तिट	कत	गदि	गन
धा	ऽ	तिट	कत

गदि	गन	धा	ऽ
तिट	कत	गदि	गन

14. Fard (फ़र्द)

Tiṭghiḍā	*ऽNadhāऽ*	*Ghiḍnag*	*Dhīnākat*
Kiṭdhin	*Ghiḍnag*	*Dhiṭdhāge*	*Tiṭtāke*
Dhaḍaऽnna	*Gaऽddī*	*Katghin*	*Dhāgendhā*
Gendhāge	*Dignāge*	*Tirkiṭtaktāऽ*	*ऽDhirdhirkiṭ*

तिटघिड़ा	ऽनधाऽ	घिड़नग	धीनाकत
किटधिन	घिड़नग	धिटधागे	तिटताके
धड़ऽन्न	गऽद्दी	कतघिन	धागेनधा
गेनधागे	दिगनागे	तिरकिटतकताऽ	ऽधिरधिरकिट

15. Mukhḍā (मुखड़ा)

Dhāऽ	*Tinnā*	*Kiḍnak*	*Tinnā*
Kiḍnak	*Tirkiṭ*	*Taktā*	*Tirkiṭ*
Dhāऽ	*Tirkiṭ*	*Taktā*	*Tirkiṭ*
Dhāऽ	*Tirkiṭ*	*Taktā*	*Tirkiṭ*

धाऽ	तिनां	किड़नक	तिंना
किड़नक	तिरकिट	तकता	तिरकिट
धाऽ	तिरकिट	तकता	तिरकिट
धाऽ	तिरकिट	तकता	तिरकिट

16. Mohrā (मोहरा)

Dhāऽ	*Tinnā*	*Kiḍnak*	*Tāऽtir*
Kiḍnak	*Tirkiṭ*	*Taktak*	*Dhingin*
Dhāऽ	*Kaऽt*	*Dhāऽ*	*Ghiऽnta*
Dhāऽ	*Takiṭ*		

धाऽ	तिंना	किड़नक	ताऽतिर
किड़नक	तिरकिट	तकतक	धिनगिन
धाऽ	कऽत	धाऽ	घिऽनत
धाऽ	तकिट		

Kaherwa Tāla-8 Beats

17. Laggī (लग्गी)

Dhāऽ	*Tin*	*Tā*	*Rā*
Tāऽ	*Tin*	*Dhā*	*Ḍā*

कहरवा ताल–8 मात्रा

धाऽ	तिन	ता	रा
ताऽ	तिं	धा	ड़ा

18. Laḍi (लड़ी)

Dhātī	*Dhāg*	*Dhātī*	*Dhāg*
Dhātī	*Dhāg*	*Dhātī*	*Dhāg*

धाती	धाग	धाती	धाग
धाती	धाग	धाती	धाग

7

Principles of Composition

A close, analytical look at the compositions of the different gharānās given in the previous chapter, and at my own repertoire, has enabled me to seize some definite principles which determine composition in the field of rhythm, without, of course, exhausting the creative potential of this art. It is precisely these principles that I propose to discuss in this chapter.

At the very outset, however, I would like to focus on an important point. A new composition can dawn upon the mind quite suddenly, instead of resulting from a long conscious effort of trial and error. Such creative flashes, however, occur only in the case of those who already possess a rich repertoire, and whose minds have become saturated with the spirit of rhythm, as a sequel to long and loving fellowship with the art. The well known aesthetician Croce, I am told, emphasized the supreme role of intuition in art-making. Now, in so far as I am not an aesthetician myself, though I *can* claim to have some aesthetic sense, I am not aware of how exactly Croce argues for his emphasis. Nor do I know what intuition really is. But if it also means suddenness of the way in which some thought, some insight, or an impulse may come to the mind, I can vouch for the truth of the emphasis in question, strictly in the light of my own humble experience of creative work in the field of rhythm. What has happened to me repeatedly is that, quite without any intention to compose, suddenly a tuft of alphabets flashes upon the mind — I do not know from where, and because of what; and then its own aesthetic demand and my own familiarity with rhythm as a *performing* art jointly make for its flowering into a whole composition *wholly in the mind*, that is, well before any try to actually play it on the tablā. And all this takes place while I am engaged in some humdrum activity, such as ambling in the market. Of course, I cannot say that sudden or immediate, effortless awareness is *confined to* art-making. Even in daily life, if two things are put side by side, do we take time in sensing whether they are similar or different? But those intutitive flashes which make for the creation of beautiful forms are surely distinctive of a life of intense, personal commitment to some art.

I indeed feel sure of one specific fact. Authentic creative work in the field of rhythm is just not possible if one has not already assimilated, over a period of years, *the essence and variform working* of rhythm. The essence, here, is not merely evenness of pace, but its active *regulation* which (also) means management of variations within an overall order. This is exactly what distinguishes time as rhythm from clock time on the one hand, and from our everyday experience of time (or lived time) on the other. The ticks of a clock occur at an even pace, *and never deviate from it*, that is, till before some mechanical defect occurs. But this is not the way of time as we actually experience it in daily life. On a particular day when we have nothing to do, time seems to pass very slowly. On a busy day, contrarily, if we have to work ceaselessly and complete many tasks, each within a prefixed time limit, the end of working hours may seem to come a bit too quickly. Similarly, in the region of rhythm, our sense of the passage of artistically created time can vary greatly; and, what is more, here too the orderly regulation of pace is both *segmental* and *overall*. The former is provided by *vibhāg*s (in the case of the basic cycle) and by *jāti*s (in the case of patterns); and the latter (that is, *overall*) by *two* factors. The first of these is the norm of the pattern's seeming *self-*completion at the *sama* — or at least an ideal indication of the focal beat through a skilfully designed avoidance of it; and the second determinant of *overall* regulation of pace is the individual player's own essential hold over the flow of *laya* as expressed in quickening a tuft of *bols* or decelerating the pace of another, *without any wobbling or harm to the basic laya.*

At this point, however, I find it necessary to make the following clarificatory remarks:

(a) The concept of *jātis* is the only thing which I am able to pick from our traditional theory of *tāla*, partly because I do not know Sanskrit, and partly because I have not seen any tablā maestro relating to his own manner of playing any such concept as that of the ten *prānas* of *tāla*.

(b) Further, I have preferred to speak of the pattern's *self*-completion, not of mere completion, at the *sama*. In saying so, I want to emphasize two points: first, the inner dynamics of the *composition* itself; and, second, the aesthetic centrality of the *sama*. The inner flow within the composition has to appear *as moving towards* an end; and the end, or the *sama*, has to appear not as the mere terminus, but as the target or aesthetic destiny of the whole composition. This gives us an important principle of composition, namely, dynamic orientation.

(c) What, however, deserves a little more emphatic mention, because it is not commonly thought of, is what I have spoken of as the individual *player's own contribution to the overall regulation of laya*. I may make the point clear by inviting attention to some of the actual compositions notated in the book:

1. See composition No. 42, a kind of *chalan* which is also called *relā* quite freely on pp. 155-56. Here, the 5th and 10th beats have four alphabets each, and so have to be played at double the pace of the basic *laya* of the whole composition. This change in pace, it is obvious, has to be managed by the player himself without letting the transition appear abrupt or awkward. Another illustration of the point in question is provided by a composition of 17 beats which *has to be played* in such a skilful manner that it may cover only 16 beats. (see no. 3 on p. 120)

Laya, however, is not the only thing in a rhythmic composition; it has a filling of *bols* too; and it is with this in mind that I put forward the following general principles:

1. Articulation

This word is here to be taken to mean the act of uttering or producing distinct sounds even where they are quite close to each other. The reference, here, is to both *paḍant* (or recitation of *bols*) and actual playing. Applied to tablā playing *paḍant* articulation would mean clarity in the *nikās* (or execution) of individual *bols*. This would require that only those *bols* are put alongside of each other which do not tend to bedim mutual distinctness.

I may also add that an important way to heighten articulateness or the mutual distinctness of *bols* is accentuation. Thus, as is common knowledge, in the following (*jhaptāla*) *ṭhekā* of 10 beats:

1	2	3	4	5
dhiṅ	*nā*	*dhiṅ*	*dhiṅ*	*nā*
6	7	8	9	10
tiṅ	*nā*	*dhiṅ*	*dhiṅ*	*nā*
1	2	3	4	5
धिन	ना	धिं	धिं	ना
6	7	8	9	10
तिंन	ना	धिं	धिं	ना

Here, every *dhiṅ* (धिं) has to be played a little forcefully, and *nā* (ना) and *tiṅ* (तिं) have to played (or spoken) a little softly, though not of course unclearly. In other words, what is here to be regulated is वज़न or the force of impact of playing at the drums. This, incidentally, applies not only to every rhythm *cycle*, but to every rhythmic *composition*. Without a proper distribution of emphases, all playing would appear anaemic or spiritless, or ठंडा, बेजान, मुर्दा, as we say in popular parlance.

2. Playability and tonal appeal of bols

Further, mere correctness in respect of the number of *mātrās* covered is not enough to ensure good playing. The collocation of *bols* has to be playable too without undue strain. Consider, for instance, the following (attempted) composition in a stretch of 16 beats:

1	2	3	4	5	6	7	8
धिट	धिट	तागे	तिट	कड़धि	तिट	तागे	तिट
9	10	11	12	13 14	15	16	
धिन	गिन	गदि	गन	तक्ध्ड़ान	कडांन	तकिट(धा: सम)	

Here, 16 *mātrās* have been duly covered by the syllabic filling; but the filling itself is *not playable in its present sequence.*

It has also to be borne in mind that the *bols* of our rhythm are not only played, but recited. They should not sound funny when uttered. So, whereas *tiṭghiḍān* (तिटघिड़ान) is all right, तिततितान and धिधधिधान (*tittitān* and *dhidhdhidhān*) are forbidden, so to say.

3. Mellowness

The norm of articulation makes another demand on the player. It is, we have said, helped by accentuation. So, naturally, some *bols* have to sound louder than others. But, however emphatic be the sound of some *bols*, the playing, as a whole, has to look effortless and controlled. *Such a look may be said to be mellow.* It comes after long years of practice. I here feel impelled to cite a remark which I have often heard from masterly tablā players of some gharānās:

> In the beginning of one's playing career, *bols* have the thickness of a rope; later, as *reyāz* progresses, they come to acquire the softness of silken threads.

However, softness may not be all along there in actual playing. A look of effortlessness is a more binding requirement.

4. Segmentation

Qualities like the softness of an individual *bol* or the intentional waywardness of the manner it may relate to the basic *laya* as perceived by the *rasika*'s ear, are however not the same thing as the ease with which a bunch of some *bols* may be comprehended by the mind. The latter calls for a proper articulation (not division or disruption) of the whole pattern into shapely segments; and it is here that the Gestalt laws of perception — such as those of proximity, similarity, contrast, and common destiny or coercive design come into play. In a *bol* like नगनग, both *similarity* and *proximity* facilitate its comprehension as a single unit, though it comprises four letters. This is very different from attending to a *word* of four letters, such as धनवान, as one, partly because the *emphasis* here, generally, is on getting the *meaning* of the word, not only on registering the *sound* of its letters. The purpose of the word — that is, conveying some meaning — can be achieved by merely reading it quietly. The purpose a *bol* of rhythm, on the other hand, is not at all achieved unless it is *sounded* for the listening ear. The principle of *contrast* here works not only as the opposition of closed and open (बन्द और खुले) *bols*, as in the case of तिटघिड़ानधा, where तिट and घि are clearly dissimilar to ड़ा and धा, but as the transposition of *bols*, as in the case of तकधिन धिनतक. Here, however the two groups not only oppose, but also balance each other, because both comprise four letters each, and are expected to take an equal length of time.

In respect of segmentation, however, the following additional points are also noteworthy:

(a) What we have called a segment — that is, not *any* part, but a section or group of *bols* having a look of some self-completeness about it — appears so only to him who is able to follow the basic *laya* of the whole pattern; otherwise, they will appear mere fragments, not *segments*, that is, such parts as are actually sensed *as making for a whole,* in virtue of the very *laya* at which they are played. The *rasika* cannot afford to slacken his grip over the basic *laya* even for a moment. In a single, undivided act of attention he has to follow both the temporal (that is, relating to time) *extent* and manner of flow (and varying sound!) of the *bols and* the unheard — because not here played as a matrix — but always remembered basic pace or *laya*. From this point of view, discriminating perception of the play of our rhythmic patterns may be said to be bifocal, in a way.

(b) This at once makes a heavy demand on the playing artist too. He has to keep the relation between the pace of the pattern and the basic pace (initially established by the *ṭhekā*) identifiably clear (in principle) all along. Otherwise, the very essential condition of our relish of the *varying design* of our patterns will disappear; and the listener will have to content himself with, and admire only such merely heard and seen (not understood) and superficial (if necessary) features as sheer fluency, nimble movements of fingers, and occasional alternation of loud with whispering sounds. The *ṭhekā* is a *ṭhekā* not merely because it can be straight away made to open a solo recital, not even because it just provides rhythmic support to a musician at work, but because it is the *anchor* of our entire artistic creation and aesthetic enjoyment of rhythm. *Composition* is here the vital requirement; and, in the case of our rhythm, *it* is not simply a matter of what *bol*s are put together and how, but of how the whole collocation of *bol*s (as a pattern) relates to the basic *laya*.

(c) Segmentation of a long collocation of *bol*s may also be helped by the use of what may be called rhythmic end-rhymes (or *quāfiyā radeef*) as in the case of an authentic *quāyedā*. To take an example, in the case of composition No. 56 on (p. 163), all the four lines end with the same bunch of *bol*s, namely, *trakdhiṅgin* (त्रकधिनगिन). This is likely to remind readers of end-rhymes in poetry.

But, at this point, we may mark a difference too. Where a poem builds upon blank verse, quite a few of its lines do not appear *clearly complete* in meaning, though they surely get rolled into the unity of the poem's overall import. In our rhythm, on the other hand, *every* pattern has either to end sharply at the *sama* — that is, the focal beat — or to slightly overstep or fall short of it so designedly that the very incompliance of the end of the pattern as played may heighten a knowledgeable listener's sense of the set location of the beat in question. My reference, here, is to patterns of *ateet* and *anāgat* variety.

Outer completeness and distinctness of properly disposed *bol*s on the inside are so necessary features of our rhythm that the definition of beauty as unity in variety is perhaps nowhere as aptly applicable as here. The definition I speak of is, of course, *not* relevant to every case of beauty. A ruby may strike us as irresistibly beautiful; but will this impression reveal any inner differences in the gem-stone?[1] Not at all. The case of rhythm is different; and it is not without reason that our Ustads of old, unlettered though they might have been, would always insist on the supreme importance of wholeness of design and clarity of inner accents, and would therefore abstain from playing at hectic speed where *clarity and manifest wholeness of form* both give way to fuzziness.

Today, on the other hand, even regular critics seem to prefer sheer fluency to other excellences of the art of rhythm. They seem to be oblivious of the truth that if rhythm is an art, which (I have argued) it assuredly is, it is primarily because of its emphasis on the two excellences I have just put in italics, in the previous para. But, I hasten to add, rhythm is just *not* covered by the view which regards art as essentially an expression, be it organized or just a spontaneous spill-over, of the artist's immediate or recollected *emotions*. Our rhythm as such is at no point an expression of any designable emotion, such as joy, sorrow or anger, though it can certainly be adapted to heighten the emotive look of vocal music where such music seeks to express some emotion. For instance, where what is being sung is a composition in *rāgā adānā*, which is expected to evoke a semblance of valour, the tablā player may well add to the overall effect by resorting to a forceful manner of playing. Yet, we may note, our rhythm does not build upon sounds which express some feeling, as a wail may express grief. It *is* possible to so pick, organize and play some syllables that the whole pattern may resemble, more or less, the characteristic chirping of a bird. But that would be representation, not expression; and even representation cannot be regarded as essential to rhythm. Those who seek to regale lay audiences

1. The reference here is to a point made by John Hospers in his essay, "Hartshorne's Aesthetics" in *The Philosophy of Charles Hartshorne*, edited by L.E. Hahn, La Salle, Illinois, 1991, p. 128.

by playing in a way which resembles the start, acceleration and cessation of the movement of a railway train, are mere entertainers, not tablā *artists*. Be that as it may, in my fifty years' fellowship with this art I have never seen a good solo tablā recital acclaimed because it has been very expressive of an emotion or truly representative of a fact, activity, or situation.

At the same time, however, our experience of rhythm is no mere listening. A segment is what it is, partly because there is an interval of quiet, however brief, before the next one appears. This interval helps assimilation of what has just been heard and generates a looking-forward-to what is to come next — an expectation which is directed by the basic *laya*-flow.[2] So, a *rasikā*'s listening is at once contemplation.

5. Structural Orientation

The looking-forward-to, which I have just spoken of, can be helped by a measure of structural orientation in the composition one is listening to. It is noteworthy that the requisite wholeness of form to which I referred a little earlier is no inert completeness. Rhythm is an occurrent art; we see it being made; passage is its very life; but this passage has to look targeting, and not merely to end at the *sama*. Further, this passage is not uniform in respect of the impact of its constituent *bols*. Some of these are accented; others are just cut out clearly. It is this variation of emphasis in the cutting of *bol*s which, along with some other structural features, gives to our patterns of rhythm a look of aiming at, and making for the *sama*, instead of merely ending at it tamely, if correctly. The most common way to evoke this

2. In this respect, the form of rhythm may be said to actualize itself more or less like form in literature. See, in this context, the following:

   "A work [of literature] has form in so far as one part of it leads a reader to anticipate another part, to be gratified by the sequence" Cited by Edward Cone in his essay, "Music and Form" in *What is Music*? (edited by Philip Alperson, The Pennsylvania State University Press, Pennsylvania, 1994 PB, p.134.

aesthetic semblance is to make a pattern end with a *tihāī*. Aesthetically, I repeat, the *sama* has to appear as the destiny rather than as the mere terminal point of a pattern. As I say so, I have in mind the Gestalt principle of coercive design. What I here wish to emphasize is the look of orientation and the varying distribution of emphases over the *bols* of a composition which give to rhythm some semblance of life. In everyday life too we do not utter every word with equal force; and the listener's attention is directed, if in part, by the emphases and pauses that we introduce in our talk.

6. Aesthetic resilience

But there is something more subtle that a player can do to make his rhythmic work appear 'alive.' He can make a pattern appear to lapse for a moment from the basic pace *and then make immediate amends*, somewhat like the way a speaker may quickly replace a word just used with a better one. But let me clarify the point with the help of an example. On p. 120 I have notated a *quāyedā* which actually comprises 17 beats but has to be played in a (slightly shorter) range of just 16 beats. The *bol* which closes the first line in the frame of 17 beats is *dhiṭdhāge* (धिटधागे); and in the 16-beat setting, it is *dhiṭdhāgenā* (धिटधागेना). So the *Nā* (ना) of *dhāgenā* which occurs at the 5th beat (in notation) has to be covered (during playing) in the 4th beat itself, which means that the *bol, dhiṭdhāgenā* (धिटधागेना), must be played a little more quickly, so that *Nā* (ना) may be duly assimilated through the quickening of pace, and the normal pace of *laya* may promptly re-assert itself.

8

Creativity at Work
Some of
Author's Own Compositions

THIS chapter, which presents a part of my own creative work in the field of rhythm, may be taken as an attempt to verify almost all that I have said (in the previous chapter) about the principles of composition.

Note: In some of the notated compositions that follow (*in Hindi*) some beats have been bisected as ½ + ½ = 1, with small lines underrunning them. This has been done with a view to induce the practice of paying close attention to *laya*. In other cases, this has not been done. Everywhere, however, whatever is there in each column is to be regarded as making one *bol* (or mnemoinc letter or bunch of such letters) and as occupying just one *mātrā* (or beat). All this, however, relates only to the *Hindi* version of notations, becuase notations in English have not been underlined.

नोट: अब जो 'कम्पोज़ीशन्स' (यां बोलों की बन्दिशें) आगे आयेंगी (हिन्दी में) उनमें से कुछ के बोलों के नोटेशन के नीचे की लाइन को दो भागों में बांट दिया गया है, ऐसे: ½ + ½ = १ मात्रा। बाक़ी जगह ऐसा नहीं किया गया है। लेकिन हर column में जो कुछ भी है उसे एक बोल ही समझना है, और केवल एक मात्रा का बोल। एक मात्रा का विभाजन इसलिये किया गया है कि लय पर सूक्ष्म रूप से ध्यान देने की आदत पड़े।

1. Peshkār : Tritāla, Tisrā-Jāti (पेशकार: त्रिताल, तिस्त्र जाति)

Dhīkḍa dhiṅ	*Tā dhiṅtā*	*Dhāti dhā*	*Dhā dhiṅtā*
Tiṭ Dhāg	*Dhā dhiṅtā*	*Dhāti dhā*	*Dhā dhiṅtā*
Kiḍnak tiṅ	*Tinākin tāke*	*Tiṭkiṭ tāke*	*Trak tinnākin*
Tiṭ Dhāg	*Dhā dhiṅtā*	*Dhāti dhā*	*Dhā dhiṅtā*

धीक्ड़ धिन	ता धिन्ता	धाति धा	धा धिन्ता
तिट धाग	धा धिन्ता	धाति धा	धा धिन्ता

किड़नक तिं	तिनाकिन ताके	तिटकिट ताके	त्रक तिन्नाकिन
तिट धाग	धा धिंता	धाति धा	धा धिन्ता

2. Peshkār-Quāyedā: (32 beats, Tisrā-Jāti) पेशकार-कायदा (तिश्र जाति, ३२ मात्रा)

Dhakḍ dhā	*Ti dhāऽ*	*Ginā dhā*	*Ge dhinnā*
Ginā dhiṅ	*Nā ginā*	*Dhāge dhiṅ*	*Nā ginā*
Ginā dhiṅ	*Nā ginā*	*Dhāge dhiṅ*	*Nā ginā*
Ghinā dhiṅ	*Nā ginā*	*Dhāge tiṅ*	*Nā kinā*
Tākḍ Tā	*Tītāऽ*	*Kin tā*	*Ke tinnā*
Kinā tiṅ	*Nā kinā*	*Tāke tiṅ*	*Nā kinā*
Ginā dhiṅ	*Nā ginā*	*Dhāge dhiṅ*	*Nā ginā*
Ghinā dhiṅ	*Nā ginā*	*Dhāge dhiṅ*	*Nā ginā*

धाक्ड़ धा	ति धाऽ	गिना धा	गे धिन्ना
गिना धिन	ना गिना	धागे धिन	ना गिना
गिना धिन	ना गिना	धागे धिन	ना गिना
घिना धिन	ना गिना	धागे तिन	ना किना
ताक्ड़ ता	तीताऽ	किन ता	के तिन्ना
किना तिन	ना किना	ताके तिन	ना किना
गिना धिन	ना गिना	धागे धिन	ना गिना
घिना धिन	ना गिना	धागे धिन	ना गिना

Note: The following point deserves notice in respect of both the compositions notated above:

1. Not merely in respect of recitation, but in actual execution the difference between *gi* and *ghi* has to be duly brought out. The proper playing of *gi* requires just a soft touch on the *bānyā* (the left drum). On the other hand, *ghi* has to be produced by using a little force.

नोट:- ऊपर नोटेशन की हुई दोनों रचनाओं में एक बात पर ध्यान देना आवश्यक है:-

बोलते और बजाते समय *गि* और *घि*, दोनों में अन्तर रखना आवश्यक है। *गि* के निकास में बांये को हल्के से काम में लाना है और *घि* के निकास में बायें पर तनिक अधिक वज़न रखना है।

Some *Quāyedās* Set to *Tritāla,* and in *Chatusra Jāti*
कुछ क़ायदे, त्रिताल और चतुस्त्र जाति में निबद्ध

3. (32 Beats, ३२ मात्रा)

Dhi kḍa	*Dhiṅ dhā*	*ऽGhiḍ*	*Nag dhiṅ*
Tiṭ ghiḍ	*Nag dhiṅ*	*Dhāge trak*	*Dhinnā ginā*
Tak tadhiṅ	*ऽTa kat*	*Dhiṅऽ ta*	*Kat dhiṅ*
Tiṭ ghiḍ	*Nag dhiṅ*	*Dhāge trak*	*Tinnā kinā*
Ti kḍ	*Tiṅ ta*	*ऽkiḍ*	*Nak tiṅ*
Tiṭ kiḍ	*Nak tiṅ*	*Tāke trak*	*Tinnā kinā*
Takat dhiṅ	*ऽTakat*	*Dhi ऽnta*	*Kat dhiṅ*
Tiṭ ghiḍ	*Nag dhiṅ*	*Dhāge trak*	*Dhinnā ginā*

धी क्ड़	धिं धा	ऽ घिड़	नग धिं
तिट घिड़	नग धिं	धागे त्रक	धिंना गिना
तक तधिं	ऽत कत	धिंऽ त	कत धिं
तिट घिड़	नग धिं	धागे त्रक	तिंना किना
ती क्ड़	तिं ता	ऽ किड़	नक तिं
तिट किड़	नक तिं	ताके त्रक	तिंना किना
तकत धिं	ऽ तकत	धिऽन्त	कत धिं
तिट घिड़	नग धिं	धागे त्रक	धिंना गिना

4. (16 Beats, १६ मात्रा)

Dhāऽ Gin	*Dhāti ṭadhā*	*Gin dhāge*	*Dhinnā tiṭ*
Dhāge Dhinnā	*Dhāti ṭadhā*	*Gin dhāge*	*Tinnā kinā*
Tāऽ kin	*Tāti ṭatā*	*Kin tāke*	*Tinnā tiṭ*
Dhāge Dhinnā	*Dhāti ṭadhā*	*Gin dhāge*	*Dhinnā Ginā*

धाऽ गिन	धाति टधा	गिन धागे	धिंना तिट
धागे धिंना	धाति टधा	गिन धागे	तिंना किना
ताऽ किन	ताति टता	किन ताके	तिंना तिट
धागे धिंना	धाति टधा	गिन धागे	धिंना गिना

5. (16 Beats, १६ मात्रा)

Dhāऽ Tiṭ	*Dhāge Nati*	*Ṭa Dhāgen*	*Dhinnā Kḍedhā*
Tiṭ Ghin	*Dhāti ṭadhā*	*Tiṭ Dhāge*	*Tinnā kinā*

Tāऽ Tiṭ	*Tāke Nati*	*Ṭatā kena*	*Tinnā Kḍetā*
Tiṭ Ghin	*Dhāti ṭadhā*	*Tiṭ Dhāge*	*Dhinnā Ginā*

धाऽ तिट	धागे नति	टधा गेन	धिंना क्ड़ेधा
तिट घिन	धाति टधा	तिट धागे	तिंना किना
ताऽ तिट	ताके नति	टता केन	तिंना क्ड़ेता
तिट घिन	धाति टधा	तिट धागे	धिंना गिना

6. (16 Beats, १६ मात्रा)

Ghin dhā	*Ghin tiṭ*	*Ghin dhāge*	*Dhinnā tiṭ*
Dhāge dhinnā	*Tiṭ Ghin*	*Dhātī dhāge*	*Tinnā Kinā*
Kin Tā	*Kin tiṭ*	*Kin tāke*	*Tinna tiṭ*
Dhāge dhinnā	*Tiṭ Ghin*	*Dhāti dhāge*	*Dhinnā Ginā*

घिन धा	घिन तिट	घिन धागे	धिंना तिट
धागे धिंना	तिट घिन	धाती धागे	तिंना किना
किन ता	किन तिट	किन ताके	तिंना तिट
धागे धिंना	तिट घिन	धाती धागे	धिंना गिना

7. (16 Beats, १६ मात्रा)

Dhāti dhāge	*Dhinnā dhādhā*	*Tidhā gena*	*Dhinnā Ghinā*
Dhinnā Ginā	*Dhādhā tidhā*	*Gena dhāge*	*Tinnā Kinā*
Tāti tāke	*Tinnā tātā*	*Titā Kena*	*Tinnā Ghinā*
Dhinnā Ginā	*Dhādhā tidhā*	*Gena dhāge*	*Dhinnā Ginā*

धाती धागे	धिंना धाधा	तिधा गेन	धिंना घिना
धिंना गिना	धाधा तिधा	गेन धागे	तिंना किना
ताति ताके	तिंना ताता	तिता केन	तिंना घिना
धिंना गिना	धाधा तिधा	गेन धागे	धिंना गिना

8. (32 Beats, ३२ मात्रा)

Dhātra kadhi	*Naga dhiṅ*	*Dhāऽ ghi*	*Naga dhinn*
Ghinā gaghi	*Naga dhiṅ*	*Dhāge trak*	*Dhinnā Ginā*
Ghinā gadhiṅ	*ऽGhi nag*	*Dhin ऽghi*	*Naga dhiṅ*
Ghinā gadhā	*Trak dhiṅ*	*Dhāge trak*	*Tinnā Kinā*
Tātra kati	*Naka tiṅ*	*Tā ऽki*	*Naka tiṅ*
Kinā kaki	*Naka tiṅ*	*Tāke trak*	*Tinnā Kinā*

Ghinā gadhiṅ	*ऽGhi nag*	*Dhiṅ ऽGhi*	*Naga dhiṅ*
Ghinā gadhā	*Traka Dhiṅ*	*Dhāge trak*	*Dhinnā Ginā*

धात्र कधि	नग धिन	धा ऽघि	नग धिंन
घिना गघि	नग धिन	धागे त्रक	धिंना गिना
घिना गधिन	ऽघि नग	धिन ऽघि	नग धिन
घिना गधा	त्रक धिन	धागे त्रक	तिंना किना
तात्र कति	नक तिन	ता ऽकि	नक तिन
किना ककि	नक तिन	ताके त्रक	तिंना किना
घिना गधिन	ऽघि नग	धिन ऽघि	नग धिन
घिना गधा	त्रक धिन	धागे त्रक	धिंना गिना

9. (16 Beats, १६ मात्रा)

Ghin dhāऽ	*Ghin dhāge*	*Trak dhinnā*	*Ghin dhāge*
Dhinnā Ginā	*Dhāge tiṭ*	*Dhāge trak*	*Tinnā kinā*
Kin tāऽ	*Kin tāke*	*Trak Tinnā*	*Kin dhāge*
Dhinnā Ginā	*Dhāge tiṭ*	*Dhāge trak*	*Dhinnā Ginā*

घिन धाऽ	घिन धागे	त्रक धिंना	घिन धागे
धिंना गिना	धागे तिट	धागे त्रक	तिंना किना
किन ताऽ	किन ताके	त्रक तिंना	किन धागे
धिंना गिना	धागे तिट	धागे त्रक	धिंना गिना

10. (32 Beats, ३२ मात्रा)

Dhāge tir	*Kiṭ dhāge*	*Tir kiṭ*	*Dhāge trak*
Dhiṅ ऽ	*ऽ Dhāge*	*Tir kiṭ*	*Dhiṅ ऽ*
Dhāge tir	*Kiṭ dhāge*	*Tir kiṭ*	*Dhāge trak*
Dhinnā Ginā	*Dhāge tiṭ*	*Dhāge trak*	*Tinnā kinā*
Tāke tir	*Kit tāke*	*Tir kiṭ*	*Tāke trak*
Tiṅ ऽ	*ऽ Tāke*	*Tir kiṭ*	*Tiṅ ऽ*
Dhāge tir	*Kiṭ dhāge*	*Tir kiṭ*	*Dhāge trak*
Dhinnā Ginā	*Dhāge tiṭ*	*Dhāge trak*	*Dhinnā Ginā*

धागे तिर	किट धागे	तिर किट	धागे त्रक
धिं ऽ	ऽ धागे	तिर किट	धिं ऽ
धागे तिर	किट धागे	तिर किट	धागे त्रक
धिंना गिना	धागे तिट	धागे त्रक	तिंना किना

ताके तिर	किट ताके	तिर किट	ताके त्रक
तिं ऽ	ऽ ताके	तिर किट	तिं ऽ
धागे तिर	किट धागे	तिर किट	धागे त्रक
धिंना गिना	धागे तिट	धागे त्रक	धिंना गिना

11. (16 Beats, १६ मात्रा)

Dhāg Dhāg	*Dhāti ṭdhā*	*Ginā Dhāge*	*Dhinnā Ginā*
Dhinnā Ginā	*Dhāti ṭdhā*	*Ginā Dhāge*	*Tinnā Kinā*
Tāk Tāk	*Tātiṭ tā*	*Kinā Tāke*	*Tinnā Ginā*
Dhinnā Ginā	*Dhatiṭ dhā*	*Ginā Dhāge*	*Dhinnā Ginā*

धाग धाग	धाति टधा	गिना धागे	धिंना गिना
धिंना गिना	धाति टधा	गिना धागे	तिंना किना
ताक ताक	ताति टता	किना ताके	तिंना गिना
धिंना गिना	धाति टधा	गिना धागे	धिंना गिना

12. (32 Beats, ३२ मात्रा)

ऽ *Ghiḍ*	*Nag dhiṅ*	*Dhāge trak*	*Dhiṅ Ghiḍ*
Nag dhiṅ	*Dhāge tiṭ*	*Dhāge trak*	*Dhinnā Ginā*
Tiṭ Ghiḍ	*Nag dhiṅ*	*Dha* ऽ*ḍ*	*Ghiḍ nag*
Dhiṅ Ghiḍ	*Nag dhiṅ*	*Dhāge trak*	*Tinnā kinā*
ऽ *kiḍ*	*Nak tiṅ*	*Tāke trak*	*Tin kiḍ*
Nak tiṅ	*Tāke tiṭ*	*Tāke trak*	*Tinnā Kinā*
Tiṭ Ghiḍ	*Nag dhiṅ*	*Dhā* ऽ*ḍ*	*Ghiḍ nag*
Dhiṅ Ghiḍ	*Nag dhiṅ*	*Dhāge trak*	*Dhinnā Ginā*

ऽ घिड़	नग धिन	धागे त्रक	धिन घिड़
नग धिन	धागे तिट	धागे त्रक	धिंना गिना
तिट घिड़	नग धिन	धा ऽड़	घिड़ नग
धिन घिड़	नग धिन	धागे त्रक	तिंना किना
ऽ किड़	नक तिन	ताके त्रक	तिन किड़
नक तिन	ताके तिट	ताके त्रक	तिंना किना
तिट घिड़	नग धिन	धा ऽड़	घिड़ नग
धिन घिड़	नग धिन	धागे त्रक	धिंना गिना

13. (32 Beats, ३२ मात्रा)

Dhāti dhāge	*Dhinnā dhādhā*	*Tīdhā gena*	*Dhinnā Ghinā*
Dhinnā Ghinā	*Dhādhā tidhā*	*Gena dhāge*	*Dhinnā Ghinā*
Dhādhā Dhādhā	*Dhāti Dhāge*	*Dhinnā Dhāti*	*Dhāge dhinnā*
Ghinā dhinnā	*Dhādhā tidhā*	*Gena dhāge*	*Tinnā kinā*
Tāti tāke	*Tinnā tātā*	*Tiṭā kena*	*Tinnā kinā*
Tinnā kinā	*Tātā titā*	*Kena tāke*	*Tinnā kinā*
Dhādhā Dhādhā	*Dhāti dhāge*	*Dhinnā dhāti*	*Dhāge dhinnā*
Ghinā dhinnā	*Dhādhā tīdhā*	*Gena dhāge*	*Dhinnā Ghinā*

धाती धागे	धिंना धाधा	तीधा गेन	धिंना घिना
धिंना घिना	धाधा तिधा	गेन धागे	धिंना घिना
धाधा धाधा	धाती धागे	धिंना धाती	धागे धिंना
घिना धिंना	धाधा तिधा	गेन धागे	तिंना किना
ताति ताके	तिंना ताता	तिटा केन	तिंना किना
तिंना किना	ताता तिता	केन ताके	तिंना किना
धाधा धाधा	धाती धागे	धिंना धाती	धागे धिंना
घिना धिंना	धाधा तीधा	गेन धागे	धिंना घिना

14. (32 Beats) (३२ मात्रा)

Dhāऽ tiṭ	*Kiṭ dhā*	*Ghiḍ nag*	*Dhiṅ dhā*
Tiṭ kiṭ	*Dhāऽ ghiḍ*	*Nag dhiṅ*	*Dhinnā ginā*
Tak dhiṅ	*Dhāऽ tiṭ*	*Ghiḍ nag*	*Dhin dhā*
Tiṭ kiṭ	*Dhāऽ ghiḍ*	*Nag tiṅ*	*Tinnā kinā*
Taऽ tiṭ	*Kiṭ tā*	*Kiḍ nak*	*Tintā*
Tiṭ kiṭ	*Tāऽ kiḍ*	*Nak tiṅ*	*Tinnā kinā*
Tak Dhiṅ	*Dhaऽ tiṭ*	*Ghiḍ nag*	*Dhinn dhā*
Tiṭ kiṭ	*Dhaऽ Ghiḍ*	*Nag dhiṅ*	*Dhinnā Ginā*

धाऽ तिट	किट धा	घिड़ नग	धिन धा
तिट किट	धाऽ घिड़	नग धिन	धिंना गिना
तक धिन	धाऽ तिट	घिड़ नग	धिन धा
तिट किट	धाऽ घिड़	नग तिन	तिंना किना
ताऽ तिट	किट ता	किड़ नक	तिन ता
तिट किट	ताऽ किड़	नक तिन	तिंना किना
तक धिन	धाऽ तिट	घिड़ नग	धिंन धा
तिट किट	धाऽ घिड़	नग धिन	धिंना गिना

15. (32 Beats, ३२ मात्रा)

Dhin dhinnā	*Trak dhinnā*	*Tiṭ dhāge*	*Dhinnā Ginā*
Dhinnā Ghinā	*Dhāti ṭadhā*	*Gena dhāge*	*Dhinnā Gina*
Dhinnā Ginā	*Tiṭ dhāge*	*Dhinnā dhādhā*	*Tiṭ dhāge*
Dhinnā Ginā	*Dhāti ṭadhā*	*Gena dhāge*	*Tinnā kinā*
Tiṅ tinnā	*Trak tinnā*	*Tiṭ tāke*	*Tinnā kinā*
Tinnā kinā	*Tāṭi ṭatā*	*Ken tāke*	*Tinnā kinā*
Dhinnā Ginā	*Tiṭ dhāge*	*Dhinnā dhādhā*	*Tiṭ dhāge*
Dhinnā Ginā	*Dhāti ṭadhā*	*Gen dhāge*	*Dhinnā Ginā*

धिन धिंना	त्रक धिंना	तिट धागे	धिंना गिना
धिंना घिना	धाती टधा	गेन धागे	धिंना गिना
धिंना गिना	तिट धागे	धिंना धाधा	तिट धागे
धिंना गिना	धाति टधा	गेन धागे	तिंना किना
तिन तिंना	त्रक तिंना	तिट ताके	तिंना किना
तिंना किना	ताति टता	केन ताके	तिंना किना
धिंना गिना	तिट धागे	धिंना धाधा	तिट धागे
धिंना गिना	धाति टधा	गेन धागे	धिंना गिना

16. (16 Beats, १६ मात्रा)

Dhāऽ katā	*Ghinā tinnā*	*Kḍadhā katā*	*Ghinā tinnā*
Katā tādhā	*Tidhā gena*	*Dhāti dhāge*	*Tinnā kinā*
Taऽ katā	*Kinā tinna*	*Kḍatā katā*	*Kinā tinā*
Katā tādhā	*Tidhā gena*	*Dhāti dhāge*	*Dhinnā Ginā*

धाऽ कता	घिना तिंना	क्ड़धा कता	घिना तिंना
कता ताधा	तिधा गेन	धाति धागे	तिंना किना
ताऽ कता	किना तिंना	क्ड़ता कता	किना तिना
कता ताधा	तिधा गेन	धाती धागे	धिंना गिना

17. (32 Beats, ३२ मात्रा)

Dhāऽ dhāti	*Dhāge dhinnā*	*Tiṭ dhāge*	*Dhinnā Ghinā*
Dhinnā Ghinā	*Dhāti ṭadhā*	*Gina dhāge*	*Dhinnā Ginā*
Tiṭ dhāge	*Dhinnā Dhādhā*	*Tiṭ dhāge*	*Dhinnā Tiṭ*
Dhāge dhinnā	*Dhāti ṭadhā*	*Gina dhāge*	*Tinnā kinā*
Tāऽ tāti	*Tāke tinnā*	*Tiṭ tāke*	*Tinnā kinā*

Tinnā kinā	*Tāti ṭatā*	*Kin tāke*	*Tinnā kinā*
Tiṭ dhāge	*Dhinnā dhādhā*	*Tiṭ dhāge*	*Dhinnā tiṭ*
Dhāge dhinnā	*Dhāti ṭadhā*	*Gina dhāge*	*Dhinnā Ginā*

धाऽ धाति	धागे धिंना	तिट धागे	धिंना घिना
धिंना घिना	धाति टधा	गिन धागे	धिंना गिना
तिट धागे	धिंना धाधा	तिट धागे	धिंना तिट
धागे धिंना	धाति टधा	गिन धागे	तिंना किना
ताऽ ताति	ताके तिंना	तिट ताके	तिंना किना
तिंना किना	ताति टता	किन ताके	तिंना किना
तिट धागे	धिंना धाधा	तिट धागे	धिंना तिट
धागे धिंना	धाति टधा	गिन धागे	धिंना गिना

18. (32 Beats, ३२ मात्रा)

Dhā ऽ	ऽ *Ghiḍ*	*Nag Dhin*	ऽ ऽ
ऽ *Ghiḍ*	*Nag Dhiṅ*	*Dhāge Trak*	*Dhiṅ Ghiḍ*
Nag Dhiṅ	ऽ ऽ	ऽ *Ghiḍ*	*Nag Dhiṅ*
Dhāge Trak	*Dhiṅ Ghiḍ*	*Nag Tiṅ*	*Tinnā kinā*
Ta ऽ	ऽ *kiḍ*	*Nag Tiṅ*	ऽ ऽ
ऽ *kiḍ*	*Nag Tiṅ*	*Tāke Trak*	*Tiṅ kiḍ*
Nag Tiṅ	ऽ ऽ	ऽ *Ghiḍ*	*Nag Dhiṅ*
Dhāge Trak	*Dhiṅ Ghiḍ*	*Nag Dhiṅ*	*Dhinnā Ginā*

धा ऽ	ऽ घिड़	नग धिन	ऽ ऽ
ऽ घिड़	नग धिन	धागे त्रक	धिन घिड़
नग धिन	ऽ ऽ	ऽ घिड़	नग धिन
धागे त्रक	धिन घिड़	नग तिन	तिंना किना
ता ऽ	ऽ किड़	नग तिन	ऽ ऽ
ऽ किड़	नग तिन	ताके त्रक	तिन किड़
नग तिन	ऽ ऽ	ऽ घिड़	नग धिन
धागे त्रक	धिन घिड़	नग धिन	धिंना गिना

Quāyedās-Tisra-Jāti

19. (16 Beats, १६ मात्रा)

Dhātiṭkiṭ	*Dhāghiḍnag*	*Dhindhinnāginā*	*Dhāghiḍnag*
Dhindhinnāginā	*Dhātiṭkiṭ*	*Dhāghiḍnag*	*Tintinnākinā*

Tātiṭkiṭ	*Tākiḍnak*	*Tintinnākinā*	*Dhāghiḍnag*
Dhindhinnāginā	*Dhātiṭkiṭ*	*Dhāghiḍnag*	*Dhindhinnāginā*

धातिटकिट	धाघिड़नग	धिनधिंनागिना	धाघिड़नग
धिनधिंनागिना	धातिटकिट	धाघिड़नग	तिनातिंनाकिना
तातिटकिट	ताकिड़नक	तिनतिंनाकिना	धाघिड़नग
धिनधिंनागिना	धातिटकिट	धाघिड़नग	धिनधिंनागिना

20. (16 Beats, १६ मात्रा)

Dhātidhā	*Dhādhinnā*	*Ghiḍnagdhiṅ*	*Nāghiḍnag*
Tirkiṭtak	*Dhirdhirkiṭ*	*Dhātidhā*	*Dhātinnā*
Tātītā	*Tātinnā*	*Ghiḍnagdhiṅ*	*Nāghiḍnag*
Tirkiṭtak	*Dhirdhirkiṭ*	*Dhatidhā*	*Dhādhinnā*

धातिधा	धाधिंना	घिड़नगधिं	नाघिड़नग
तिरकिटतक	धिरधिरकिट	धातिधा	धातिंना
तातीता	तातिंना	घिड़नगधिं	नाघिड़नग
तिरकिटतक	धिरधिरकिट	धातिधा	धाधिंना

21. (16 Beats, १६ मात्रा)

Dhāghiḍnag	*Dhinghiḍnag*	*Tirkiṭtak*	*Dhirdhirkiṭ*
Dhāghiḍnag	*Dhinghiḍnag*	*Tirkiṭtak*	*Tintinnākinā*
Tākiḍnak	*Tinkiḍnak*	*Tirkiṭtak*	*Tirtirkiṭ*
Dhāghiḍnag	*Dhinghiḍnag*	*Tirkiṭtak*	*Dhindhinnāginā*

धाघिड़नग	धिनघिड़नग	तिरकिटतक	धिरधिरकिट
धाघिड़नग	धिनघिड़नग	तिरकिटतक	तिनतिंनाकिना
ताकिड़नक	तिनकिड़नक	तिरकिटतक	तिरतिरकिट
धाघिड़नग	धिनघिड़नग	तिरकिटतक	धिनधिंनागिना

22. (32 Beats, ३२ मात्रा)

Dhākḍa	*Dhitiṭ*	*Tiṭkḍa*	*Dhitiṭ*
Dhātrak	*Dhiṅdhāti*	*Dhāgdhiṅ*	*Nāginā*
Trakdhi	*Ṭghin*	*Dhātighi*	*Nādhāti*
Dhātrak	*Dhiṅdhāti*	*Dhāgetiṅ*	*Nākinā*
Tākḍ	*Titiṭ*	*Tiṭkḍa*	*Tiṭiṭ*
Tātrak	*Tiṅtātī*	*Tāketiṅ*	*Nākinā*

Trakdhi	*Ṭaghin*	*Dhātighi*	*Nādhāti*
Dhātrak	*Dhiṅdhāti*	*Dhāgedhiṅ*	*Nāginā*

धाक्ड़	धितिट	तिटक्ड़	धितिट
धात्रक	धिंधाति	धागधिं	नागिना
त्रकधि	टघिन	धातीघि	नाधाति
धात्रक	धिंधाति	धागेतिं	नाकिना
ताक्ड़	तितिट	तिटक्ड़	तितिट
तात्रक	तिंताती	ताकेतिं	नाकिना
त्रकधि	टघिन	धातिघी	नाधाति
धात्रक	धिंधाती	धागेधिं	नागिना

23. (16 Beats, १६ मात्रा)

Dhātidhā	*Genadhā*	*Tirkiṭdhiṅ*	*Nāginā*
Dhātidhā	*Gedhāti*	*Dhāgetiṅ*	*Nākinā*
Tātitā	*Kentā*	*Tirkiṭdhiṅ*	*Nāginā*
Dhātidhā	*Gedhāti*	*Dhāgedhiṅ*	*Nāginā*

धातिधा	गेनधा	तिरकिटधिं	नागिना
धातिधा	गेधाती	धागेतिं	नाकिना
तातिता	केनता	तिरकिटधिं	नागिना
धातिधा	गेधाती	धागेधिं	नागिना

24. (16 Beats, १६ मात्रा)

Dhagattakiṭ	*Dhāgetiṭkiṭ*	*Dhagetiṭdhāge*	*Trakdhinnāginā*
Takdhingin	*Dhāgetiṭkiṭ*	*Dhāgetiṭdhāge*	*Trakdhinnākinā*
Takattakiṭ	*Tāketiṭkiṭ*	*Tāketiṭtāke*	*Traktinnākinā*
Takdhingin	*Dhāgetiṭkiṭ*	*Dhāgetiṭdhāge*	*Trakdhinnāginā*

धगततकिट	धागेतिटकिट	धागेतिटधागे	त्रकधिंनागिना
तकधिनगिन	धागेतिटकिट	धागेतिटधागे	त्रकधिंनाकिना
तकततटिक	ताकेतिटकिट	ताकेतिटताके	त्रकतिंनाकिना
तकधिनगिन	धागेतिटकिट	धागेतिटधागे	त्रकधिंनाकिना

25. (16 Beats, १६ मात्रा)

Dhāgdhādhāghiḍ	*Nagdhinnā*	*Dhingindhāge*	*Trakdhināginā*
Takiṭtakiṭ	*Takdhingin*	*Dhagetiṭdhāge*	*Traktinnākinā*

Tāktātākiḍ	*Naktinnā*	*Tinkintāke*	*Traktinnākinā*
Takiṭṭakiṭ	*Takdhingin*	*Dhagetiṭdhāge*	*Trakdhinnāginā*

धागधाधाघिड़	नगधिंना	धिनगिनधागे	त्रकधिनागिना
तकिटतकिट	तकधिनगिन	धागेतिटधागे	त्रकतिंनाकिना
ताकताताकिड़	नकतिंना	तिनकिनताके	त्रकतिंनाकिना
तकिटतकिट	तकधिनगिन	धागेतिटधागे	त्रकधिंनागिना

26. (16 Beats, १६ मात्रा)

Dhāgedhāgeऽnna	*Dhāgdhāgeऽnna*	*Dhāgetiṭdhāge*	*Trakdhinn āgina*
Dhāgenadhiṅऽnna	*Dhāgdhāgeऽnna*	*Dhāgetiṭdhāge*	*Traktinn ākinā*
Tāktākeऽnna	*Tāktākeऽnna*	*Taketiṭṭāke*	*Traktinnākinā*
Dhāgendhiṅऽnna	*Dhāgdhāgeऽnna*	*Dhāgetiṭdhāge*	*Trakdhinn āginā*

धागधागेऽन्न	धागधागेऽन्न	धागेतिटधागे	त्रकधिंनागिना
धागेनधिंऽन्न	धागधागेऽन्न	धागेतिटधागे	त्रकतिंनाकिना
ताकताकेऽन्न	ताकताकेऽन्न	ताकेतिटताके	त्रकतिंनाकिना
धागेनधिंऽन्न	धागधागेऽन्न	धागेतिटधागे	त्रकधिंनाकिना

Gat-Quāyedā

27. (32 Beats, ३२ मात्रा)

Dhāghiḍnag	*Dhinnāghiḍ*	*Nagdhindhāge*	*Trakdhinnāginā*
Ghiḍnagdhin	*Nāghiḍnag*	*Dhingindhāge*	*Trakdhinnāginā*
Ghinaktiṅऽna	*Tāketiṭkiṭ*	*Tāketiṭṭāke*	*Traktinnākinā*
Ghiḍnagdhiṅ	*Nāghiḍnag*	*Dhingindhāge*	*Traktinnākinā*
Tākiḍnak	*Tinnākiḍ*	*Naktintāke*	*Traktinnākinā*
Kiḍnaktin	*Nākiḍnak*	*Tinkintāke*	*Traktinnākinā*
Ghinakdhiṅऽna	*Dhāgetiṭkiṭ*	*Dhāgetiṭdhāge*	*Trakdhinnāginā*
Ghiḍnagdhiṅ	*Nāghiḍnag*	*Dhingindhāge*	*Trakdhinnāginā*

धाघिड़नग	धिंनाघिड़	नगधिनधागे	त्रकधिंनागिना
घिड़नगधिन	नाघिड़नग	धिनगिनधागे	त्रकधिंनागिना
घिनकतिंऽन	ताकेतिटकिट	ताकेतिटताके	त्रकतिंनाकिना
घिड़नगधिन	नाघिड़नग	धिनगिनधागे	त्रकतिंनाकिना
ताकिड़नक	तिंनाकिड़	नकतिनताके	त्रकतिंनाकिना
किड़नकतिन	नाकिड़नक	तिनकिनताके	त्रकतिंनाकिना

घिनकधिंऽन	धागेतिटकिट	धागेतिटधागे	त्रकधिंनागिना
घिड़नगधिन	नाघिड़नग	धिनगिनधागे	त्रकधिंनागिना

28. (32 Beats, ३२ मात्रा)

Dhātidhā	*Dhātirkiṭ*	*Ghinādhī*	*Nāginā*
Dhātidhā	*Dhātirkiṭ*	*Dhātidhā*	*Dhādhinnā*
Tirkiṭdhā	*Dhātirkiṭ*	*Dhātidhā*	*Dhātirkiṭ*
Tirkiṭdhā	*Dhātirkiṭ*	*Dhātidhā*	*Dhatinnā*
Tātitā	*Tātirkiṭ*	*Kinātī*	*Nākinā*
Tātitā	*Tātirkiṭ*	*Tātitā*	*Tātinnā*
Tirkiṭdhā	*Dhātirkiṭ*	*Dhātidhā*	*Dhātirkiṭ*
Tirkiṭdhā	*Dhātirkiṭ*	*Dhātidhā*	*Dhādhinnā*

धातीधा	धातिरकिट	घिनाधी	नागिना
धातीधा	धातिरकिट	धातिधा	धाधिंना
तिरकिटधा	धातिरकिट	धातिधा	धातिरकिट
तिरकिटधा	धातिरकिट	धातिधा	धातिंना
तातिता	तातिरकिट	किनाती	नाकिना
तातिता	तातिरकिट	तातिता	तातिंना
तिरकिटधा	धातिरकिट	धातीधा	धातिरकिट
तिरकिटधा	धातिरकिट	धातिधा	धाधिंना

Relās (Chatusra-Jāti)
रेले-चतुश्र जाति

30. (16 Beats, १६ मात्रा)

*Dha*ऽ	ऽ*Ghiḍnag*	*Dhātirghiḍnag*	*Dhirdhirghiḍnag*
Dhingindhātir	*Ghiḍnagdhingin*	*Dhātirghiḍnag*	*Tatirkiḍnag*
*Tā*ऽ	ऽ*kiḍnag*	*Tātirkiḍnag*	*Tirtirkiḍnag*
Dhingindhātir	*Ghiḍnagdhingin*	*Dhātirghiḍnag*	*Dhātirghiḍnag*

धाऽ	ऽघिड़नग	धातिरघिड़नग	धिरधिरघिड़नग
धिनगिनधातिर	घिड़नगधिनगिन	धातिरघिड़नग	तातिरकिड़नग
ताऽ	ऽकिड़नग	तातिरकिड़नग	तिरतिरकिड़नग
धिनगिनधातिर	घिड़नगधिनगि	धातिरघिड़नग	धातिरघिड़नग

31. (32 Beats, ३२ मात्रा)

Dhāgetir	*Kiṭdhāge*	*Tirkiṭ*	*Dhāgetrak*
Dhiṅऽ	*ऽDhāge*	*Tirkiṭ*	*Dhiṅऽ*
Dhāgetir	*Kiṭdhāge*	*Tirkiṭ*	*Dhāgetrak*
Dhingin	*Dhagetiṭ*	*Dhāgetrak*	*Tinkin*
Tāketir	*Kiṭtāke*	*Tirkiṭ*	*Tāketak*
Tiṅऽ	*ऽTāke*	*Tirkiṭ*	*Tiṅऽ*
Dhāgetir	*Kiṭdhāge*	*Tirkiṭ*	*Dhāgetrak*
Dhingin	*Dhāgetiṭ*	*Dhāgetrak*	*Dhingin*

धागेतिर	किटधागे	तिरकिट	धागेत्रक
धिनऽ	ऽधागे	तिरकिट	धिनऽ
धागेतिर	किटधागे	तिरकिट	धागेत्रक
धिनगिन	धागेतिट	धागेत्रक	तिनकिन
ताकेतिर	किटताके	तिरकिट	ताकेतक
तिनऽ	ऽताके	तिरकिट	तिनऽ
धागेतिर	किटधागे	तिरकिट	धागेत्रक
धिनगिन	धागेतिट	धागेत्रक	धिनगिन

32. (32 Beats, ३२ मात्रा)

Dhātir	*Ghiḍnag*	*Dhingin*	*Dhātir*
Ghiḍnag	*Dhātir*	*Ghiḍnag*	*Dhingin*
Dhingin	*Dhātir*	*Ghiḍnag*	*Dhātir*
Ghiḍnag	*Dhingin*	*Dhātir*	*Kiḍnag*
Tātir	*Kiḍnag*	*Tinkin*	*Tātir*
Kiḍnag	*Tātir*	*Kiḍnag*	*Tinkin*
Dhingin	*Dhātir*	*Ghiḍnag*	*Dhātir*
Ghiḍnag	*Dhingin*	*Dhātir*	*Ghiḍnag*

धातिर	घिड़नग	धिनगिन	धातिर
घिड़नग	धातिर	घिड़नग	धिनगिन
धिनगिन	धातिर	घिड़नग	धातिर
घिड़नग	धिनगिन	धातिर	किड़नग
तातिर	किड़नग	तिनकिन	तातिर
किड़नग	तातिर	किड़नग	तिनकिन
धिनगिन	धातिर	घिड़नग	धातिर
घिड़नग	धिनगिन	धातिर	घिड़नग

33. (16 Beats, १६ मात्रा)

Dhātir	*Kiṭdhā*	*Dhirdhir*	*Ghiḍnag*
Dhātir	*Ghiḍnag*	*Tīnnā*	*Kiḍnag*
Tātir	*Kiṭdhā*	*Dhirdhir*	*Ghiḍnag*
Dhātir	*Ghiḍnag*	*Dhīnnā*	*Ghiḍnag*

धातिर	किटधा	धिरधिर	घिड़नग
धातिर	घिड़नग	तींना	किड़नग
तातिर	किटधा	धिरधिर	घिड़नग
धातिर	घिड़नग	धींना	घिड़नग

(Tisra Jāti)

34. (16 Beats, १६ मात्रा)

Tiṭghiḍaऽn	*Dhinghiḍnag*	*Dhingindhāge*	*Trakdhingin*
Dhagattakiṭ	*Takdhingin*	*Dhingindhāge*	*Traktinkin*
Tiṭkiḍāऽn	*Tinkiḍnak*	*Tinkintāke*	*Traktinkin*
Dhagattakiṭ	*Takdhingin*	*Dhingindhāge*	*Trakdhingin*

(तिश्र जाति)

तिटघिड़ाऽन	धिनघिड़नग	धिनगिनधागे	त्रकधिनगिन
धगत्तकिट	तकधिनगिन	धिनगिनधागे	त्रकतिनकिन
तिटकिड़ाऽन	तिनकिड़नक	तिनकिनताके	त्रकतिनकिन
धगत्तकिट	तकधिनगिन	धिनगिनधागे	त्रकधिनगिन

35. (16 Beats, १६ मात्रा)

Dhagatdhaऽḍ	*Dhāgenagdhiṅ*	*Dhāgetiṭdhāge*	*Trakdhiṅgin*
Tiṭghiḍnag	*Dhagatdhaऽḍ*	*Dhingindhāge*	*Traktinkin*
Takattaऽḍ	*Tākenaktin*	*Taketiṭtāke*	*Traktinkin*
Tiṭghiḍnag	*Dhagatdhaऽḍ*	*Dhingindhāge*	*Trakdhiṅgin*

धगतधाऽड़	धागेनगधिन	धागेतिटधागे	त्रकधिनगिन
तिटघिड़नग	धगतधाऽड़	धिनगिनधागे	त्रकतिनकिन
तकतताऽड़	ताकेनकतिन	ताकेतिटताके	त्रकतिनकिन
तिटघिड़नग	धगतधाऽड़	धिनगिनधागे	त्रकधिनगिन

36. (16 Beats, १६ मात्रा)

Dhingintak	*Takdhiṅgin*	*Dhingindhāge*	*Trakdhiṅgin*
Taktaktak	*Takdhiṅgin*	*Dhingindhāge*	*Traktinkin*
Tinkintak	*Taktinkin*	*Tinkintāke*	*Traktinkin*
Taktaktak	*Takdhiṅgin*	*Dhingindhāge*	*Trakdhiṅgin*

धिनगिनतक	तकधिनगिन	धिनगिनधागे	त्रकधिनगिन
तकतकतक	तकधिनगिन	धिनगिनधागे	त्रकतिनकिन
तिनकिनतक	तकतिनकिन	तिनकिनताके	त्रकतिनकिन
तकतकतक	तकधिनगिन	धिनगिनधागे	त्रकधिनगिन

37. (16 Beats, १६ मात्रा)

Takiṭtakiṭ	*Takdhiṅgin*	*Dhingindhāge*	*Trakdhiṅgin*
Dhingintak	*Takdhiṅgin*	*Dhingindhiṅ*	*Gintinkin*
Takiṭtakiṭ	*Taktinkin*	*Tinkintāke*	*Traktinkin*
Dhingintak	*Takdhiṅgin*	*Dhingindhiṅ*	*Gindhiṅgin*

तकिटतकिट	तकधिनगिन	धिनगिनधागे	त्रकधिनगिन
धिनगिनतक	तकधिनगिन	धिनगिनधिन	गिनतिनकिन
तकिटतकिट	तकतिनकिन	तिनकिनताके	त्रकतिनकिन
धिनगिनतक	तकधिनगिन	धिनगिनधिन	गिनधिनगिन

38. (16 Beats, १६ मात्रा)

Dhindhiṅdhiṅ	*Dhindhāgetrak*	*Dhingindhāge*	*Trakdhigin*
Dhingindhāge	*Trakdhiṅgin*	*Dhāgetrakdhiṅ*	*Gintinkin*
Tintintin	*Tintāketrak*	*Tinkintāke*	*Traktinkin*
Dhingindhāge	*Trakdhiṅgin*	*Dhāgetrakdhiṅ*	*Gindhiṅgin*

धिनधिनधिन	धिनधागेत्रक	धिनगिनधागे	त्रकधिगिन
धिनगिनधागे	त्रकधिनगिन	धागेत्रकधिन	गिनतिनकिन
तिनतिनतिन	तिनताकेत्रक	तिनकिनताके	त्रकतिनकिन
धिनगिनधागे	त्रकधिनगिन	धागेत्रकधिन	गिनधिनगिन

39. (16 Beats, १६ मात्रा)

Ghiḍnagtiṭ	*Kiṭdhātiṭ*	*Ghiḍnagtiṭ*	*Ghiḍnag*ऽ
Tiṭghiḍnag	*Dhādhātiṭ*	*Dhāghiḍnag*	*Tiṭkiḍnak*

Kiḍnaktiṭ	*Kiṭtātiṭ*	*Kiḍnaktiṭ*	*Kiḍnakऽ*
Tiṭghiḍnag	*Dhādhātiṭ*	*Dhāghiḍnag*	*Tiṭghiḍnag*

घिड़नगतिट	किटधातिट	घिड़नगतिट	घिड़नगऽ
तिटघिड़नग	धाधातिट	धाघिड़नग	तिटकिड़नक
किड़नकतिट	किटतातिट	किड़नकतिट	किड़नकऽ
तिटघिड़नग	धाधातिट	धाघिड़नग	तिटघिड़नग

Chalan or Chālā Chatusra-Jāti

40. (16 Beats, १६ मात्रा)

Ghiḍnag	*Dhingin*	*Dhāgetrak*	*Dhingin*
Dhinghiḍ	*Nagdhiṅ*	*Dhāgetrak*	*Dhingin*
Dhagetiṭ	*Kiṭdhiṅ*	*Dhaऽऽ*	*Ghiḍnag*
Tiṭghiḍ	*Nagdhiṅ*	*Dhāgetrak*	*Dhingin*

चलन अथवा चाला चतुश्र जाति

घिड़नग	धिनगिन	धागेत्रक	धिनगिन
धिनघिड़	नगधिन	धागेत्रक	धिनगिन
धागेतिट	किटधिन	धाऽऽ	घिड़नग
तिटघिड़	नगधिन	धागेत्रक	धिनगिन

41 (16 Beats, १६ मात्रा)

Ghiḍnag	*Ghiḍnag*	*Dhindhāge*	*Trakdhiṅ*
Ghiḍnag	*Dhingin*	*Dhāgetrak*	*Dhingin*
Dhāgetrak	*Dhinghiḍ*	*Nagdhiṅ*	*Dhāgetrak*
Dhinghiḍ	*Nagdhiṅ*	*Dhāgetrak*	*Dhingin*

घिड़नग	घिड़नग	धिनधागे	त्रकधिन
घिड़नग	धिनगिन	धागेत्रक	धिनगिन
धागेत्रक	धिनघिड़	नगधिन	धागेत्रक
धिनघिड़	नगधिन	धागेत्रक	धिनगिन

42. (16 Beats, १६ मात्रा)

Tak	*Dhiṅ*	*Gin*	*Dhādhā*
Kiṭtak	*Tak*	*Dhiṅ*	*Gin*

Dhādhā	*Kiṭṭak*	*Tak*	*Dhiṅ*
Gin	*Tak*	*Dhiṅ*	*Gin*

तक	धिन	गिन	धाधा
किटतक	तक	धिन	गिन
धाधा	किटतक	तक	धिन
गिन	तक	धिन	गिन

Chalan (Tisra-Jāti)

43. (16 Beats, १६ मात्रा)

Taktaktak	*Takdhiṅgin*	*Dhingindhāge*	*Trakdhiṅgin*
Ghinaṭghiḍ	*Nagdhiṅgin*	*Dhingintak*	*Takdhiṅgin*
Dhagattakiṭ	*Takdhiṅgin*	*Dhingindhāge*	*Trakdhiṅgin*
Taktaktak	*Takdhiṅgin*	*Dhingintak*	*Takdhiṅgin*

चलन (तिश्र जाति)

तकतकतक	तकधिनगिन	धिनगिनधागे	त्रकधिनगिन
घिनऽतघिड	नगधिनगिन	धिनगिनतक	तकधिनगिन
धगततकिट	तकधिनगिन	धिनगिनधागे	त्रकधिनगिन
तकतकतक	तकधिनगिन	धिनगिनतक	तकधिनगिन

44. (16 Beats, १६ मात्रा)

Tiṭghiḍāsn	*Dhinghiḍāsn*	*Dhingindhāge*	*Trakdhiṅgin*
Ghiḍāsntak	*Takghiḍasn*	*Dhingindhāge*	*Trakdhiṅgin*
Tiṭghiḍāsn	*Tiṭghiḍāsn*	*Dhingindhāge*	*Trakdhiṅgin*
Ghiḍāsntak	*Takdhiṅgin*	*Dhingindhiṅ*	*Gindhiṅgin*

तिटघिड़ाऽन	धिनघिड़ाऽन	धिनगिनधागे	त्रकधिनगिन
घिड़ाऽनतक	तकघिड़ाऽन	धिनगिनधागे	त्रकधिनगिन
तिटघिड़ाऽन	तिटघिड़ाऽन	धिनगिनधागे	त्रकधिनगिन
घिड़ाऽनतक	तकधिनगिन	धिनगिनधिन	गिनधिनगिन

Chatusra-Jāti

45. (16 Beats,१६ मात्रा)

Dhāgenag	*Dhindhāge*	*Trakdhiṅ*	*Ghintā*ऽ
Dhāgetrak	*Dhingin*	*Dhāgetrak*	*Ghintā*ऽ
*Ghintā*ऽ	*Ghintiṭ*	*Ghindhāge*	*Trakdhiṅ*
Tiṭghin	*Dhāghin*	*Trakdhiṅ*	*Ghintā*ऽ

चतुश्र जाति

धागेनग	धिनधागे	त्रकधिन	घिनताऽ
धागेत्रक	धिनगिन	धागेत्रक	घिनताऽ
घिनताऽ	घिनतिट	घिनधागे	त्रकधिन
तिटघिन	धाघिन	त्रकधिन	घिनताऽ

Chatusra-Jāti

46. (32 Beats, ३२ मात्रा)

Takdhiṅ	*Gintak*	*Takdhiṅ*	*Gintak*
Tak tak	*Dhingin*	*Dhāgetrak*	*Dhingin*
Dhintak	*Dhintak*	*Takdhiṅ*	*Taktak*
Takdhiṅ	*Gindhiṅ*	*Dhāgetrak*	*Dhingin*
Taktak	*Taktak*	*Dhintak*	*Takdhiṅ*
Takdhiṅ	*Taktak*	*Tiṭkata*	*Kiḍnag*
Dhintak	*Dhintak*	*Takdhiṅ*	*Taktak*
Takdhiṅ	*Gindhiṅ*	*Dhāgetrak*	*Dhingin*

चतुश्र जाति

तकधिन	गिनतक	तकधिन	गिनतक
तकतक	धिनगिन	धागेत्रक	धिनगिन
धिनतक	धिनतक	तकधिन	तकतक
तकधिन	गिनधिन	धागेत्रक	धिनगिन
तकतक	तकतक	धिनतक	तकधिन
तकधिन	तकतक	तिटकत	किड़नग
धिनतक	धिनतक	तकधिन	तकतक
तकधिन	गिनधिन	धागेत्रक	धिनगिन

Tukḍas-From *Sama* to *Sama* and ending with a *tihāī* *Chatusra-Jāti*

47. (32 Beats, ३२ मात्रा)

Takdhiṅ	*Takdhiṅ*	*Natakghi*	*Takdhiṅ*
Ghitakan	*Takdhiṅ*	*Dhāgetrak*	*Dhinnāginā*
Natakghi	*Taknata*	*Kaghitak*	*Dhingin*
Natakghi	*Takdhiṅ*	*Dhāgetrak*	*Dhinnāginā*
Dhirdhirkiṭṭak	*Dhātirkiṭṭak*	*Takghḍāsndhā*	*Dhinnāghiḍnag*
Tirkiṭṭakdhir	*Dhirkiṭdhāti*	*Dhās*	*sDhāti*
Dhā dhāti	*Dhā dhāti*	*Dhā dhāti*	*Dhā dhāti*
Dhā dhāti	*Dhā dhāti*	*Dhā dhāti*	*Dhā dhāti*

टुकड़े-सम से सम तक: तिहाई द्वारा सम्पन
(चतुश्र जाति)

तकधिन	तकधिन	नतकघि	तकधिन
घितकन	तकधिन	धागेत्रक	धिंनागिना
नतकघि	तकनत	कघितक	धिनगिन
नतकघि	तकधिन	धागेत्रक	धिंनागिना
धिरधिरकिटतक	धातिरकिटतक	तकघ्डाऽनधा	धिंनाघिड़नग
तिरकिटतकधिर	धिरकिटधाती	धाऽ	ऽधाती
धाधाती	धाधाती	धाधाती	धाधाती
धाधाती	धाधाती	धाधाती	धाधाती

48. (16 Beats, १६ मात्रा)

Dhātidhā	*sGhin*	*Dhātighin*	*Dhātighin*
Dhās	*Kḍedhetdhi*	*Tiṭghin*	*Dhātighin*
Dhātighin	*Dhāskiḍnag*	*Tās*	*skiḍnag*
Tiṅs	*sKiḍnag*	*Tāskiḍnag*	*Tāskiḍnag*
Tiṅkiḍnag	*Tiṅkiḍnag*	*Tirkiṭṭaktā*	*Tirkiṭdhāge*
Dhātiṅsna	*Dhāgedhātī*	*snadhāge*	*Dhātiṅsna*

धातीधा	ऽघिन	धातिघिन	धातिघिन
धाऽ	क्ड़ेधेतधि	तिटघिन	धातिघिन
धातिघिन	धाऽकिड़नग	ताऽ	ऽकिड़नग
तिंऽ	ऽकिड़नग	ताऽकिड़नग	ताऽकिड़नग

तिंकिड़नग	तिंकिड़नग	तिरकिटतकता	तिरकिटधागे
धातींऽन	धागेधाती	ऽनधागे	धातींऽन

Note:- The above composition comprises 24 beats. Hence, it has to be played at double the speed of the *ṭhekā;* and is to be covered in three rounds of the *tāla* (16x3 = 48)

नोट:- ऊपर की रचना २४ मात्रा की है। इसलिये इस बन्दिश को ठेके की दुगुनी लय में बजाना होगा, जिससे कि यह ताल के तीन आवर्तनों में पूरी हो जायेगी। (१६x३=४८)

49. (16 Beats, १६ मात्रा)

Dhātīdhā	*ऽGhin*	*Dhātī Ghin*	*Dhināऽ*
Dhāgenkat	*Dhātighin*	*Dhīnāऽ*	*Kiḍnagtā*
Tākiḍnag	*Tākiḍnag*	*TāऽTāऽ*	*Kiḍnagtirkiṭ*
Taktātirkiṭ	*Dhātidhāgen*	*Dhātidhāgen*	*Dhātidhāgen*

धातीधा	ऽघिन	धातीघिन	धिनाऽ
धागेनकत	धातिघिन	धीनाऽ	किड़नगता
ताकिड़नग	ताकिड़नग	ताऽताऽ	किड़नगतिरकिट
तकतातिरकिट	धातिधागेन	धातिधागेन	धातिधागेन

50. (16 Beats, १६ मात्रा)

Dhinghiḍnag	*Ghiṅtarāऽn*	*ऽTakiṭdhiṅ*	*Ghiḍnagtiṅ*
Taktakiṭghiḍā	*ऽNghiḍnagdin*	*Tiṭkiṭkiḍ*	*Naktinkin*
Ghiṅtarāऽn	*Dhiṭghiṅऽnta*	*Rāऽntakiṭdhā*	
ऽDhirdhirkiṭṭaktakiṭ	*Dhātakiṭdhā*	*ऽDhirdhirkiṭṭaktakiṭ*	
Dhātakiṭdhāऽ	*Dhirdhirkiṭṭaktakiṭ*		

धिनघिड़नग	घिंतराऽन	ऽतकिटधिन	घिड़नगतिं
तकतकिटघिड़ा	ऽनघिड़नगदिन	तिटकिटकिड़	नकतिनकिन
घिंतराऽन	धिटघिंऽनत	राऽनतकिटधा	
ऽधिरधिरकिटतकतकिट	धातकिटधा	ऽधिरधिरकिटतकतकिट	
धातकिटधाऽ	धिरधिरकिटतकतकिट		

51. (16 Beats, १६ मात्रा)

Takiṭdhitiṭ	*Ghiṅtarāऽn*	*Dhāऽdinntā*	*Katktiṭkat*
Ghiṅtarāऽn	*Dhāऽdinntā*	*Takiṭdhitiṭ*	*Ghiṅtarāऽn*
Dhāऽkāऽt	*Dhātakiṭ*	*Dhitiṭghiṅऽnta*	*Rāऽndhā*
Kaऽṭdhā	*Takiṭdhitiṭ*	*Ghiṅtarāऽn*	*DhāऽKaऽt*

तकिटधितिट	घिंतराऽन	धाऽदिंता	कतकिटकत
घिंतराऽन	धाऽदिंता	तकिटधितिट	घिंतराऽन
धाऽकऽत	धातकिट	धितिटघिंऽनत	राऽनधा
कऽतधा	तकिटधितिट	घिंतराऽन	धाऽकऽत

52. (64 Beats, ६४ मात्रा)

Dhin tak	*Dhiṅ Tak*	*Tak tak*	*Dhiṅ tak*
Tak dhiṅ	*Tak tak*	*Dhiṅ tak*	*Dhiṅ tak*
Tak tak	*Dhiṅ tak*	*Dhiṅ tak*	*Tak tak*
Dhiṅ tak	*Dhiṅ tak*	*Tak tak*	*Dhiṅ tak*
Dhirdhir	*Ghiḍnag*	*Dhiṅtak*	*Ghiḍnag*
Dhintak	*Dhirdhir*	*Ghiḍnag*	*Dhintak*
Tiṭkatā	*Kiḍnag*	*Tin tak*	*Kiḍnag*
Tintak	*Tiṭkatā*	*Kiḍnag*	*Tintak*
Katdhirdhir	*Kiṭṭaktakiṭ*	*Dhāऽtakiṭ*	*Dhāऽkat*
Dhirdhirkiṭṭak	*Takiṭdhāऽ*	*Takiṭdhāऽ*	*Katdhirdhir*
Kiṭṭak takiṭ	*Dhāऽtakiṭ*	*Dhāऽ*	*Katdhirdhir*
Kiṭṭak takiṭ	*Dhāऽtakiṭ*	*Dhāऽkat*	*Dhirdhirkiṭṭak*
Takiṭ dhāऽ	*Takiṭ dhāऽ*	*Katdhirdhir*	*Kiṭṭaktakiṭ*
Dhāऽtakiṭ	*Dhāऽ*	*Katdhirdhir*	*Kiṭṭaktakiṭ*
Dhāऽtakiṭ	*DhāऽKat*	*Dhirdhirkiṭṭak*	*Takiṭdhāऽ*
Takiṭdhāऽ	*Katdhirdhir*	*Kiṭṭaktakiṭ*	*Dhāऽtakiṭ*

धिनतक	धिनतक	तकतक	धिनतक
तकधिन	तकतक	धिनतक	धिनतक
तकतक	धिनतक	धिनतक	तकतक
धिनतक	धिनतक	तकतक	धिनतक
धिरधिर	धिड़नग	धिनतक	घिड़नग
धिनतक	धिरधिर	घिड़नग	धिनतक
तिटकता	किड़नग	तिनतक	किड़नग
तिनतक	तिटकता	किड़नग	तिनतक
कतधिरधिर	किटतकतकिट	धाऽतकिट	धाऽतक
धिरधिरकिटतक	तकिटधाऽ	तकिटधाऽ	कतधिरधिर
किटतकतकिट	धाऽतकिट	धाऽ	कतधिरधिर

किटतकतकिट	धाऽतकिट	धाऽकत	धिरधिरकिटतक
तकिटधाऽ	तकिटधाऽ	कतधिरधिर	किटतकतकिट
धाऽतकिट	धाऽ	कतधिरधिर	किटतकतकिट
धाऽतकिट	धाऽकत	धिरधिरकिटतक	तकिटधाऽ
तकिटधाऽ	कतधिरधिर	किटतकतकिट	धाऽतकिट

Deepchandi Ang:- (Misra-Jāti) 3,4; 3.4

53. (48 Beats, *deepchandi ang misrajāti* : 3,4; 3,4)
(४८ मात्रा, दीपचंदी अंग, मिश्र जाति: ३,४; ३,४)

Dhingintak	*Dhingintaktak*	*Dhingintak*	*Dhingintāऽ*
Taktaktak	*Dhingintaktak*	*Dhingintak*	*Dhingintāऽ*
Dhingintak	*Dhingintaktak*	*Dhingintak*	*Dhingintaktak*
Dhingintak	*Dhingintaktak*	*Dhingintak*	*Dhingintāऽ*
Kḍedhiṅ	*Nānākiḍnag*	*Tirkiṭtak*	*Dhirdhirkiṭtak*
Dhāऽtī	*Dhāऽऽ*	*Kḍedhiṅ*	*Nānākiḍnag*
Tirkiṭtak	*Dhirdhirkiṭtak*	*Tirkiṭtak*	*Dhirdhirkiṭtak*
Tirkiṭtak	*Dhirdhirkiṭtak*	*Dhāऽऽ*	*Kḍedhiṅ*
Nānākiḍnag	*Tirkiṭtak*	*Dhirdhirkiṭtak*	*Tirkiṭtak*
Dhirdhirkiṭtak	*Tirkiṭtak*	*Dhirdhirkiṭtak*	*Dhāऽऽ*
Kḍedhiṅ	*Nānākiḍnag*	*Tirkiṭtak*	*Dhirdhirkiṭtak*
Tirkiṭtak	*Dhirdhirkiṭtak*	*Tirkiṭtak*	*Dhirdhirkiṭtak*

धिनगिनतक	धिनगिनतकतक	धिनगिनतक	धिनगिनताऽ
तकतकतक	धिनगिनतकतक	धिनगिनतक	धिनगिनताऽ
धिनगिनतक	धिनगिनतकतक	धिनगिनतक	धिनगिनतकतक
धिनगिनतक	धिनगिनतकतक	धिनगिनतक	धिनगिनताऽ
क्ड़ेधिन	नानाकिड़नग	तिरकिटतक	धिरधिरकिटतक
धाऽती	धाऽऽ	क्ड़ेधिन	नानाकिड़नग
तिरकिटतक	धिरधिरकिटतक	तिरकिटतक	धिरधिरकिटतक
तिरकिटतक	धिरधिरकिटतक	धाऽऽ	क्ड़ेधिन
नानाकिड़नग	तिरकिटतक	धिरधिरकिटतक	तिरकिटतक
धिरधिरकिटतक	तिरकिटतक	धिरधिरकिटतक	धाऽऽ
क्ड़ेधिन	नानाकिड़नग	तिरकिटतक	धिरधिरकिटतक
तिरकिटतक	धिरधिरकिटतक	तिरकिटतक	धिरधिरकिटतक

(*Chatusra-Jāti*)

54. (48 Beats, ४८ मात्रा)

Nānānā	*Tāऽkiṭṭak*	*Tirkiṭṭātir*	*Kiṭṭaktakiṭ*
Dhāऽ	*ऽkiṭṭak*	*Tirkiṭṭātir*	*Kiṭṭaktakiṭ*
Dhākiṭṭak	*Tirkiṭṭātir*	*Kiṭṭaktakiṭ*	*Dhikiṭṭak*
Tirkiṭṭātir	*Kiṭṭaktakiṭ*	*Dhāऽ*	*ऽऽ*
Katkat	*Ghiḍāऽn*	*Katkat*	*Ghiḍaऽn*
Katghiḍā	*ऽnkat*	*Ghiḍāऽn*	*Gadigan*
Dhā dhirdhir	*Kiṭṭaktakiṭ*	*Dhāऽ*	*Katkat*
Ghiḍāऽn	*Katkat*	*Ghiḍāऽn*	*Katghiḍā*
ऽnkat	*Ghiḍāऽn*	*Gadigan*	*Dhā dhirdhir*
Kiṭṭaktakiṭ	*Dhāऽ*	*Katkat*	*Ghiḍāऽn*
Katkat	*Ghiḍāऽn*	*Katghiḍā*	*ऽnkat*
Ghiḍāऽn	*Gadigan*	*Dhā dhirdhir*	*Kiṭ tak takiṭ*

(चतुश्र जाति)

नानाना	ताऽकिटतक	तिरकिटतातिर	किटतकतकिट
धाऽ	ऽकिटतक	तिरकिटतातिर	किटतकतकिट
धाकिटतक	तिरकिटतातिर	किटतकतकिट	धाकिटतक
तिरकिटतातिर	किटतकतकिट	धाऽ	ऽऽ
कतकत	घिड़ाऽन	कतकत	घिड़ाऽन
कतघिड़ा	ऽनकत	घिड़ाऽन	गदिगन
धाधिरधिर	किटतकतकिट	धाऽ	कतकत
घिड़ाऽन	कतकत	घिड़ाऽन	कतघिड़ा
ऽनकत	घिड़ाऽन	गदिगन	धाधिरधिर
किटतकतकिट	धाऽ	कतकत	घिड़ाऽन
कतकत	घिड़ाऽन	कतघिड़ा	ऽनकत
घिड़ाऽन	गदिगन	धाधिरधिर	किटतकतकिट

(*Gat Chār Bāgh Tisra - Jāti*)

55. (16 Beats, १६ मात्रा)

Dhātīdhā	*Gadhātī*	*Dhāgdhi*	*Nāgin*
Tirkiṭṭak	*Dhirdhirkiṭ*	*Dhāgdhi*	*Nāgin*
Taktiṅ	*Nākiḍnak*	*Tirkiṭṭak*	*Dhirdhirkiṭ*
Tirkiṭṭak	*Dhirdhirkiṭ*	*Dhāgdhi*	*Nāgin*

(*गत चारबाग़*) तिश्र-जाति

धातीधा	गधाती	धागधि	नागिन
तिरकिटतक	धिरधिरकिट	धागधि	नागिन
तकतिं	नाकिड़नक	तिरकिटतक	धिरधिरकिट
तिरकिटतक	धिरधिरकिट	धागधि	नागिन

56. (16 Beats, १६ मात्रा)

Tak Ghḍāऽn	*Dhāghiḍnag*	*Dhingindhāge*	*Trakdhiṅgin*
Dhinginnag	*Takdhiṅgin*	*Dhāgetiṭdhāge*	*Trakdhiṅgin*
Dhāgetiṭkiṭ	*Dhindhagetiṭ*	*Dhāgetiṭdhāge*	*Trakdhiṅgin*
Ghināऽtghiḍ	*Nagdintak*	*Tiṭkiṭdhāge*	*Trakdhiṅgin*

तकघ्ड़ाऽन	धाघिड़नग	धिनगिनधागे	त्रकधिनगिन
धिनगिननग	तकधिनगिन	धागेतिटधागे	त्रकधिनगिन
धागेतिटकिट	धिनधागेतिट	धागेतिटधागे	त्रकधिनगिन
घिनाऽतघिड़	नगदिनतक	तिटकिटधागे	त्रकधिनगिन

57.(16 Beats, १६ मात्रा)

Dhagat takiṭ	*Tak din tak*	*Dhir dhir ghiḍ*	*Nag din tak*
Dhirdhirghiḍ	*Nagdhirdhir*	*Dhirdhirghiḍ*	*Nag din tak*
Tak din tak	*Din tak tak*	*Dhirdhirghiḍ*	*Nag din tak*
Takiṭdhāऽd	*Dhāghiḍnag*	*Dhirdhirghiḍ*	*Nag din tak*

धगततकिट	तकदिनतक	धिरधिरघिड़	नगदिनतक
धिरधिरघिड़	नगधिरधिर	धिरधिरघिड़	नगदिनतक

तकदिनतक	दिनतकतक	धिरधिरघिड़	नगदिनतक
तकिटधाऽड़	धाघिड़नग	धिरधिरघिड़	नगदिनतक

58. (16 Beats, १६ मात्रा)

Takiṭ dhitiṭ	*Takiṭ dhitiṭ*	*Ghiṅtarsn*	*Ghiṅtarāsn*
Dhātrakdhitiṭ	*Dhātrakdhitiṭ*	*Katgadigan*	*Katgadigan*
Ghindhātīghin	*Dhātīdhāgdhiṅ*	*Dhingadigan*	*Dhingadigan*
Katiṭtagan	*Dhiṭ dha ḍāsn*	*Dhātrakdhitiṭ*	*katgadigan*
तकिटधितिट	तकिटधितिट	घिंताराऽन	घिंताराऽन
धात्रकधितिट	धात्रकधितिट	कतगदिगन	कतगदिगन
घिनधातीघिन	धातीधागधिन	धिनगदिगन	धिनगदिगन
कतिटतगन	धिटधड़ाऽन	धात्रकधितिट	कतगदिगन

Gats (Tisra - Jāti)

59. (16 Beats, १६ मात्रा)

Takghḍāsn	*Dhādhiṅnag*	*Tirkiṭtak*	*Dhāsdhinnā*
Nagan nagan	*Katkatghin*	*Dhinnāskasta*	*Dhāss*
Katkatghin	*Katkatghin*	*Nagtiṭtā*	*Tiṭtāghin*
Takiṭ takiṭ	*Kat kat kat*	*Ghinakatakiṭ*	*Dhāskast*

गत (तिश्र जाति)

तकघ्ड़ाऽन	धाधिननग	तिरकिटतक	धाऽधिंना
नगननगन	कतकतघिन	धिंनाऽकऽत	धाऽऽ
कतकतघिन	कतकतघिन	नगतिटता	तिटताघिन
तकिटतकिट	कतकतकत	घिनकतकिट	धाऽकऽत

(Chatusra Jāti) Dumui - Gat

60. (16 Beats, १६ मात्रा)

Dhāgetiṭ	*Kiṭdhiṅ*	*Dhāgetrak*	*Dhingin*
Dhinghiḍ	*Nagdhāge*	*Tiṭkiṭ*	*Dhingin*
Dhinghiḍ	*Nagdhāge*	*Tiṭkiṭ*	*Dhingin*
Dhagetiṭ	*Kiṭdhiṅ*	*Dhāgetrak*	*Dhingin*

(*चतुश्र जाति*) दुमुई-गत

धागेतिट	किटधिन	धागेत्रक	धिनगिन
धिनघिड़	नगधागे	तिटकिट	धिनगिन
धिनघिड़	नगधागे	तिटकिट	धिनगिन
धागेतिट	किटधिन	धागेत्रक	धिनगिन

61. (16 Beats, १६ मात्रा)

Ghiḍnag	*Dhindhāge*	*Trakdhiṅ*	*Ghiḍnag*
Dhindhag	*Dhagdhiṅ*	*Dhāgetrak*	*Dhinghiḍ*
Nagdhiṅ	*Dhinnāginā*	*Tāghiḍ*	*Nagdhiṅ*
Dhāgetrak	*Dhinghiḍ*	*Nagdhiṅ*	*Dhinnāginā*

(चतुश्र जाति)

घिड़नग	धिनधागे	त्रकधिन	घिड़नग
धिनधग	धगधिन	धागेत्रक	धिनघिड़
नगधिन	धिंनागिना	ताघिड़	नगधिन
धागेत्रक	धिनघिड़	नगधिन	धिंनागिना

(Tisra - Jāti) Dumui-*Gat*

62. (16 Beats, १६ मात्रा)

Dhagat takiṭ	*Dhāgetiṭkiṭ*	*Dhagdhinnag*	*Tiṭkatāsn*
Tiṭkatāsn	*Dhāgetiṭkiṭ*	*Dhagdhinnag*	*Tiṭkatāsn*
Taktaktak	*Tiṭkatāsn*	*Dhagdhinnag*	*Tiṭkatāsn*
Dhagat takiṭ	*Dhāgetiṭkiṭ*	*Dhagdhinnag*	*Tiṭkatāsn*

(*तिश्र जाति*) (दुमुई-गत)

धगत्तकिट	धागेतिटकिट	धगधिन्नग	तिटकताऽन
तिटकताऽन	धागेतिटकिट	धगधिन्नग	तिटकताऽन
तकतकतक	तिटकताऽन	धगधिन्नग	तिटकताऽन
धगत्तकिट	धागेतिटकिट	धगधिन्नग	तिटकताऽन

(Chatusra - Jāti) Dumui - Gat

63. (16 Beats, १६ मात्रा)

Dhāghiḍ	*Nagdhiṅ*	*Nāsḍ*	*Ghiḍnag*
Dhingin	*Dhāgetrak*	*Dhinnāginā*	*Tāketrak*

Tinnākinā	*Dhāghiḍ*	*Nagdhiṅ*	*Nāsḍ*
Ghiḍnag	*Dhingin*	*Dhāgetrak*	*Dhinnāginā*

(*चतुश्र जाति*) *दुमुई-गत*

धाघिड़	नगधिन	नाऽड़	घिड़नग
धिनगिन	धागेत्रक	धिंनागिना	ताकेत्रक
तिंनाकिना	धाघिड़	नगधिन	नाऽड़
घिड़नग	धिनगिन	धागेत्रक	धिंनागिना

64. (16 Beats, १६ मात्रा)

Dhāgetiṭ	*Ghiḍāsn*	*Dhingin*	*Dhāgetrak*
Dhināginā	*Dindinā*	*Gindhāge*	*Tiṭkiṭ*
Dhāgetiṭ	*Dhāgetrak*	*Dhinnāginā*	*Tiṭghiḍā*
snghiḍ	*Nagdhiṅ*	*Dhāgetrak*	*Dhinnāginā*

(चतुश्र जाति)

धागेतिट	घिड़ाऽन	धिनगिन	धागेत्रक
धिनागिना	दिनदिना	गिनधागे	तिटकिट
धागेतिट	धागेत्रक	धिंनागिना	तिटघिड़ा
ऽनघिड़	नगधिन	धागेत्रक	धिंनागिना

65. (16 Beats, १६ मात्रा)

Dhirdhirdhir	*Dhirghiḍnag*	*Dhirdhirghiḍ*	*Nagdintak*
Tiṭghiḍāsn	*Dhāghiḍnag*	*Dhirdhirghiḍ*	*Nagdintak*
Tiṭghiḍāsn	*Dhitghiḍāsn*	*Ghiḍnagdhir*	*Dhirghiḍnag*
Takiṭdhāsḍ	*Dhādiṅtā*	*Dhirdhirghiḍ*	*Nagdintak*

(तिश्र जाति)

धिरधिरधिर	धिरघिड़नग	धिरधिरघिड़	नगदिनतक
तिटघिड़ाऽन	धाघिड़नग	धिरधिरघिड़	नगदिनतक
तिटघिड़ाऽन	धिटघिड़ाऽन	घिड़नगधिर	धिरघिड़नग
तकिटधाऽड़	धादिंता	धिरधिरघिड़	नगदिनतक

Chakradār - Tukḍās

66. (81 Beats, ८१ मात्रा)

Tādhā	*Tādhā*	*Gadigan*	*Dhittā*
Kiḍdhit	*Tākat*	*Gadigan*	*Dhāstiṭ*
Dhās	*TāsDhā*	*Dhirdhir-kiṭtak*	*Dhā dhirdhir*
Kiṭtakdhā	*Dhirdhirkiṭtak*	*Dhās*	*Tāsdhā*
Dhirdhir kiṭtak	*Dhādhirdhir*	*Kiṭtak dhā*	*Dhirdhir-kiṭtak*
Dhās	*Tāsdhā*	*Dhirdhir-kiṭtak*	*Dhās Dhirdhir*
Kiṭtak dhās	*Dhirdhir-kiṭtak*	*Dhās*	

(27x3 = 81)

ताधा	ताधा	गदिगन	धित्ता
किड्धित	ताकत	गदिगन	धाऽतिट
धाऽ	ताऽधा	धिरधिरकिटतक	धाधिरधिर
किटतकधा	धिरधिरकिटतक	धाऽ	ताऽधा
धिरधिरकिटतक	धाधिरधिर	किटतकधा	धिरधिरकिटतक
धाऽ	ताऽधा	धिरधिरकिटतक	धाऽ धिरधिर
किटतकधाऽ	धिरधिरकिटतक	धाऽ	

67. (27x3 = 81, २७ x ३=८१)

Takghḍasndhā	*Dhinnāghidnag*	*Tirkiṭtakdhir*	*Dhirkiṭdhātī*
Dhāss	*sGhiḍnag*	*Tirkiṭtakdhir*	*Dhirkiṭdhātī*
Dhāsghesnt	*Dhāskat*	*Dhāstā*	*Dhāsghiḍnag*
Tirkiṭtakdhir	*Dhirkiṭdhātī*	*Dhāsdhāti*	*Dhāsdhātī*
Dhāsghiḍnag	*Tirkiṭtakdhir*	*Dhirkiṭdhātī*	*Dhāsdhātī*
Dhās dhātī	*Dhāsghiḍnag*	*Tirkiṭtakdhir*	*Dhirkiṭdhātī*
Dhāsdhātī	*Dhāsdhātī*	*Dhās*	

तकघ्डाऽनधा	धिंनाघिड्नग	तिरकिटतकधिर	धिरकिटधाती
धाऽऽ	ऽघिड्नग	तिरकिटतकधिर	धिरकिटधाती
धाऽघेऽन्त	धाऽकत	धाऽता	धाऽघिड्नग
तिरकिटतकधिर	धिरकिटधाती	धाऽधाती	धाऽधाती
धाऽघिड्नग	तिरकिटतकधिर	धिरकिटधाती	धाऽधाती
धाऽधाती	धाऽघिड्नग	तिरकिटतकधिर	धिरकिटधाती
धाऽधाती	धाऽधाती	धाऽ	

68. (27 x 3 = 81, २७ x ३=८१)

Takiṭdhā	*Trakdhiṅ*	*Dhāsghi*	*Nakdhiṅ*
Dhātrakdhi	*Nakdhiṅ*	*Dhirdhirkiṭtak*	*Tātirkiṭtak*
Katiṭtā	*Gandhiṅ*	*Natakghi*	*Takdhiṅ*
Dhinnata	*Kaghitak*	*Dhirdhirkiṭtak*	*Tātirkiṭtak*
Dhāsdhir	*Dhirdhir*	*Kiṭtak*	*Dhās*
skat	*Dhāsdhir*	*Dhirdhirkiṭtak*	*Dhās*
skat	*Dhāsdhir*	*Dhirdhirkiṭtak*	*Dhās*

तकिटधा	त्रकधिन	धाऽघि	नकधिन
धात्रकधि	नकधिन	धिरधिरकिटतक	तातिरकिटतक
कतिटता	गनधिन	नतकघि	तकधिन
धिननत	कघितक	धिरधिरकिटतक	तातिरकिटतक
धाऽधिर	धिरधिर	किटतक	धाऽ
ऽकत	धाऽधिर	धिरधिरकिटतक	धाऽ
ऽकत	धाऽधिर	धिरधिरकिटतक	धाऽ

9

Epilogue

Now that the art of rhythm *as such* has been discussed at fair length, a little thought may be given to it *from some major points of view*. To make for the requisite fulness of concern we have indeed to give some thought to what we actually find it related to. This context is variform; and if only in brief, it requires us to look at the following: rhythm and allied concepts; the principle of figure and ground; rhythm *in music*; evaluating performances; types of audience; and players, past and present.

Rhythm and allied Concepts

To begin with a point that we have already dealt with in the opening chapter, whether it is played as solo or as accompaniment, rhythm (or *tāla*) may well be defined as regularly recurring movement isolated, identified and measured (with the help of *mātrā*s or beats) in respect of its manner and speed. Measurement (in *tāla*) of *laya* (or aesthetic pace) from the viewpoint of its manner (called *andāz*) gives us the distinctive idiom (or *chalan*) of the various *ṭhekā*s (rhythm cycles) such as *tritāla* and *ektāla*; and measurement of *laya* in respect of its pace gives us such concepts as *vilambit, madhya, drut*, and *atidrut*.

From the viewpoint of music, unattended flow is not itself *laya*. It becomes *laya* only when the mind begins to flow in accord with it, without as yet interposing any mathematical measure into it. In the region of music *laya* as such is found in *ālāpa* of the *dhruvapada* singer. Here, he is surely mindful of the pace of melodic passages and of the duration of abidance at individual notes; but this is done only to evoke some effects — say, of tranquillity and repose, or of mergence or emergence — but quite without measuring the pace with the help of *mātrās*. When it is measured in the way just referred to, *laya* becomes *tāla*. *Tāla* is to *laya* what a yard is to distance; in both cases, the former is a measure of the latter. Again, just as a yard possesses clear internal distinctions — say, inches and their further sub-divisions — so a *tāla* has its own inner accents, namely, the *khāli* and the *bhari* and the individual *mātrās*. Now, *tāla* (or rhythm) taken with its own internal distinctions, number of *mātrās*, manner of movement, and as organized around the first beat (called the *sama*), and not merely in the general sense of just being a measured cross-section of *laya*, is called *ṭhekā*, or the rhythmic anchor of *tāla* in its entirety.

The *ṭhekā*, therefore, first points to something other than itself, that is, to that of which it itself is a mere measure, say, *laya*; and secondly, it is possessed of, and *establishes* its own character, which is precisely why it is better to speak of ठेका क़ायम करना; as against ठेका बजाना. Here, however, a question may be put. Why should we at all talk of *mātrās*, *khāli*, and *bhari*, and *sama* of the *ṭhekā*? Why can't we make do with *laya* alone? The answer to both these questions is provided by a simple psychological truth. Whatever is quite formless and without any distinct features cannot be attended to without some extra effort. The *mātrās*, the *khāli* and *bhari*, and the *sama* lend internal variety and distinctness to the *ṭhekā*. This, in turn, helps concentration. Any vocalist will testify to the fact that he quickly becomes impatient with a tablā player whose *ṭhekā* is not distinctly articulated in its parts, not merely because he (the vocalist) finds it difficult to pick up *laya* if the *khāli* is not shown properly (though that too is sometimes the main cause), but because the design (or the *shape*, as they say) of a *ṭhekā* thus executed is neither conducive to concentration nor satisfying aesthetically.

I may add that the point I have just tried to make is warranted by the very feel of real life. Experience, even as it comes originally, is neither a characterless continuity nor a mosaic of chaotic bits, but an 'articulated' field of view. Distinct *objects* appear as original wholes against a *background*, the latter being at once essential to, yet distinct from, the exact perceived character of the former. The same holds true of music as presented or appreciated. Here, whether it is present in the way of pure *laya*, as it is seen in *ālāpa*, or in the more definite shape of a *ṭhekā* which accompanies singing according to beat-measured *tāla* — rhythm is marked by distinct sounds, be it in the form of individual *swara-samoohas* or in that of *layakāri*. How rhythm (in the form of *tāla*) facilitates attention can be easily illustrated by appealing to the evidence of both listening to music and of a detail of the practice of religion.

Only highly trained listeners enjoy *ālāpa* in vocal and instrumental music. The average listener responds positively only to *sthāyi*-singing or *gatkāri*, both of them being set to definite *tālas* with obvious dependence on the *ṭhekā* as marked by the tablā player. Even the average *performer* may sometimes appear to become impatient with *ālāpa*, and to breathe a sigh of relief, so to say, when tablā accompaniment begins. And to turn to the practice of religion, the beads of the rosary which help the devotee to concentrate on the act of praying are all discrete accents that occur successively.

Rhythm and the figure-ground principle

Considered in comparative isolation from music in general, the charm of rhythm consists essentially, though surely not entirely, in its conformity with an important psychological law, the law of repetition with variation, or the law of figure and ground. As we have defined it initially, rhythm is regularly recurring or repetitive movement. Repetition itself attracts attention. But, as used in music, rhythm is not merely repetitive movement, such as is seen in the swinging pendulum of a clock; it is repetition interspersed, or rather studded with subtle variations. The repetitive part, which is also the more inclusive one, furnishes the background against which the variations appear as delightfully discrete figures. The general patternings of the tablā player are variations upon the ground of the *ṭhekā*, even as the *gatkāri* of the sitār or sarod player conjures up variegated beauty upon the basic *gat* which serves as the ground.

Here, however, I may be allowed to make two observations which do not easily strike the average listener, but which are of profound aesthetic value; and which may easily cast a spell over him without his knowing the secret of the charm. Firstly, the crisper and more unexpected the *variation*, and the more inclusive and steadfast the *background*, the quicker and more irresistible will be the effect of the former (provided, of course, the listener's attention has been following it closely), so readily appealing, indeed, that the listener may be impelled to acclaim it spontaneously. This explains why perhaps the most deeply *satisfying*, though not *dazzling* thing in the art of solo tablā playing is a *quāyedā*, that is, a methodically repetitive timing-pattern having clearly marked subdivisions, in and through which the passage of *laya* meanders in the form of delightfully different curls of grace, technically called *bul khulnā* or the unwinding (so to say) of the pattern's subtle turns. Second, the law of figure and ground operates not only in the patternings which are often wrongly thought to be merely extraneous to the *ṭhekā*, but in the latter itself. And here, incidentally, I get a chance to indicate how the merely psychological is transmuted into the patently aesthetic.

The proper execution of a *ṭhekā* shows its different accents as the self-differentiation of a pervasive continuity. Just as the perceptual field of view is not broken up, but is only articulated (so to say) by the distinct objects which it contains, so the different *mātrā*s or sub-sections (or *vibhāg*s) of a *ṭhekā* — that is, its *khāli* and *bhari* — should appear as accents, howsoever distinct, in (or of) a continuity. The continuity is provided (in part) by the proper use of the *bānyā* (or the left hand drum) which produces, as I have already said, a resonance that covers or unites the individual sounds of the right drum, and prevents the latter from appearing as completely separate from the left drum. The other aspect of *individuated sharpness* is provided by clearly executed strokes: hence the importance of using the *chānt* (or the rim) of the right drum correctly. Only when these two conditions have been met can the law of figure and ground become operative in the *ṭhekā* itself, and invest the latter with a charm of its own. And once the law becomes operative — the left one providing a little continuity and so some ground, because of which perhaps it is called *the male one* — the separate strokes begin to look as accents in a flow, or as the self-differentiation of the *ṭhekā*'s own flow. The *ṭhekā* now appears as a thing of instrinsic beauty; the mind cannot help bowing to it; and the felt charm of the playing looks *grounded in an object*, and is therefore aesthetic, not merely psychological.

Rhythm in Music

We may now consider how, besides being interesting in itself, rhythm lends charm to music as a whole. Speaking quite generally, it does so in at least three clear ways. First, by virtue of its cyclic quality as a *ṭhekā*, it makes *the singing or playing* appear well formed, as against a mere series of *swaras*; and, second, whether it is symmetrical or asymmetrical — say, in the form of cycles like *tritāla* and *roopak* — it helps both the performer and the listener in getting attuned to what is being made and presented, that is, the run of music. In the case of *ālāpa*, however — I mean, *ālāpa* of the traditional *dhruvapada*-singer, where there is no *tāla* as such — it is what *tāla* measures and projects as a cycle, that is, *laya* which enlivens the music and engages the listener by making greater demands on his patience and wilful attention than are made by *tāla*-bound music. In *ālāpa*, we may note, *laya* is present in two controlled ways, namely, as the pace of passage from one *swara* to another, *and* as the duration of abidance of voice at individual notes, neither of which is regulated with the help of beats. The supreme regulative power, here, is the musician's own aesthetic sense. Thirdly, rhythm adds to our aesthetic relish by inducing us to sense the skill of those passages where the ongoing music deviates just for a moment, and designedly, from the pace as set and marked by the *ṭhekā* of the rhythm chosen, and lapses back to this pace with alacrity and unerring accuracy.

At this point, however, a note of caution may be sounded. Ideally, both in its seamless purity (as in *ālāpa*) and as embodied in *tāla*, *laya* should permeate music *through and through*. Where a performer chooses, at a particular moment, to 'show' *layakāri*, that is, as an isolated element of music, the aesthetic effect suffers, as a rule. This is specially true of quite a few *dhruvapada* singers of today. *Laya* and *swara* are the life-breath of music, even like word-bound images and the very sound and disposition — not merely the meaning — of words in the case of poetry; and just as good poetry is importantly a blend of the factors just distinguished, so music too should never appear as a mere *alternation* of the melodic with the rhythmic.

Valuing recitals

But, turning to tablā rhythm, how exactly can we evaluate a particular exposition of it? Is one to go by the judgment of authentic maestros or by the reactions of those who make the audience, and most of whom cannot distinguish a *dhiṭ* from a *tiṭ*? In olden days, a maestro of tablā would never hesitate to take the opinion of other masterly players regarding the quality of his own or anybody else's performance. They were so broad-minded that they never felt small if any knowledgeable player, of equal eminence, pointed out some fault in their recitals. What is more, if they found the quality of any one's performance below par, they would quietly discuss the matter among themselves and adjudge the player in question as *'be-peerā'* (बे-पीरा), that is, one who did not have the privilege of learning at the feet of an acknowledged Ustad. (*Be*, means *without*; *peer*, an authentic teacher; and *ā* added to *peer* means 'one who is.') However, they would never reveal their opinion to the player in question, just to avoid discouraging him. Today, however, everything seems to depend on reactions *of the audience*. So we may give some thought to:

Types of Audience

Before the advent of Independence, music programmes were mostly held at royal courts, in camera, for personal enjoyment of the royalty. Audiences at such concerts comprised a few chosen courtiers, artists and aristocracy who would mostly be conversant with the subtle beauties of our *saṅgeet*. No big music conferences were organized in those days for one and all. But with the passage of years, as music came to be accepted as a part of our everyday culture, and the common man began to get frequent opportunities to listen to great masters who were earlier leading a sheltered life under the wings of royal patrons, the restriction of music to select audiences disappeared; and this led at once to a wider propagation of the art; *and, at the same time, to a relative fall in the quality of audience-reactions.*

Speaking quite generally, audiences can be divided into four main types. The first one may be said to comprise the aristocratic elite of society who go to listen to renowned artistes as a matter of fashion or social prestige. Many of them have hardly any sense of the high seriousness of good classical music; and therefore quite a few of them are impressed only by the gorgeous and colourful dresses of good-looking musicians. They prefer to sit in the first few rows, and take care to applaud and clap with the *rasika*s (or knowledgeable listeners) if there are any around. What one sees in their faces is mere wonder or excitement at something in the recital, never the subdued, yet genuine delight of discriminating approval. They are often thrilled by a sudden emphatic stroke on the drums, even if it is not suitably related to the general tenor of playing, or by a merely loud way of playing, as when the tablā player may, so to say, fall at the *sama* with a clumsy thud. Unfortunately, however, such audiences are indispensable; for, as the astute organizers clearly see, big programmes cannot survive without the financial assistance of such patrons of music. A peculiar thing about the members of such an audience is that they do not hesitate to leave the hall if the performing artist somehow fails to tickle their fancy. Further, they lend little listener-support to an artist who is yet to create a name for himself, even if he is intrinsically very good.

The second type of modern audience consists of listeners who, on the basis of their scanty knowledge of some very popular *rāga*s and *tāla*s, deceive themselves into believing that they have become connoisseurs of the art, and so keep enlightening their friends on either side about the calibre of the performing artist *right during the course of the recital,* Such people are sometimes very disturbing to the artist at work, and annoying to the genuine *rasika*s who may prefer to listen to and enjoy the playing wholly undisturbed.

The third type of audience, we may say, consists wholly of musicians who may either be participating in the same conference or attending the recital in question as special invitees of the organizers, and so seem to be obliging them, in a way. Such an audience, consisting mostly of professional musicians, generally remains unconcerned with, and appears quite unmoved by the tablā player's creative work. They manage to present a blank expression even where they are inwardly impressed, and do not acclaim openly, probably because they think it to be below their dignity to appreciate any performance except their own or of some pupil or member of their own gharānā; and when, at the end of the recital, they go to the green room to congratulate the performer as a mere formality, they do so in such a casual and unfeeling way that the artist's acknowledgement of their compliments becomes just as insincere.

The fourth and the last type of audience is of those who have somehow managed, but do not really deserve to become critics. On the basis of what they know, say, about the grammar of some *rāga*s and *tāla*s, they assume, mostly very wrongly, that they can judge a tablā recital too. They feed their critical ability by browbeating (so to say) some lesser known artist who may meekly succumb to the belief that his whole future depends on how *they* (the critics) react; and the critics manage to retain their own position by studiously avoiding to make adverse comments on the top artists. The ability to write impressively, if quite indiscriminately, is a further aid to their continuing sway. It is a pity that such critics are openly patronized and encouraged by some of the most eminent artists with an eye to their own aggrandizement.

Here, I think it necessary to point to a grievous lacuna in our cultural life. There is hardly any competent critic of the art of solo tablā in the country today. Our present critics are technically ill-equipped. If they cannot distinguish a तिरकिट (*Tirkiṭ*) from a धिरकिट (*Dhirkiṭ*), and have to content themselves with such general comments as that the recital which they have written on was sweet and very fluent, how can they be expected to mark that the norm of 'काफ़िया रदीफ़' (say, the end-rhyme) is met by similar, but not identical *'bols'* — say, तिना किना and धिंना गीना — in a *quāyedā*? How can they be expected to check if the way of using fingers *was surreptitiously* altered when a particular composition was, so to say, thrown up from बराबर की लय to its दुगुन or double pace?

The result naturally is that it is not always the best tablā player who wins 'critical' acclaim. Is there any way to rectify the situation? I believe there is, and so I venture to make the following suggestions:

First, the senior tablā players, some of whom are still living, must take a vow not to misguide and intentionally teach faulty ways of playing to those who come to them for instruction. They should be honest enough to make the youngsters alive to the value and character of authentic compositions, so that posterity may not be denied the privilege of listening to truly artistic tablā. At the same time, the younger players too should be receptive to the expert guidelines given by the seniors. Further, the eminent players of today should also resolve to play authentic compositions every time they are required to present a solo recital. If *they* do not thus refine the taste of audiences, who else will? Is not *dhruvapada ālāpa* showing a kind of resurgence today *simply because of the resolution of its exponents to stick to tradition*? Finally, it would also be of help if, before starting the actual execution of a subtle and beautiful composition, every performer not only recites, but explains the aesthetic character of what he is going to present. A proper response from the audience surely presupposes some *understanding* of what they are reacting to.

Players — Past and Present

But one has also to take into account the state of tablā playing today. Has it been improving since the advent of our political Independence? How do our present-day luminaries, distinguished as much by frequent trips to the West as by their gorgeous *kurtās*, compare with the Ustads of old? Not very favourably, I regret to say. I do not, of course, maintain that the old is necessarily superior to the new. But, on the other hand, I cannot help going by the evidence of facts and the demands of time-honoured principles of artistic practice; and I can *argue* for my somewhat negative judgement. Playing with technical precision and yet effortlessly is one thing; playing to the gallery, quite another. The former can refine our taste, making it a little more discriminating. The latter only caters to the vulgar demand for mere speed and virtuosity. Our Ustads of old, who had the requisite skill, repertoire, and feeling for perfection, always performed with the confidence that they could sway audiences with playing based on definite principles; they would never resort to random strokes or mere showmanship. Technical perfection, a cultivated sense of artistic form, and *regard for the orderly sequence of compositions* were so unremitting determinants of their recitals that they could often quite easily repeat, with almost perfect accuracy, a particular solo performance of theirs. Nor would they grow unduly tense while playing; the thoroughness of their training gave them the requisite poise. Today, randomness freely pays if it can be coupled with sheer *tayyāri* (or fluency). Every modern player has developed his own style, and is seen to perform in the way of his choice, his overriding aim being simply to impress the audience. I do not deny that players today have brains and stamina, are devoted to *reyāz* (practice), and can play quite fluently. But, I regret to say, their repertoire of compositions is not quite adequate; and it is importantly because of this defect that their playing tends to be rather haphazard. Why should they not seek to remedy this defect by learning from those genuine maestros of old who are still living and quite willing to pass on the riches of the art to any one who is eager and able to receive them? Like every other performing art, our rhythm too has two types of beauty: one arising from *how* one presents (or plays) what he knows, and the other from the quality of *what* one presents. The *how* here covers not only how neatly and fluently one plays, but how methodically he does it all; and the *what* here signifies the repertoire of compositions. Most of our players today may be admirable in respect of (a facile kind of) fluency, and a neatness born of rigorous practice; but from the viewpoint of method and compositional variety, their playing has yet to go a long way. It is important to remember that fluency in tablā playing *as an art* is no mere nimbleness of fingers, but facility in executing some *shapely bol or bunches of bols*. Our audiences today cannot see this difference. It is for the tablā players to heed it, to profit thereby, and so to train the audience, if incidentally.

Above all, commitment to a particular gharānā is essential for thoroughness in basic training. Only then can one venture to benefit from the riches of *other* gharānās, without being swept off one's feet. At the same time, congenial conditions must be provided to *every* gharānā for continuing abidance and progress; for each one of them has something valuable to offer. I see this very clearly, and this indeed is why I have tried, in this book, to give almost equal attention to every major gharānā.

The kind of rhythm that the gharānās have given us distinguishes our country from the rest of the world. We should not let the roots of this pre-eminence wither.

Glossarial Index

I. TERMS

(Quite a few of the technical terms that make the substance of this book have already been explained in the text, at page numbers duly underlines in this index. So they are listed without explanatory comments.)

Ālāpa, Singing (or playing) without words, but necessarily in conformity with a *rāga*. In the case of *ālāpa* which precedes the dhruvapada composition even *tāla* (or beat-measured rhythm) is abstained from: 169-170, 173, 177

Āmad, That distinct segment of a rhythmic pattern (or of a *sthāyī* in vocal music) which wears a look of heading for the *sama*, the focal beat of a rhythm-cycle: 81

Anāgat, A rhythmic pattern which is so designed (and played) that it ends just a little *before* the *sama*, 58

Anguṣṭhānā: 57-58

Atāi: 59

Ateet, A rhythmic pattern which is so designed (and played) that it ends just a tittle *after* the set location of the *sama*: 58

Baaj, Distinctive style of playing an instrument, stringed or percussive: 75, 78, 79, 81, 90, 104, 116, 119

Bānyā, The left hand drum: 7, 10, 14, 17, 117

Bol, In the region of rhythm a *bol* is a letter or a tuft of letters (alike meaningless) which serves as the material of rhythm-cycles and patterns: 2, 7, 8, 9, 15, 16, 18, 21-26, 40, 58, 62, 67, 104, 116, 119, 132-34, 137

Chalan: 54, 78, 80

Chakradār: 35, 40, 51-52, 68, 78, 81, 99, 104

Chaupalli: 50, 78

Dānyā, The right hand drum: 117

Dhruvapada, The oldest extant genre of North Indian classical vocal music in which the pre-*layakāri* part of singing proceeds as a set, orderly succession of four distinct segments (*sthāyi, antarā, samcāri, āthog*), and the relation of which to its accompanying rhythm is essentially parallel: 76, 78, 98, 169, 173, 177

Dhrupadāngi, Sharing the idiom of *dhruvapada* in respect of abstention from flirtatious embellishments and

II. NAMES

a. Maestros

b. Others